FLORIDA STATE
UNIVERSITY LIBRARIES

APR 11 1996

TALLAHASSEE, FLORIDA

The Other City

The Other City

People and Politics in New York and London

EDITED BY

Susanne MacGregor

and

Arthur Lipow

HUMANITIES PRESS
NEW JERSEY

First published 1995 by Humanities Press International, Inc.,
165 First Avenue, Atlantic Highlands, New Jersey 07716

©This collection 1995 by Humanities Press International, Inc.

©1995 by the individual authors

Library of Congress Cataloging-in-Publication Data

The Other City : people and politics in New York and London / edited
  by Susanne MacGregor and Arthur Lipow.
    p. cm.
    Includes bibliographical references and index.
    ISBN 0-391-03852-4. — ISBN 0-391-03885-0 (pbk.)
    1. New York (N.Y.)—Economic conditions. 2. London (England)—
Economic conditions. 3. New York (N.Y.)—Social conditions.
4. London (England)—Social conditions. 5. Urban policy—New York
(N.Y.) 6. Urban policy—England—London. I. MacGregor, Susanne.
HC108.N7086   1995
307.76'09421—dc20   94-24212
                                                                  CIP

A catalog record for this book is available from the British Library.

All rights reserved. No part of this book may be reproduced
or transmitted, in any form or by any means, without written
permission from the publisher.

Printed in the United States of America

For Michael Harrington

It is as if Disraeli's famous remark about the two nations of the rich and the poor had come true in a fantastic fashion. At precisely that moment in history when for the first time a people have the material ability to end poverty, they lack the will to do so. They cannot see: they cannot act. The consciences of the well off are the victims of affluence; the lives of the poor are the victims of a physical and spiritual misery.

Michael Harrington
The Other America

CONTENTS

Illustrations xi
Preface xiii

1 Bringing the People Back In:
   Economy and Society in London and New York
   Susanne MacGregor and Arthur Lipow   1

2 New York under Siege
   William Kornblum   28

3 Soup Kitchen Blues: Postindustrial Poverty in Brooklyn
   William DiFazio   40

4 Poverty in London
   Carey Oppenheim   61

5 City of Darkness, City of Light:
   Crime, Drugs, and Disorder in London and New York
   Geoffrey Pearson   85

6 Inner-City Crisis and Drug Dealing:
   Portrait of a New York Drug Dealer and His Household
   Eloise Dunlap   114

7 Urban Regeneration, Economic Restructuring, and
   Community Response in London Docklands
   Andrew Church   132

8 Bust, Baby, Bust: Coming of Age in America
   with Inflated Expectations and Diminished Options
   Donna Gaines   153

9 Race and Housing: Politics and Policy in London
   John Solomos   165

10 Fiscal Crisis and the New Class Politics:
    Managing Inequality in an Age of Decline
    Eric Lichten   183

11 Enabling or Empowering: Local Democracy in a
    Fragmenting Society
    Sue Goss   202

12 Turning the Clock Back One Hundred Years:
    The Problems of Getting Reliable Information
    and of Developing New Social Policies in the
    New Economic Order
    Peter Townsend   214

Contributors   231
Index   233

ILLUSTRATIONS

TABLES

4.1	Sources of Income, Single-Person Households in 1991	66
4.2	Rises and Falls in Employment by Sector between 1982 and 1990 in Greater London, Rest of the Southeast, and Great Britain (ooos and % Changes)	67
4.3	Changes in Employment Patterns between 1982 and 1990 in Greater London, Rest of the Southeast, and Great Britain (ooos and % Changes)	68
4.4	Numbers and Proportion of Greater London on Supplementary Benefit/Income Support between 1971 and 1988	71
4.5	Proportion of All School Children Receiving Free School Meals between 1979 and 1990	71
4.6	Number and Proportion of Individuals and Children Living in Poverty (Below 50 Percent of Average Income) by Region in 1980–82 and 1983–85	72
4.7	Unemployment Rates of London Boroughs in May 1991 (Percentages)	73
4.8	Unemployment Rates by Ethic Origin in Greater London (Aged 16 and Over)	74
4.9	U.K. Unemployment in Spring 1990	
4.10	Proportions of Different Groups Experiencing High Material and Social Deprivation	75
4.11	Income and Material and Social Deprivation by Ethnic Group in Islington in 1987	76

| 4.12 | Weekly Earnings for Men and Women in 1986 in London by "Race" | 77 |
| 4.13 | Benefits of Full-Time Workers by "Race" in 1986 in London | 78 |

FIGURES

1	The Risk of Poverty by Economic Status in 1988/89	65
2	The Risk of Poverty by Family Status in 1988/89	65
3	London Docklands	135

PREFACE

The city has long symbolized the best and the worst in humanity's search for new and improved forms of social organization. Wordsworth's joy in "escaping from the vast city" to the tranquility of the Lake District touches deep chords in the English psyche. For students of English local government, much can be gained from comparisons of the needs and spending patterns of metropolitan and shire authorities. Small-town America too, as in both 1950s films and Tennessee Williams's pain, is at once both image and reality when set against the "fear and loathing" and turbulence of cities like Los Angeles and Miami. Most compellingly, in the 1990s, Sarajevo came to symbolize the test of the cosmopolitan, cultured, multiethnic city besieged by the dark forces of nationalism and racism. This was not all or only image.

Debates about people and politics in London and New York thus connect to wider debates about policy and practice in the nation as a whole and link with analyses and prescriptions for international relations.

The utopias and dystopias which have structured intellectual thought and political practice in the twentieth century, as much on the left as on the right, have included representations of the city as a central item in their accounts. Arthur Lipow has shown how much that was taken to be socially progressive on the left in this period was heavily ingrained with antidemocratic, authoritarian principles wherein the solutions to social problems would best be managed by enlightened elites doing to and for others in the interests of the "whole."

In futuristic science fiction worlds, a central categorization has often been between those who are insiders and those who are outsiders—outside the city wall, where the dead are buried and the crosses fixed. Those above and those below: those within and those without. The city on the hill and the dark groups huddled round fires on the plain. Who gets to eat whom? Progress and decay. Hope and disillusion.

In writing *The Other America*, Michael Harrington linked into these images of us and them, the included and the excluded, in a book which marked the beginning of the 1960s War on Poverty. We have called this collection *The Other City* in respect for the tradition of Michael Harrington's work which in our modest way we celebrate here. Michael Harrington was a scholar and an activist, a democratic socialist who wrote about, among other things, poverty in America and internationally (as in *The Vast Majority*). He chose to link his work to the Democratic Party of America through the Democratic Socialists of America (DSA). Not every contributor to this collection shares all his political views or the early optimism of some DSAers at the election of a Democratic president. But they do all share his belief in the value of theory *and* practice, thinking *and* doing, not being content to remain ivory tower intellectuals, idolizing Theory in the comfort of the Academy.

The contributors to this collection were drawn together through the activities of the Michael Harrington Centre, and the book grew out of contacts made at its first London conference. This conference, inaugurating the establishment of the Michael Harrington Centre at Birkbeck College (University of London), was held in January 1991 and was supported by funds from Harkness Fellowships of the Commonwealth Fund NY, Nuffield Foundation, Baring Foundation, New Statesman and Society, the University of London, the Center for Social Research CUNY, and the Michael Harrington Center (Queens College CUNY). The link between London and New York, especially through Arthur Lipow of the University of London and Ray Franklin of City University of New York, has been critical to its activities, but the network of contacts spreads more widely to include people from other walks of life: trade unionists, journalists, policy makers, practitioners, political activists, and a whole range of others.

One principle that is shared by those who admired Michael Harrington and by contributors to this book is a belief in the potentially beneficial role of public policy in regulating and reshaping life chances and experiences. To say this seems commonplace, but it is often denied by those believers in the free market who want to limit the role of public policy. The important questions are, of course, in what direction to regulate and reshape, to what ends and for whose benefit—and who will decide? And here we answer, for the benefit of working people, men and women, using means which are determinedly democratic, secular, and nonracist.

The authors are social researchers and writers from London and New York who share a common democratic and humanistic perspective on social life and politics. We would expect readers to be people who share with them a worry about the failure of urban planners, politicians, and businesspeople to come up with solutions and who recoil from the tendency to talk about the city as though it were made up only of real estate and development opportunities. The essays are based on detailed analyses of social data, ethnographic studies, and participant observation.

Running through the collection is the theme that the problem is one of political failure. No party in the United Kingdom or the United States yet has a program that addresses fundamental social inequalities.

Two central changes have occurred with the economic transformation of global cities: a large segment of the manufacturing labor force has been displaced; and the structure of opportunity has changed for those entering the labor force. Those particularly affected include some young people, some women, some ethnic minorities, and some recent migrants. Paralleling this has been the burgeoning of an underground economy, especially surrounding drugs.

The belief in democratic egalitarian politics and policy was unfashionable for many years in the United States and the United Kingdom in the years dominated by Reagan-Thatcher thinking. Profound transformations were made in this period in public life and social institutions which impacted severely on those living in the great cities of London and New York.

Poverty and inequality increased in most Western democracies during the 1980s. But there were substantially greater increases in both Britain and the United States. Research findings from Washington's Joint Center for Political and Economic Studies have shown that the configuration of poverty in Britain, previously similar to that of other European welfare states, is now much closer to the North American pattern. This, said Roger Lawson of Southampton University, is one of the saddest features of the "special relationship."

By the mid-1980s, the U.S. poverty rate was double that of every continental European country. The poverty rate of black Americans was ten times that of foreigners in West Germany. In sharp contrast to other countries, U.S. government policies did not reduce overall levels of poverty in the 1980s.

By the mid-1980s, U.K. levels of poverty were markedly higher than in other European countries. Under the impact of Thatcherism, twin sister to America's Reaganism, Britain moved rapidly from a social democratic form of welfare state toward a more residual one, coming to share some of the features of the U.S. pattern. The two countries also adopted similar economic policies. They share problems of relative economic decline—a phenomenon coming to be described as the Anglo-American model.

But no sooner had the world started to celebrate the triumph of the free market and the collapse of the Soviet bloc ("socialism") than fear and loathing reappeared to challenge complacency about a new world order. In an ironic celebration of May Day 1992, economic collapse, violence, and ethnic warfare worldwide were mirrored in civil disorder and rioting in the cities of the United States. "One of the world's richest cities [Los Angeles] has torn itself apart," wrote Martin Walker of the *Guardian* (May 2, 1992). "America's free market has its costs, its democracy fails to embrace so many of its poor, and the high temple of consumer capitalism has been pillaged by its own excluded worshippers."

It is in this context that the contributors to this volume felt it legitimate and of value to come together to look critically at what has been happening in their cities. Much has been written on global cities, megacities, and the metropolis. This book concentrates on the people who live in New York and London, especially poor people. While the two cities are monuments to past achievements and unique expressions of the power of human creativity, offering excitement and opportunities and the rich swirling mix of cultures of talented people from far and wide, they also share common problems of decline and transformation. What are the implications for their citizens?

The writers have aimed to tell it as it is, to try in part to describe how people really live their lives in London and New York as distinct from the images portrayed in the media, where the city is predominantly a metaphor for all current ills and is, in the classic twist, also blamed for the very problems it has to try to deal with.

The Reagan-Thatcher years were a period in which the people were pushed out from decision making as the market was given greater priority over representative politics. Deliberate restructuring of social institutions in an attempt to change the culture and behavior of people took place. In the cities, the fragmentation and polarization produced by these policies are becoming clearer and made more prominent in a context of economic decline and fiscal crisis. Is the concept of a "civic culture" also then a thing of the past? Some efforts to re-create these values can be glimpsed in the Clinton program and in the stress on citizenship in center-left discussions in Britain, but it is unclear how inclusive the concept of "citizen" is intended to be in all these visions.

Two key features provide the context for our current concerns: changes in the economy and labor market, especially continuing high levels of unemployment and the return of casualization of the workforce; and changes in the welfare state, together with fears about the appearance of a surplus population in a postindustrial economy.

While fragmentation is a constant reference in the chapters in this book, wider forces are indicated as explaining the developments that are described, which affect whole generations, whole genders, whole ethnic groups in systematic ways. The complexity of the situation is part of the analysis and explanation. The vitality of the inner city can be opposed to the gray wastelands of suburbia, as much as the decay of the inner city can be contrasted with the comfort of the suburbs. The message is the need to look at how people are living, to let people talk for themselves, even if what they say and do is not always comforting or necessarily in accord with preconceived views of either a liberal or a conservative nature. Poverty can be brutalizing, but crises bring out the worst and the best in human beings.

And here too the writers share one other feature: they care about these cities and the people, their fellow citizens who live there—not just the playmates and the successful but those who make up the "others," the "strangers," especially those whose suffering is most acute and increasing. And if care for the stranger is part of the basis of an altruistic welfare state, then such are the policies to be promoted.

From all this (and more—we do not pretend to comprehensiveness) we may be moved to understand a little more and condemn a little less.

The collection is also in its way perhaps, and unwillingly, "postmodern"—fragments of a reality, a variety of shafts, perspectives on the whole. The theme of the book is poverty and inequality, contrasts of rich and poor, power and powerlessness, and how to challenge these contrasts and differences and the decisions about who is to be included in and who excluded from the feast.

Chapter 1, by MacGregor and Lipow, presents an overview of the two cities and of themes in the book. This is followed by chapters from Kornblum, DiFazio, and Oppenheim which focus on poverty and homelessness, explanations of differences in life chances, and proposals for political and policy responses. Pearson and Dunlap in their chapters deal with the issues of image and reality and the impact of social forces and perceptions on urban lives, especially with regard to drugs and crime. Church discusses the London Docklands redevelopment and its impact especially on local communities, young people, and ethnic minorities. Chapters by Gaines and Solomos follow up related themes; Gaines considers the opportunities and life chances of young people, and Solomos looks at policy interventions to redress ethnic and racial differences in access to housing. In chapters by Goss, Lichten, and Townsend, the account moves out again from the particular to the general; they present analyses of economic change and fiscal crisis, relating these to changing forms of the state and discussing the possibilities for action in a situation where the local, the national, and the global are increasingly intertwined.

In an age of profound political and intellectual shifts, too much coherence might be viewed with suspicion. The attempt to grasp a changing scene will be partial and miss some key features. The focus is maintained, however, and it is on poverty, unemployment, and underlying economic change and how these impact on people's lives. Will the fragmentation so frequently referred to eventually produce a shattered city? Or will the city prove to be a living being, organic, constantly renewing through inward flows of new life—migrants and visitors—and through the new young blood of the next generation?

Response, resistance, and adaptation to change are the themes of the essays in this book. The value of continuing resistance, opposition to what is wrong, even when we are less sure of what is right or what different policies might be proposed, is important and is affirmed in some of the examples in the book. Pushing back the boundaries of the possible, resisting the attempt to push you out, demanding that the issues be on the agenda, articulating alternatives: these are the stuff of the critical politics described here. Strategies to link these resistances through networks and campaigns all add to rebuilding a civic democratic politics and may overcome defeatism and despair.

This collection would not have been put together without the assistance of many people; they are too numerous to mention individually, but I thank them all. However, I should like to give special thanks to the women who assisted me in mobilizing contributions from two sides of the Atlantic: Harriet Lodge, Angela Kerkhoff, Valerie Mann, Shirley Angel, Sarah Lyons, and Hedi Petri.

Susanne MacGregor
Middlesex University

1

Bringing the People Back In: Economy and Society in London and New York

Susanne MacGregor and Arthur Lipow

The property giant Olympia and York was one of the prime architects of changes in the shape of both London and New York during the 1980s. Their giant office projects in New York's Battery Park City and London's Canary Wharf symbolize the commonalities between these two financial global cities. At its height in 1990, Olympia and York owned forty million square feet of offices in North America alone. "In the 1980s, if you wanted to be taken seriously as a player in the international urban big league you had to have O&Y in town." Later, however, "caught in the grip of the sharpest property slump in a generation on both sides of the Atlantic, the company's global reach ... turned out to be more of a handicap than an advantage, leaving them vulnerable rather than spreading the risk from local difficulties" (Sudjic 1992, 32).

London and New York are global cities. They are highly concentrated command points in the organization of the world economy; they are key locations for the finance and specialized service firms which have replaced manufacturing as the leading economic sectors; they are sites of production, including the production of innovation; and they act as markets for these products and innovations. With this go changes in their economic base, spatial organization, and social structure (Sassen 1991, 3–4).

What is the impact of such global economic and financial developments on the lives of people, especially poor people, living in London and New York? In London and New York, for some time now, there has been a feeling that "things fall apart, the centre cannot hold." Uncertainty and insecurity for some, howling pain for others, the whirlpool of the city, the bonfire of the vanities have long been familiar themes. But how much of our present concern is really new and how much the familiar disquiet of each generation on seeing its old certainties fall before the fashions and tastes of the succeeding one?

The shock felt by visitors to the big city is nothing new. Engels had this to say as he commented on a London of two and a half million inhabitants in the early nineteenth century:

> I know nothing more imposing than the view one obtains of the river when sailing from the sea up to London Bridge. . . . All this is so magnificent and impressive that one is lost in admiration. The traveller has good reason to marvel at England's greatness even before he steps on English soil.
>
> It is only later that the traveller appreciates the human suffering which has made all this possible. He can only realise the price that has been paid for all this magnificence after he has tramped the pavements of the main streets of London for some days and has tired himself out by jostling his way through the crowds and by dodging the endless stream of coaches and carts which fills the streets. . . . Hundreds of thousands of men and women drawn from all classes and ranks of society pack the streets of London. Are they not all human beings with the same innate characteristics and potentialities? . . . Yet they rush past each other as if they had nothing in common. . . . The more that Londoners are packed into a tiny space, the more repulsive and disgraceful becomes the brutal indifference with which they ignore their neighbours and selfishly concentrate upon their private affairs. We know well enough that this isolation of the individual—this narrow-minded egotism—is everywhere the fundamental principle of modern society. But nowhere is this selfish egotism so blatantly evident as in the frantic bustle of the great city. The disintegration of society into individuals, each guided by his private principles and each pursuing his own aims has been pushed to its furthest limits in London. (Engels 1971, 30–31)

One hundred and fifty years later, the common view is that those limits are now to be found pushed even further out in the teeming streets of New York. Now it is in that city that Engels's "social conflict—the war of all against all—is fought out in the open" (ibid.).

LONDON AND NEW YORK

Glancing at the two cities of London and New York, what is striking is that both have so much going for them but both have underperformed so dismally. They share many features but in other ways are very different.

Londoners are blind to racism, New Yorkers blinded by it. In New York, the police are accused of having given up on some neighborhoods; in London, the complaint is that policing is too heavy-handed. One is a capital city, the other the gateway to the nation. Making money, getting money, is a prime part of each city's ethos—more genteel in one than in the other but the bottom line for both.

In both too, the bottom third live in poverty and insecurity. Homelessness and begging have returned to an extent undreamed of in postwar years. The mentally ill wander the streets looking for community care.

But in New York, poverty means death and violence and incarceration; young black men in poor neighborhoods are killing each other at ever-increasing rates, lowering their life expectancies to third world levels.

New Yorkers will say "You ain't seen nothing yet" to Londoners who complain; they will smile in wry amusement when the English point to the homeless under Waterloo Bridge or fuss about the litter. Manhattan's streets by contrast are overwhelming for the tourist: human and material debris discarded and rotting while busy people pass by stony-faced, occasionally throwing quarters into extended paper cups.

Everyday racism is a reality of New York life. One young woman of our acquaintance, an Ethiopian student, told us in moving detail of the daily insults to which she is subjected, merely because of her skin color: no chip on the shoulder here, just a person from another society, another world, discovering what American blacks know and experience every day. Such racism was given legitimacy by George Bush's exploitation of Willie Horton in his 1988 presidential campaign. In the spring of 1992 this produced its own reaction in the riots which followed the acquittal of L.A. police officers on trial for beating up Rodney King.

Public Problems, Private Strategies

A minor accident at 42nd Street: one car has bumped another. A plainclothes police officer gets involved, trying to sort it out; a crowd gathers. Suddenly, the police officer turns on the watching crowd and yells in fury: "I really hate being white. Every time something happens they yell racism." A common little incident, an everyday example of the tension, the explosiveness, and the pent-up resentment only just beneath the surface of life in New York.

And the seeming intractability of the problems creates another problem. The second or third time around, people are no longer shocked; they grow bored, brutalized, unable to contemplate further change, unable to think up solutions when all the obvious ones, they think, have failed. When you stop even talking about the problem you are really in trouble. Private survival strategies flourish: finding your own routes through the chaos; traveling only at certain times; locking your door at dusk and never answering it; never sitting at the window seat in a restaurant in case the faces pressed up against the glass put you off your meal; acting slightly mad to frighten off marauders; drugging or drinking yourself into a protective cocoon; plugging in the Walkman, switching on the telly, turning off the news.

What can be learned by each city from the other? Can multiethnic cities retain a vital pluralism without degenerating into separatism? How can tolerance of difference, even enjoyment and celebration of difference, be built into the political and cultural life of the city—especially in this age of renewed nationalism?

MATURE WORLD CITIES

In many senses, London now dominates Britain, not only as the capital and financial and administrative center. London and the rest of the southeast have 40 percent of the population of England and Wales and over one-third of the population of the entire United Kingdom. All but three of the twenty new 1992 Tory cabinet posts were held by representatives of southern constituencies. In the early 1990s London and the southeast experienced the sharpest rises in unemployment as the worst recession since the 1930s hit the new service industries.

Signs of poverty and insecurity are found in increasing indebtedness, due to interest repayments, unemployment, and the almost unique British policy of shifting homeownership down the income scale to encompass those on lower and less stable incomes. Between April 1993 and April 1994, the rise in average earnings in Greater London was the second lowest of all British regions at 1.8 percent. Still, weekly wages for full-time workers there are well above those of other regions. Workers in Greater London were paid 127.6 percent of the British average. But while pay in London is higher than the average, there is no significant trickle-down effect. The earnings of the lowest paid 10 percent at that time in Greater London averaged £197.40 compared to £682.90 per week for the top 10 percent.

So in both London and New York, quality of life is the dominant issue. Both cities have experienced decline compared to other cities in the rest of the United States and Europe.

A London Weekend Television survey in November 1990 found that 48 percent of those living in London wanted to leave while only 39 percent said they liked living there. (A few years later, this seemed less impressive in the light of a *Daily Telegraph* survey which found 67 percent of people wanted to leave the country!)

World cities are based on knowledge, information, technology, and services. As such, their survival depends upon being internationally competitive. The Lord Mayor of London sees the City of London as unmatched anywhere in the world—as the world's leading international financial center.

Fifty percent of Stock Exchange business is reported to be in shares in foreign business, earning £14 billion net income for the United Kingdom in one year. Financial and business services now employ one-quarter of all employees in London, dominating London's economy to an extent not found in other world cities such as New York and Tokyo. More than a third of London's Gross Domestic Product comes from this sector.

"The key to sustained competitiveness as a world city is human ability and creativity in a network of interlocking and supportive firms and organizations whose business is supplying the world market" (Kennedy 1991, 63). The same survey concluded that there are three essential interlinked components to a successful city: wealth creation, job generation, and the quality of life. Underpinning each of these is the enabling infrastructure, which includes transport and communications, commercial and residential accommodation, and the provision of education, training, and skills.

In both London and New York, manufacturing (traditionally defined) is particularly weak. This reflects in each case national weakness in manufacturing and the failure to revive this sector as older industries declined. By the late 1980s, manufacturing accounted for only 9 percent of employment in New York and 12 percent in London compared to 21 percent in Tokyo and 18 percent in Frankfurt. The growth in the share of finance within total employment in London since the early 1970s has been 80 percent compared to Tokyo's 75 percent and New York's 20 percent (Coopers and Lybrand Deloitte 1991). However, as Sassen has pointed out, it is important to get beyond the dichotomy between manufacturing and services. "The 'things' a global city makes are services and financial goods" (Sassen 1991, 5).

New York to its credit is now seen as the leading world cultural center, at least as far as its contribution to wealth creation goes. Apart from this, however, when compared with Frankfurt, Berlin, Paris, and Tokyo, both London and New York appear relatively poor in most infrastructural areas. Especially singled out continuously for adverse comment are their internal transport systems, London's being particularly bad.

The critical factors in cities' economies are intracity mobility, education and training, and access to a diverse set of skills. In the past twenty years, the labor markets of all world cities have become more complex. Underlying problems, with their related economic inefficiencies and human costs, remain, such as long-distance commuting, skills mismatches, and the growth of an "underclass"—those who are marginalized in both the labor and the housing markets and who risk social and political exclusion. Polarization and multiple deprivation grow alongside the burgeoning of city economies.

It is in the two most mature world cities, London and New York, that these problems are most acute. A research project co-sponsored by the London Planning Advisory Committee concluded that the 1980s' renewed growth of employment opportunities in these cities was met not so much from remaining inner-city residents but by labor imported from the increased populations on the periphery. "The consequences of this increased commuting were additional costs to employers (disruption costs), to the commuter (stress and fatigue), to the public purse (the costs of transport provision) and to the overall environment (air pollution and noise)" (Coopers and Lybrand Deloitte 1991, 5). The report concluded that polarization is most pronounced in London and New York and that London and New York are far less likely to generate jobs and income over the next fifteen years than are Tokyo and particularly the other European cities.

Changing Social Economies

By the year 2000, London's population is expected to reach over seven million. After falling from its level of 4.3 million in the early 1960s, the labor force is expected to increase to slightly over 3.6 million (partly influenced by increasing employment of women and a growing number of self-employed workers) (Kennedy 1991, 70). For about one-third of the workforce, their skills are marketable and in demand virtually anywhere in London. These workers are predominantly skilled, white, middle class, high earning, and living on the fringes of London or beyond (ibid., 71). "But for another major component (of the order of a fifth) of the labor force, London comprises a large number of ill-defined (though by no means mutually exclusive) local labor markets, each with its own distinct characteristics" (ibid.).

These local labor markets show signs of weakness and mismatch, a reflection partly of poor training infrastructure. "London's training provision appears to be quite inadequate to meet the scale of the needs of those who have become marginalized from the labor market or, indeed, have been thrust outside it. This implies not only a waste of resources and the creation of social polarisation and tension but also requires an expensive solution—through commuting—to meet the labor requirements of central London businesses" (ibid., 72).

The type of work carried out in London has changed more rapidly than in the rest of Britain. "In 1990 a full 80 percent of London's workforce was engaged in financial and business services, public administration and education. The decline in manufacturing employment has been dramatic and it is projected that by the year 2000 only 6 percent of London's workforce will be engaged in manufacturing" (ibid., 73).

This London: World City research project concluded:

> An urban policy framework must consider the dangers posed by widening social divisions in a city where job opportunities are polarised between high status producer service jobs for the qualified 'insiders' and unstable

consumer service employment for the rest. These social and employment tensions were a key factor in New York's period of economic crisis in the 1970s and the flight of headquarters from the city." (ibid., 75)

The responses from below have taken many forms—the most obvious being the urban riots which characterized the 1980s: Brixton in 1981; Broadwater Farm in 1985; Trafalgar Square in 1990. There were serious street disorders every year throughout the 1980s. There are frequent crowd disturbances and Saturday night brawls, phenomena in which policing tactics play a major role. Crime figures rose relentlessly in the 1980s: recorded crime increased by 79 percent during Mrs. Thatcher's period in office. Relations between the police and young people are particularly poor.

On the other side of the Atlantic, on one day, February 2, 1992, eight killings were reported in the *New York Times*. A young man, ordering a hamburger at a White Tower, gets into a dispute with other customers over their place in line. One pulls out a gun and shoots him through the head as he leaves the restaurant. In Bedford-Stuyvesant, a man walks into a grocery store, shoots two people, killing one, and sets fire to the building. Ten people are hospitalized for smoke inhalation (Bennet 1992).

In Morris Heights, the Bronx, Police Officer Hilario Serrano, off duty, is mugged and shot in an elevator on his way to visit his mother. "Officer Serrano's relatives and friends struggled to understand how a man who faced danger on duty could be slain at his mother's doorstep.... We never thought it would be like this," said Hilario Serrano's cousin, Jose Diaz Jr. The residents of Morris Heights are terrified by the continuing violence. Wanda Pagan, a resident of the same building as Officer Serrano's mother, tells how her brother-in-law was shot by more than twenty bullets two years earlier. The people responsible for the violence, drug gangs who sell crack and cocaine, "don't care," Ms. Pagan says. "They shoot whoever is there. Every night there is a shooting. Now, it's people that we know that are getting killed. There are more than 10 shootings a month" (Newman 1992).

The population of New York was 7.3 million by 1986 and is now around 8 million. By September 1990, New York's workforce was around 3.3 million, an increase after its absolute decline during the 1970s from 3.7 to 3 million (thus a smaller proportion [41.25 percent] of its population is in the labor force than is the case in London [51.4 percent]). Manufacturing now accounts for only 9 percent of the total employment. "New York—like London—is suffering an unhealthy polarization of its workforce, the repercussions of which are almost certain to be an increasingly inefficient labor market and rising unemployment—or at the very least, the further development of the city's 'hidden economy'" (Kennedy 1991, 76). New York has a similar but much more marked social and employment polarization and tension to that in London. One-fifth of the New York population live below the poverty line.

> There are three points of uncomfortable similarity between New York and London which we feel obliged to note. First, both cities have a low percentage of their employment in manufacturing—in 1989 both cities employed about 10 percent in this sector compared with over 15 percent in the other world cities. Second, the public education and training system in both cities is poorly regarded internationally.... Third, the intracity mobility provision in both cities is deemed by resident businesses to be poor. (ibid., 77)

The flight to the suburbs and the concentration of problems and poverty in particular neighborhoods and estates is also found in both. And past and present migration into the cities from more deprived areas nationally and internationally shows up in their demographic profiles.

But the ethnic mix in the two cities is very different. While Britain bears the fruits of its imperial past, the United States bears the scars of slavery. It also stands on the edge of the Spanish-speaking world. In New York, with its large Spanish-speaking population, there is now a challenge to the linguistic dominance of English. Migrants from Asia and the Caribbean compete with African Americans and Puerto Ricans for the bottom rungs of the ladder in this "classless society."

In London, 180 home languages are spoken in inner London schools. Yet the second language used by commentators in the two cities is similar. In each the talk is of crime waves, drugs, AIDS, the poor transport system, homelessness, the impossibility of community care when there is no community, and worries about the inadequacies of the schools and, overridingly, about the fiscal crisis.

Both cities now face severe problems in paying for services: in London, this results from reforms to local government finances, the squeeze on central allocations, and the shift of responsibility for care for the most vulnerable from central to local budgets with the introduction of community care in April 1993; in New York, the city had to adopt an austerity budget to confront a fiscal crisis far more serious than the one which brought the city to its knees in the 1970s.

The fiscal crisis of each city in the 1990s is a crisis made at the center—in Whitehall for London and in Albany for New York. In London, this results from a decade of deliberate undermining of the power and financial stability of local government. In New York, it reflects the imbalance of political power between the suburbs and upstate New York and New York City. It is also a crisis made in Washington. Far from reaping the "peace dividend" which the end of the cold war was supposed to bring, there were more budget cuts directly affecting the states and the hard-up cities where the social needs are greatest, partly brought about also by deep recession in the international economy.

WHAT NEEDS TO BE DONE?

New York with its mayor has the administrative but not the political infrastructure. In London, it is the reverse with a hole in the center of the administration—no one agency or person to act as champion in the way New York's mayor can. But there are strong party traditions and organizations that connect leaders and grass roots and offer alternatives to voters—something lacking in the United States, which, however, secures more forceful political representation of ethnic groups.

There is widespread agreement that a strategic authority is needed for London but disagreement over whether that authority should be elected. Some believe democracy works too slowly to provide the dynamic and flexible responses needed. Others think that in the long run a nonelected leader would encounter even more problems: it would prove impossible to make decisions stick—as happened with the infamous poll tax.

Most urgently provision is needed in both London and New York to meet the most visible problems of youth, crime, homelessness, and begging. Weeping about the decay of religious and family values will not be enough. What is needed is income support and job programs for young people, radical improvements in education at every level, especially in the schools, and expansion of real training programs with jobs at the end.

The lesson from New York for London is that if you don't spend money, if you don't have social intervention policies and planning, you will get social rot. New York's problems, moreover, cannot be solved by New Yorkers alone. They are the same problems found in other major cities, such as Washington, Detroit, Los Angeles. The mayors of all the big cities complain of crime and drugs, but no one in Washington seems to have any answers.

In December 1990, in a London Weekend Television "London Lecture" Sir Ralf Dahrendorf began by saying, "I love London," but he went on to say, "London is no longer such fun.... It is going through a bad patch.... Now one feels morally assaulted as one moves about the town." The main problem, he thinks, has been the transformation of the comfortable middle class from "citizens" into "commuters." Without the middle class, cities become the preserve of the very wealthy and the underclass, and the contribution of the middle classes to civic life is lost.

WHERE ARE THE MIDDLE CLASSES?

Head up the Great North Road out of London and you soon encounter an entirely different world: a world of leafy lanes, tennis courts, varying-sized houses—some quite large, but all having an air of comfort and well-being. Families are much in evidence, playing football or cricket, riding horses, golfing, walking dogs, shopping in huge shopping malls and do-it-yourself centers, the temples of the new consumer culture.

It is impossible to understand the life of London without seeing this other side of Greater London, the world of the suburbs, the Home Counties, Kent, and Surrey. London is a vast megacity seen from the air. But most people live in quite small neighborhoods (some see London as a series of urban villages). People travel in rat runs to and from their work; these routes they know well, but there are other parts of London with which they are completely unacquainted other than through television, radio, and newspapers or from talk among friends and colleagues.

While the contrast between "inner city" and "suburb" is a crude one, ignoring the familiar problems of outer estates and leafy central villages, such as Blackheath and Hampstead, overall the census figures do show clear differences: for example, 34 percent of children in Inner London in 1991 were growing up in a household where no adult was in paid employment; this was the case for 17 percent of Outer London children.

How visible, then, are the problems of poverty? Is poverty a low priority on the agenda because people do not know about it, do not encounter it in their own lives? Are those in the suburbs, the commuters moving regularly between their leafy comfortable residences and centrally heated offices, unaware of the growing poverty of the communities beneath the bridges and to the side of the railway lines?

Of critical importance is a person's relation to work and family—the key institutions of contemporary society. Poverty in any society can be explained by the way work and the family are organized. Whatever the principles of organization, they are maintained by excluding those people whose lives do not accord with these principles.

Poverty and marginalization are sometimes described today as reflecting a lack of *attachment* to these key areas of production and reproduction. There is a danger in this phraseology—even Charles Murray can agree with it—for it implies it is all a question of poor people's values and attitudes: they don't have the work ethic or the right moral fiber or values. But the idea is useful if we stress the element of *exclusion* from the family and from work, possibly in spite of sharing the values and the desire to work.

Who makes the decision to be poor? Who to blame? Did she fall or was she pushed? Often what we see is a mixture—involving choices made between limited available opportunities. What, then, were the choices available? How wide or how limited were they in the real situations people encounter?

For example, when we think of poverty, we often think of its most extreme manifestations in the form of homelessness and destitution. The Conservative governments in Britain in the 1980s were very successful in their housing policies: by cutting subsidies, raising rents, and restricting building, expenditure was cut by more than 60 percent in those ten years. The sale of 1.5 million council houses was the most lucrative of all the many privatization programs, cutting public sector borrowing by £33 billion and expanding owner occupation from 55 percent to nearly 70 percent. At the same time, however, raising council rents meant that nearly two-thirds of tenants now claim housing benefit—which is paid by the Department of Social Security; thus savings for one department became expenditure for another. In the same period, the number of British households without a home of their own doubled to nearly two hundred thousand.

POOR PEOPLE AND POVERTY

Poverty is about marginalization, exclusion, powerlessness, and access to services.

Peter Townsend has provided the classic definition of poverty:

> Poverty can be defined objectively and applied consistently only in terms of the concept of relative deprivation.... Individuals, families and groups in the population can be said to be in poverty when they lack the resources to obtain the type of diet, participate in the activities and have the living conditions and amenities which are customary or at least widely encouraged or approved in the societies to which they belong. Their resources are so seriously below those commanded by the average individual or family that they are, in effect, excluded from ordinary living patterns, customs and activities. (Townsend 1979, 31)

Faith in the City put it this way:

> Poverty is not only about shortage of money. It is about rights and relationships; about how people are treated and how they regard themselves; about powerlessness, exclusion and loss of dignity. Yet the lack of an adequate income is at its heart. (Archbishop of Canterbury's Commission, 1985, 195)

The same report also argued:

> Poverty is at the root of powerlessness. Poor people in UPAs [urban priority areas] are at the mercy of fragmented and apparently unresponsive public authorities. They are trapped in housing and in environments over which they have little control. They lack the means and opportunity—which so many of us take for granted—of making choices in their lives. (ibid., xv)

So poverty is not simply to be measured in terms of numbers of poor individuals and poor households. It also means poor communities where one deprivation is stacked on top of another.

The issue of power has been brought back into the discussion of poverty with the end of the postwar period of welfare state hegemony and the collapse of its related scientistic, technical language. Debate about poverty in the past decade has been intensely ideological, especially seen in the concept of the "underclass."

The growth of an underclass is set up as a nightmare to be feared—described by newscaster Donald McCormick, for example, as "maybe the most daunting prospect facing Britain to the end of the century" (Mc Cormick, 1991).

The main theme of the right-wing approach has been to stress that the poor are different. Separate people require separate treatment. This is the essence of the underclass concept.

Seeing poor people as different, as somehow not fully human, has a long and disreputable history in social policy and politics. Small examples are found today in the treatment of the poor in London. For example, a recent report quoted a confidential document prepared for the Westminster city council which had advised that there was a need to address the "moral blackmail and increasing menace of beggars and to end the blot on the domestic and tourist landscape of the homeless sleeping rough. . . . In the interests of its residents—and poll tax payers—the council might usefully mount a campaign to clean up central London."

A similar reaction against the homeless has arisen in New York. Ordinary residents are asserting their demands to reclaim their local parks for their children to play in and their old people to sit and read in. This reaction has to be taken seriously; the competing claims of the two groups cannot be solved without the needs of each being addressed. This is where politics comes in, for this is the process through which competing claims are negotiated. But where so many people are excluded from decision making—women most markedly, also certain ethnic groups and the young and the old—the chances of a fair resolution of the issue look slim.

In most of the discussions which dominated the media in the Reagan-Thatcher years, the underclass concept was used to link poverty to a number of other issues: crime, drugs, racism, violence, lone-parent families. The phenomenon was the classic one of "blaming the victim."

Alternative approaches share some of this analysis but differ in other ways and come up with different policy proposals. W. J. Wilson, for example, in attempting to explain social breakdown and decay in poor areas (inner cities), has put stress not on the notion of a culture of poverty but on the fact of *social isolation.*

He points to the collapse of social institutions under stress in the inner city. Structural changes in the economy have led to the familiar pattern of a loss of jobs for unskilled and semiskilled men in the inner-city areas of great cities. These dislocations in the American urban economy, wiping out millions of jobs in manufacturing and related fields, have had disproportionate effects on African Americans. From his studies in Chicago, Wilson has mapped out in detail the way impoverishment and unemployment affect social organization: pointing, for example, to the way lack of transport affects job opportunities, how lack of money and of telephones affects job search, how a stigmatized address can be a justification for discrimination. In this context, an alternative economy of drugs and crime proves very attractive; Wilson points to the relative opportunities offered by legitimate and illegitimate activities—to the advantage of the latter.

Going beyond this, the urban ethnographer Philipe Bourgois has pointed to the importance of the human need for dignity and respect:

> The vast majority of the residents of East Harlem are honest and hardworking. It is a struggle to live there and they struggle honourably. Nevertheless, to many, especially the young, the underground economy beckons seductively as the ultimate "equal opportunity" employer.... The rate of unemployment for Harlem youth is at least twice the city wide rate of 8.1 percent.... Most of the people I have met are proud that they are not being exploited by "the White Man." All of them have at one time or another held the jobs—delivery boys, supermarket baggers, hospital orderlies—that are objectively recognized as among the least desirable in American society. They see the illegal, underground economy as not only offering superior wages but also a more dignified workplace. (Bourgois 1989, 34)

Bourgois goes on to comment that, based on his experience, he believes that the assertion of the culture of poverty theorists that the poor have been badly socialized and do not share mainstream values is wrong. "On the contrary, ambitious, energetic, inner city youths are attracted to the underground economy precisely because they believe in the rags-to-riches American dream," and he emphasizes "the feeling of self-worth that the street-level dealer's life-style offers" (ibid.).

So young residents in these areas are not simply lazy, and they are most definitely working—they may be working very hard, taking risks, behaving as good businesspeople should, veritable entrepreneurs. But what grows up and comes to dominate in particular local areas is a culture of violence and retribution rather than law and justice; drugs and cash become the currency; and the gang becomes the most powerful social group, often with codes which are antihumane, antidemocratic, and patriarchal and which celebrate machismo.

Some therefore argue that one way to retrieve these communities, to incorporate them, would be through an extension of conventional social institutions, of education, churches, work, training, clubs, and so on. This is the thinking behind the calls for a national "Marshall Plan" for the American cities and some of the drives like that of City Challenge for inner-city development in Britain. It would be even better if alongside these top-down, incorporating approaches there were attempts to support local community networks, to help to build from below. But such secondary structures are not "natural"—they have to be created: many which spring to life only to wither in the harsh inner-city environment could be nurtured through support and resources from other networks elsewhere in the city, especially from local governments.

Young people in poor communities get drawn into criminal activities partly because their talents are not wanted elsewhere. Note, however, that large numbers do struggle with badly paid work and bad conditions, and some go on to college. Note also that one of the most effective forces in cleaning up these neighborhoods has been the cadres of Farrakhan supporters—showing how fundamentalism and authoritarianism step in when a vacuum of legitimate democratic political and social authority is allowed to develop.

Despair and Hope

Urban regeneration schemes throughout the 1980s were mainly concerned with jobs and offices. There is now a need for wider forms of urban regeneration including cultural and public facilities and transport. Especially in the inner cities of the countries of the erstwhile "First World," and London and New York are examples, an additional problem to be addressed, along with poverty, is despair, a turning inward upon themselves of urban communities, which abuse themselves through drugs and alcohol, violence and crime. The key fact explaining this seems to be the lack of connectedness between these poor areas and the rest of the city. And the extent to which so many promises have raised hopes only to be dashed to the ground when they turn out to be mere rhetoric—as with the training schemes, youth opportunity programs, and inner-city initiatives which were offered with much trumpeting but produced little tangible change in the lives of local residents. Indeed, as with the London Docklands redevelopment schemes, the effect was to impoverish and isolate the original residents even more.

The concept of demoralization in a community is hard to define but tangible when experienced and observed. It is not difficult to appreciate the meaning of the term if we consider the situation of Native Americans on the reservations or of sections of the Australian Aborigine communities. And in those societies, as elsewhere in oppressed exploited worlds, retreat into substance abuse has been pronounced and contributed to the decay and possible loss of those cultures. The analogy has not been lost on African Americans who talk of no less than genocide in the inner cities by drugs and murder now compounded by AIDS.

Recent urban riots have been set, it has been said, in "communities that have lost hope," in "forgotten and unwanted communities" (Corbin 1991). When he was the minister with responsibility for the inner cities, Michael Heseltine blamed previous policies for creating such alienated estates—dumping grounds for problem families—and bad management of estates. Often singled out especially for blame in creating this situation are lone-parent families, especially because of the difficulties mothers face in disciplining teenage children. ("Bad mothers" get the blame once again.)

In these accounts, poverty is defined as not solely of material resources but also as a poverty of spirit, a lack of strength—of resilience, of community support—a poverty of social ties and social control. The explanation is often sought in demography: the skilled or the motivated have left, and those left behind are weak families with only one adult in charge. But is this not a denigration of the residents—the view from outside, from the top of the hill? Do the communities seem so inadequate to those who live there?

Gabrielle Cox, a resident for twenty years of Moss Side in Manchester, former councillor and worker for the Low Pay Unit, stresses the different perspective of residents of these stereotyped areas singled out for attention by a sensation-hungry media then dropped from the headlines once the alarm has ceased to sound. Areas like Moss Side, Harlem in New York, and Brixton in London have images created by the media which associate them with drugs, guns, lawlessness, and fear; people are said to be afraid to go out in the streets, which, it is said, are about to collapse into chaos. All those who work hard for their area are singled out for blame—mothers, teachers, social workers, local councillors. This feeling of being looked down on, peered into, increases the residents' feelings of isolation, contributing further to their exclusion. People's voices are not heard; no one takes any notice how hard you shout to tell it as it really is. And the images create their own reality. Insurance premiums go through the roof. It is difficult to get milk delivered or hire goods on hire purchase; doctors are afraid to visit; prejudice and racism operate against job applicants with stigmatized addresses. It becomes harder to motivate children in the schools and for parents to encourage their children to obey the rules: "Where did it get you? That's a mug's game." It is these questions that references to "feelings of self-worth and dignity" and concepts of "empowerment" are trying to address. To give them their due, this is also the aim of boosterism—the PR attempts of urban renewal agencies who try to talk up the "opportunities" and advantages of living and investing in these neglected areas.

There are real problems of social control and the dominance of peer groups in defining standards and values rather than institutions with links with the wider world. The relationship between the generations is crucial here, and not only the weakening of the ties of fathers to their children—a general phenomenon which cuts across all classes. More fundamentally, what is happening is linked to the undermining of the traditional working-class culture of manufacturing, largely a male world in which young men were socialized and disciplined through the apprenticeship system. This coincided also with the rise of youth culture. It seems to be at present an irreversible trend. The question is, what will take its place? Those traditional institutions of the pub, the workplace, and shared involvement in sport, for example, cannot easily be re-created even if we wanted to. But there is a need for some alternative forms of informal social control and socialization—i.e., youth workers, teachers, outreach community workers, a whole array of activities, most of which have ironically also been cut in the last decade due to cutbacks in public expenditure.

Importantly, new thinking is required about life chances and opportunities for those who are not academically minded, whose faces do not fit the style of the newer knowledge and information industries. This is why the stress on training is so important—not just for teaching technical skills but as an institution of integration and, yes, civilization of the young. Now this is done in other societies through military training, through compulsory national service. We may most definitely not want this, but there are alternatives in the form of real training schemes and opportunities available on a *voluntary* basis for adventurous and generous community service.

Constructive guidance and a liberal education are what is being talked about—not just narrow technical training but some introduction to the wide range of activities and experiences that are available as alternatives to the consumer culture which is the only option many of the young are presently offered. We are talking about a youth policy and a broad education—which would include all those elements of liberal education, the humanities and social sciences as well as skills training and life-skills teaching, which have also been under attack over recent decades. Of course, to be meaningful there must be jobs after the training. Training which is a revolving door of make-work and low-paid substitutes is just the opposite; real training with a real job at the end requires an active labor market policy.

Similarly with the family, we need to recognize that the nuclear family is a frail institution, particularly in the harsh climate of the big city. We need new forms of support for child care and child rearing. Perhaps in addition to nurseries and after-school clubs and groups, as a number of people including Michael Young and A. H. Halsey have suggested, the older generation, once formally retired, may be able to take on some parenting functions—share the grandparenting role. There is a need to help schools with the parenting and socializing function they now have—and we need to realize that this is a function of the school not only in the infant classes but also in the teenage years. We must also therefore be prepared to put in the resources for activities additional to those of the purely examination-oriented learning—for games, activities, music, theater, expeditions, and so on.

Real empowerment comes through access to resources. Access to public services can make an enormous difference to the poor and to poor communities. Schools could become real community resources by expanding the hours and times of the day and year when they are open. Colleges and universities could adapt to become more open to the community—as some already do in London and New York.

Public policy is the way this access is made available, and of course this all costs money. We have to recognize you don't get a better society on the cheap.

Social Justice and Social Policy

Is the issue, then, not one of the lack of technical solutions but of the lack of political will? Have we lost the will to create a new society? Are we all Thatcherites now? Have we seen the end of socialism and the end of welfarism? Given the dominance of Reagan-Thatcherism, if defined as the acceptance of a high level of private enterprise, what has happened to "social justice"?

The neoliberal intellectual attack was highly successful in reorienting social policy. Although many of their half-baked and ill-thought-out plans came to grief, most notably in Britain with the poll tax legislation, they were successful in changing the rules of the game. A real shift in culture and politics occurred. And this was arguably their main intention. Changing the language of debate, how we talk about a problem, how we imagine its solution, is the first step.

This success depended on considerable investment by the right in research and propaganda, through the Heritage Foundation, the American Enterprise Association, the Manhattan Institute, the Institute of Economic Affairs, the Centre for Policy Studies, and others, the Thatcher Foundation being perhaps the latest example. At the same time, the intellectual voices of the opposition were denigrated with attacks on the universities, public broadcasting, the teaching and social work professions, and the poverty lobby.

Theodore Marmor and William Plowden have shown how American neoconservatism had a bigger impact in Britain than in the United States. This may be one reason why the tide turned first in the United States, supported as it was by the strength of alternative thinking coming from an intellectual base in the universities. In Britain, the undermining of higher education was carried further than in the United States. This, with the continuance of some elitism in English higher education, may explain some of the timidity and feebleness of the intellectual opposition to the swing to the right in the United Kingdom. Marmor and Plowden comment on the export of ideas already discredited in the United States and their reappearance, apparently without adjustment or effective challenge, in British think tanks, lecture halls, and newspaper columns.

Charles Murray popped up again on British television screens after the 1991 riots and homed in on single mothers as a main cause of these events. In the mid-1980s, Murray had argued that unemployment benefits encouraged young men to withdraw from the labor market, young women to become pregnant outside marriage, and young fathers to decline to marry the mothers of their babies. This thesis, appealing to a mixture of common sense and prejudice, justified cuts in welfare spending and reductions in taxes and state intervention.

Marmor and Plowden wonder how and why such thoroughly discredited ideas about poverty infiltrated the British conventional wisdom. It is, they comment, as if the intellectual assault on Murray that took place in the United States was unknown to Britain. What it does show, however, they comment, is "how seriously the right—especially the libertarian and pro-market right—takes the dissemination of ideas. This is a battle in part for the heads and souls of audiences not simply appeals to the economic interests of Tory workers or ethnic Democrats." Further, "it also reveals the failure of British liberals [and by this they mean social democrats or supporters of social expenditure] in the 1980s to recapture the high ground of debate about the balance between public and private activity" (Marmor and Plowden 1991).

Although academic discussion has often refuted the empirical base of the right-wing accounts, their attack was successful because it changed the questions asked and tied up effort in trying to refute these misplaced charges rather than develop policies and practices to deal with the changing contemporary situation and the emergence of new needs and conditions. In all this, importantly, the debate about poverty, because of the form it took, was severed from discussion of the economy and society.

In New York, the counterargument is seen by some to lie with increased emphasis on specific racial disadvantage especially among the "oldest Americans" (Steinberg 1989, 50), meaning not, however, it seems, Native Americans but African Americans. But the political answer to racism and sexism is not to be found in sectarianism, the weighing of one set of sufferings against another and declaring one or the other to be preeminent (Sivanandan 1989). Action must begin with an analysis which recognizes the transformation of postindustrial economies, the development of new structures in global capitalism and the stratified labor force in the cities. Changes in political economy impact profoundly on politics and parties. As the working class is remade, politics has also to be remade to reflect these cultural and social changes. The old institutional forms and the traditional cultures of masculine labor parties and movements seem increasingly less relevant in a world where the two-income household is required for a decent standard of living and where the growth in employment is in the service sector, with "flexible" terms and conditions. The losers are the unorganized workers in the new sectors, especially those in the casual labor market, and the women and children surviving in one-parent households with only one regular income at most.

It was because it was still taken in by the notion of the comfortable, prosperous, secure working classes (the "bourgeoisified" or "affluent" worker) that the Labour party in the 1992 general election opted to propose in one fell swoop significantly increased tax and insurance contributions from those earning over £22,000 per year (a 9 percent increase in National Insurance contributions) as the main way to pay for its redistributive policies. In a period of recession and insecurity, the electorate, unhappy with the Conservatives, drew back from the risk. If the Labour party had been more in tune with the realities of daily life for working people especially in high-cost areas and in single-income households, this crude policy dividing the population into those earning above and below £22,000 per year might have been questioned and more attention paid to taxing the rich and redistributing public expenditure between different heads, especially reducing the amount spent on the military.

Where one in three marriages end in divorce within twenty years, for one in three "comfortable" households insecurity and downward mobility are very real. In a similar setting of rising insecurity and recession and the awareness that average earnings had fallen or at best remained level over a ten-year period, Clinton offered a combination of austerity and vision that seemed to show a way forward. It was at least, it seemed, worth the risk. Although the votes cast for Clinton in 1992 were actually fewer than those for Dukakis in 1988, and some of the more radical proposals would prove hard to realize, the election of a new government with new faces and some new thoughts breathed some hope for a short while into the American political scene. At least, a change of government and administration reduced the complacency and corruption that enters in when one party rules for too long. In Britain, by contrast, no one was more surprised than Mr. Major when he won the 1992 election. Indeed, for months afterwards he and his government seemed paralyzed by the shock, although the attempt at a new moral agenda was soon to take over.

Redistribution is crucial in all these political discussions. It cannot await economic change and be always secondary to policies for production. But that is not to ignore economic policy: economic and social policy, domestically and internationally, have to be taken together. And discussions of redistributive tax policies must take into account the presence or absence of inherited wealth, fringe benefits, and lifetime earnings or they will be perceived to be, and will in fact be, unfair. All these issues are especially critical for women, especially where they are the sole earner with dependents, who evaluate their options not merely in terms of their hourly rate of pay but in terms of the whole complex of demands placed on them and their children and other dependents.

The Role of Public Policy

In an impressive analysis of the role of public action in preventing hunger worldwide, Amartya Sen and Jean Dreze have pointed to key aspects of public life which favor effective public policies: civic cooperation, social criticism, and political opposition.

They argue for employment creation to protect the entitlements of vulnerable groups and attention to the mechanisms of distribution. Education and health emerge as the key policy areas for effective public action, along with employment generation and income support. The well-planned use of public support, especially the public delivery of health care and basic education, is essential. Their key conclusion is that economic growth alone will not eradicate poverty, a conclusion supported by our awareness that not only poverty, not only homelessness, but *hunger* is now in the United States a major public health problem in this most rich and powerful country.

Serious attention must also be given to thinking about and experimenting with new approaches to service delivery, which involve people in shaping responses to their needs and which do away with the restrictive, rejecting, bureaucratic, and time-wasting practices which form too large a part of many services still. Important attempts at decentralization and the involvement of the nongovernmental sector are happening in some areas and need to be encouraged.

One policy area in particular requires special attention: and that is to do with drugs. In the United States, discussion of the drugs issue is closely linked to perceptions of the condition of African American people and to the contentious concept of the "underclass." Understanding of the social problem of drugs cannot be divorced from judgments about wider sociocultural conditions and appropriate policies. In both countries, conditions in the prisons are deteriorating and the criminal justice systems losing credibility, in Britain because of racism and responses to terrorism but also in both countries partly under the weight of their need to deal with drugs. New York probably has that nation's most serious drug problem, while London is beginning to feel the effects of the targeting of Europe following the saturation of the

American market for cocaine. It is worth reminding ourselves as we discuss poverty in the global economy that illicit traffic in drugs surpasses that of worldwide trade in oil and is second only to armaments.

In the United States, discussion of drugs is a way of discussing social issues without bringing in politics. As the Americanization of British politics increases, as our welfare systems converge to a common Anglo-American model, all that would remain would be for London to move toward adopting American faith in the power of the gun for the convergence to be complete.

While the policy debate on drugs has been set between the two extremes of the war on drugs or legalization, stronger arguments are for some form of public regulation. Public regulation can range from health education through taxation to legal prohibition. The key question is, what kind of regulation?

Here careful distinctions have to be made between different substances, recognizing that there are real differences in the physical and psychological effects of different drugs. The different physiological and behavioral effects of drugs matter. Social controls are crucial in regulating toxic substances. But real prevention should be the ultimate aim. U.S. Congressman Charles B. Rangel, for example, has called for coordinated community-based efforts to address the many social and economic conditions that are at the root of serious drug addiction and drug crime, and he cited homelessness, unemployment, lack of education, lack of health care, lack of family, and above all poverty (*New York Times*, December 26, 1989).

In the end, the debate is about the nature of contemporary society and politics.

POLITICS AND THE POOR

To the astonishment of outsiders, New Yorkers, even those of a liberal or left-wing persuasion, insist on discussing the economic and social problems of New York City as if it were a self-contained society. This myopia is not just a result of the powerful magnetic force which any city of eight million exerts on its inhabitants, nor because of its continuing role as America's financial and cultural capital. It stems at least as much from the sense of impotence which New Yorkers have, along with the rest of the American population, about the possibility of seriously challenging and changing the existing distribution of power and wealth in America. Even with a Democratic president, it seems hard to imagine a program for economic and social reconstruction which goes beyond the city or even beyond the individual.

In the election year of 1992, such was the poverty of American politics and so debased the discourse which passes for political debate that into the vacuum came the politics of racial hatred, ethnic division, and plain fear.

David Duke and his more respectable brother, Pat Buchanan, may have faded away during the 1992 campaign, but their political legacy lives on.

In the absence of a politics of social and economic change and of a new politics and party, race and charges of "racism," real and imagined, sincere and demagogic, have become the central issue. On the occasion of his retirement, in early 1992, after thirty years of writing for the *New York Times*, columnist Tom Wicker observed sadly that racial animosity and fears in New York City were far greater than anything he had ever known growing up in the segregated South (Logan 1992).

Having turned many young black men into criminals and gangsters, middle-class America then beats them down on the basis that they are unpredictable and violent and not to be trusted. Given one trigger of justification, those who are excluded and oppressed predictably rise up in rage, as happened with the riots of 1992.

We speak of "minorities," but the 1990 census confirms that New York is now 43 percent white, 28 percent black, 24 percent Hispanic, and 7 percent "other"—largely Asian. From one perspective, it is "whites" who are the minority in New York. But it is a perspective deeply mired in the very racism which it sometimes decries. "White" is, as Andy Logan (ibid.) points out, taken by the largely self-appointed leaders of "minority groups" to mean non-Hispanic whites; half of all Hispanics, however, call themselves "white." The conflict between blacks and Korean shopkeepers and other "Asians"—once again a category usually referred to as a "community" but which is itself internally diverse—and that between the blacks and those Jews who live in self-isolated communities is well known. Such are the politics of identity—from sexual to gender, from race and ethnicity to national—now sweeping the world, in which New York is only a microcosm. And just as in the rest of the world the totalitarian system which masqueraded as "socialism" sapped the politics of democratic socialism, so too in New York the earlier tradition of class politics has vanished. The result, whatever the rhetoric of identity politics may say, is the recrudescence of the old Tammany Hall–style politics. Different players, to be sure, but no more representative of the groups they claim to speak for than the ward heelers of yesterday.

Thus the city council, elected under the newly court-mandated redistricting plan (which painstakingly designed districts with majorities, or at least with significant minorities, of the groups which were underrepresented on the old city council, which was 75 percent white, mainly Jewish and Italian), is now composed of twenty-one blacks and Hispanics. Yet "in the end," Andy Logan writes perceptively, following the first days of the new council, "things did not seem very different from the old days of the powerful Tammany leaders, who knew who their friends and enemies were and acted accordingly" (ibid.).

At best, this is the politics of weakness, based on the assumption that it is not possible to build a majority around common interests, in which blacks will have the support of whites through an appeal to common interests. The potential viability of such a coalition, one based not on Tammany Hall–style cynicism, was demonstrated by Jesse Jackson in his campaigns, especially in 1988. By speaking class rather than race, Jackson was able to appeal, however momentarily, to white workers, however "racist" their attitudes. From common cause and common experience in the course of building a democratic movement of opposition, i.e., real rather than ersatz "interest group" politics, flows the moral force to undermine the self-destructive psychology of racism. This is the lesson, too, which Martin Luther King Jr. taught.

What is needed is a revival of the language of class, a linking of class and community, but a rephrasing of these ideas to reflect the changes in social and economic life which surround us, changes in the shape and condition of working people today. Until this new language is articulated, racism and nationalism will continue to fill the vacuum of local and world politics with terrifying consequences.

In Britain, it has been argued that the welfare groups need a new agenda. They were wrong-footed by the Thatcher years, pinned down into single-issue fights. But some single-issue campaigns were significant. Child benefit in particular might have been swept away without the Child Poverty Action Group's sophisticated campaigning efforts and construction of broad defensive alliances. But these alliances may now be breaking up. After fighting off the challenge from the right so well through the 1980s, to CPAG's amazement the new remodeled Labour party, aided by certain newspaper columnists, in its project to make itself "electable," began to question its commitment to universal benefits—and all under the guise of a debate on "Social Justice."

Another example of the importance and effectiveness of political action can be seen in the resistance of the "not quite poor" to the poll tax. This was arguably the crucial element that brought down Mrs. Thatcher. Similarly, coalitions against new roads have brought together a wide range of people from different backgrounds, as did the campaign against the Criminal Justice Act.

Other groups at the forefront of action are the churches in both New York and London. They have had considerable success in drawing attention to inequalities in income, the housing crisis, deteriorating public services, and unemployment, not least because their spokespeople speak with the authentic voice of experience.

But these views are easily dismissed by cynics as the pleadings of saints and do-gooders—"not a sound basis for public policy." So if policy is not dictated by altruism, then perhaps it may be by more pragmatic concerns and rational self-interest. The perspective here is that the welfare state is much more than a safety net. It can be justified not simply by any redistributive aims but because it does things which private markets either would not do at all or would do inefficiently. There are strong economic and social reasons supporting welfare states, as found, it is believed, in social democratic European welfare states, which at the same time appear to have stronger national economies. This view rests on the belief that capitalism is incapable of dealing with social questions adequately and thus there is need for public regulation of markets (Galbraith 1990).

In similar vein, Dahrendorf argues for a social state which would guarantee social citizenship rights to all. This would include not only the fight against discrimination but also a considered policy to make sure the underclass and the long-term unemployed were not in effect deprived of their citizenship rights. This may cost money; it may have to be justified not in terms of cost savings and efficiency but in terms of the benefits of social integration and social order.

Dahrendorf cites, in support of this, Rawls's second principle that we should accept social inequalities only if they involve a floor of common and decent opportunities. These questions of justice and entitlements are at the heart of current political discourse and have survived the fierce attempts made in the 1980s to change the discourse of social policy away from discussion of entitlements to discussion of behaviors.

Most of all, however, we need to galvanize the energies and creativity of the people in a move to revive the cities. For such new forces to develop, for genuine innovation to take place, it is essential that we provide a context of a strong civic society, where the rule of law prevails, where there is freedom of expression and association and freedom from fear and intimidation, fair policing, and a fair judicial system.

If we start to talk about institution building in London and New York, we are talking about building up a pluralistic society—rather than the fragmented mass society which appears as the dark shadow over the city. We should look for the possibility of a vital, robust, pluralistic life in which independent associations can thrive—intermediary associations, that vital layer supplementing the work of governmental agencies and working in partnership with them.

The innovations with which we must be concerned are to be judged by their effectiveness in improving the lives of poor people and empowering poor communities. Antipoverty innovations are those which aim to increase integration and inclusion, reduce disintegration and exclusion; they aim at the reduction of inequalities and polarization; in the end they are about shifting resources from the more privileged to the less privileged.

The projects which have the most impact are those which improve primary health and basic education—and those which help people to imagine new solutions, and here the role of the arts can be impressive. "We must recognize that art and architecture are not simply decorative but are part of the essential fabric of a city's identity" (Rogers and Fisher 1992, 225).

But can any of these problems be seriously discussed without taking on the big questions of taxation, of both income and wealth, and of changes in public spending priorities, especially the reduction of the waste of so-called defense spending?

Otherwise, in an era of austerity, the already mean and violent streets of New York will grow more violent and the dead-end politics of race and ethnic division will spread, dividing ever more effectively those who should be joined by a common program of social and economic reconstruction. More police will be hired in a futile attempt to keep in check the tide of crime or, at any rate, to protect the diminishing islands of middle-class safety engulfed by the rage of the unemployed and demoralized minority youth; more prisons will be built in upstate New York to house the same minorities and, providentially, provide employment for the subemployed upstate whites. New York faces terminal decay in the absence of a new political force.

For London the choice is different. Lessons can be learned from New York. There is growing awareness of the failures due to a lack of coherent London government. And Britain itself now stands at a crossroads. Will the choice be to continue to move down the American path, or will there be a shift of course to move closer to Europe? Recognizing that much of the gloss has worn off the European project, it is still the case that in the European Union the balance between individualism and public responsibility seems to have been struck differently.

The fundamental problem today may indeed be, as Dahrendorf has put it, that the majority does not need the minority: the two-thirds–one-third structuring of society, implicit in the Republican and Conservative social policies of the 1980s, lies behind this trend.

> The new minority [the underclass] cannot form itself into a class. . . . This growth of semi-citizens who are marginalised and who cannot defend themselves is a most serious development. . . . Here I see [says Dahrendorf] a major role for private initiative in the widest sense . . . philanthropic foundations, local initiatives, community projects, churches, voluntary organisation and even "charismatic" local leaders. (Dahrendorf 1990).

While we may hold many reservations about the concept of the underclass and feel that it is impossible to use the term without accepting the ideological baggage it carries with it, we might agree with William Kornblum when he writes: "If it must be used at all, I think the term underclass ought to refer to people who have fallen or been pushed into a world of suffering they can escape only *with help from others* in the larger society." (1991, 209)

Transforming the Cities

Recession and unemployment have demonstrated the links between increasing numbers in poverty and growing insecurity for many. A combination of economic restructuring and vicious dismemberment of the welfare state has shattered lives and communities. Large numbers of people have been left with little or no protection against misfortune, unemployment, accident, ill health, divorce, or old age, those contingencies of life which it was the purpose of the welfare state to meet. At the same time, there are worries about changes in family life and community breakdown. That all these processes are connected ought to be obvious, but otherwise intelligent people still insist on discussing them as though the problem were simply one of morality, easily solved by appeals to the values of duty and obligation. Public policies based solely on appeals to the poor to behave less badly or even to the rich and comfortably off to be more generous will never work. Ranked against them are rising tides of racism, fragmentation, and mindless violence. "If not socialism, then barbarism" appears increasingly to be true.

Although it is fashionable to ridicule intellectual activity, what is sorely needed is the hard work of analysis to explain the underlying processes historically and sociologically, delineating the social, cultural, political, and economic processes which lie behind those changes in values and ways of living which are so much feared and deplored. With such an understanding of where we are now, why we live as we do, we ought to be able to build proposals for more effective and beneficial social action and public policy.

All these processes are particularly evident in the cities—arenas of accelerated social transformation, as they have been described. So it is in the cities, and especially in the great cities of London and New York, where global, national, and local forces interact, that the crisis is most acute and where action must begin.

References

Archbishop of Canterbury's Commission on Urban Priority Areas. 1985. *Faith in the City: a Call for Action by Church and Nation.* London: Church House Publishing.

Bennet, J. 1992. "Bronx Youth Shot in Restaurant: 1 of 8 Killings in New York City." *New York Times*, February 2.

Bourgois, P. 1989. "Just Another Night on Crack Street." *New York Times Magazine*, November 12, 31–6.

Coopers and Lybrand Deloitte. 1991. *London: World City Summary Report.* London: Coopers and Lybrand Deloitte.

Corbin, J. 1991. "Panorama." *BBC*, November 4.

Dahrendorf, R. 1990. "Does London Need to Be Governed?" *London Weekend Television "London Lecture,"* December 6.

Dreze, J., and A. Sen 1990. *Hunger and Public Action*. Oxford: Oxford University Press.
Engels, F. 1971 [1844]. *The Condition of the Working Class in England*. Trans. and ed. W. O. Henderson and W. H. Chaloner. Oxford: Basil Blackwell.
Galbraith, J. K. 1990. "Why the Right Is Wrong." *Guardian*, January 26, 23.
Kennedy, R. 1991. *London: World City Moving into the 21st Century*. London: HMSO.
Kornblum, W. 1991. "Who is the Underclass?" *Dissent* (spring): 202–11.
Logan, A. 1992. "Around City Hall." *New Yorker*, January 27.
Marmor, T., and W. Plowden. 1991. "Spreading the Sickness." *Higher* [Times Higher Education Supplement], October 25, 17.
McCormick, D., 1991. "Special Inquiry" *ITV* November 3.
McFate, K. 1991. *Poverty. Inequality and the Crisis of Social Policy*. Washington, D.C.: Joint Center for Political and Economic Studies.
Newman, M. 1992. "Two with Gunshot Wounds Are Charged in Shooting Death of Officer." *New York Times*, February 2.
Rogers, R. and M. Fisher. 1992. *A New London*. London: Penguin.
Sassen, S. 1991. *The Global City: New York, London, Tokyo*. Princeton: Princeton University Press.
Sivanandan, A. 1989. "All That Melts into Air Is Solid: The Hokum of New Times." *Race and Class* 31: 1–30.
Steinberg, S. 1989. "The Underclass: A Case of Color Blindness." *New Politics* 11, no. 3 (New Series): 42–60.
Sudjic, D. 1992. "Towering Ambition." *Guardian*, April 17, 32.
Townsend, P. 1979. *Poverty in the United Kingdom: A Study of Household Resources and Standards of Living*. Penguin.
Wilson, W. J. 1987. *The Truly Disadvantaged*. Chicago: University of Chicago Press.

2

New York under Siege

William Kornblum

New York City is undergoing historic changes that are not well captured by sensational news stories or "hard-hitting" cinema. Popular images of a city torn by violence and demoralized by homelessness and drug use do not adequately represent the profound alterations we are experiencing in the city's economy and in its hundreds of distinct communities. Nor do most popular accounts of life in New York, like Tom Wolfe's bestseller *Bonfire of the Vanities*, offer much insight into how New Yorkers cope with the daily stress of life in a changing city or how a wiser, less ideological federal government than that of the Reagan-Bush years might try to improve conditions inside the cities.

When members of the Bush administration attempted to blame the 1992 Los Angeles riots on urban policies of the Lyndon Johnson "Great Society" period, New Yorkers who know anything about recent history were outraged. Many of them on either side of the political spectrum know that over the years of conservative leadership (something of a laissez-faire oxymoron) urban Americans paid more money in taxes and received far less aid from government in return. On the other hand, what we received from Washington for many years, and in generous supply, was verbal abuse. New Yorkers were told over and again that they failed to make their economy work, failed to protect their citizens, failed to house their poor adequately, and failed to educate their children in the public schools. During the 1992 presidential season, for example, Dan Quayle said all of this and more to a crowd of well-heeled conservatives gathered at a fund-raising dinner in Manhattan. Since the Democrats would be holding their nominating convention in New York, the vice-president of all the people promised to make the failures of "liberal" cities like New York a central feature of the Republican presidential campaign.

My purpose in this essay is not to mount a counterattack but to try, at least on a number of issues, to set the record straight. New York City has always been a laboratory for social change and social policy in the United States. It is well to ask, therefore, how the institutions built by those who took the idea of the commonweal to heart are faring in these times of severe urban crisis. New York's success with public schooling, public housing, and community development (to name only three areas one might describe) has much to offer in the way of examples to a less selfish nation. One finds in these rather critical areas of New York life some alternatives to the tiresome stalemate of American contemporary politics. Too few believe in these alternatives now, however, because of the massive attack on the city's social institutions over the past decade or more. Public schooling, public housing, and community development: each is an area of urban policy where New Yorkers were pioneers. One cannot do justice to their historic efforts in a brief essay. What follows instead are some of the most salient facts about the changes occurring in the city, seen primarily through their effect on schools, housing, and communities. A final warning: aside from the facts themselves, the perceptions and opinions are those of a native New Yorker whose parents and grandparents helped build the communal institutions that are now under such severe attack.

PUBLIC SCHOOLING IN THE IMMIGRANT CITY

Under great pressure from the nation's business classes, and with no opposition from Democrats who feared alienating their immigrant constituents, at the end of the 1980s, Congress approved an increase in legal immigration to the United States from about 450,000 per year to 650,000, with quotas projected to increase to 850,000 per year by the end of the 1990s. The majority of the newcomers enter through New York, Miami, and Los Angeles. Few will leave to establish themselves elsewhere in the United States for at least a generation. Every year, for example, at least thirty thousand Dominicans arrive in New York; fewer than four hundred find their way to Philadelphia, only one hour and a half to the south.

Conservatives make no concessions to the cities for the extra effort they make to educate the immigrants and care for their health and well-being. Certainly, as they frequently argue, there are also benefits to the city from immigration. One sees these benefits in hundreds of immigrant shops and restaurants and small businesses all over the city. But there is also much additional poverty and social stress associated with immigration. These problems the city's agencies and schools are left alone to struggle with. Although immigration policy is established by the federal government, the amount of assistance from the federal government to the public schools of New York and other cities decreased steadily in the 1980s (a point to which I will return).

The deep recession of the early 1990s wiped out almost half a million of the city's jobs, sweeping away all the employment gains made during the decade of the 1980s. Still the immigrants from Latin America and Asia and the Caribbean continue to pour into the city. Of New York's primary school children, at least 45 percent come from homes where English is not the language spoken at the dinner table. Eighty percent of the city's Italians were born here and 67 percent of its Jews, but only 38 percent of its blacks and 30 percent of its Hispanics. And now New York is a "minority-majority" city in which white residents of all national backgrounds comprise 42 percent of the population. Once again, as was true in the late nineteenth century and in the early decades of the twentieth, this is a city of newcomers where terms like "black and white" or "have and have not" demand ethnic and immigrant qualifiers. So the much trumpeted "failure of the public schools" needs to be evaluated in view of the tremendous demands that immigration and increasing poverty place on the city's schools.

What actually does ail our public schools? One hears endless chatter about how U.S. students do not measure up on math or reading or writing and that Chinese and Koreans and Indians will soon be the only ones in our science graduate schools. In New York City, however, school performance has been improving slowly over the past few years. Far too many children (approximately 19 percent) will not finish high school before the age of eighteen, but, high as it might be, the dropout rate has decreased slowly for all groups over the past two decades. Reading and math scores are still far too low, and the violence which plagues the ghettos and slums of the central city affects the schools as well. In 1992, a record number of children were shot inside New York schools or outside on school grounds. But one almost never hears about the miracle of what is actually accomplished. In the average New York City primary school classroom, about half the children are not native English speakers. A teacher can expect about 40 percent of the students to leave and be replaced with new students during the year as the parents seek adequate housing or safer neighborhoods. The curriculum is often a hodgepodge of required material reflecting different interest groups' ideas about what children need to know. Yet slowly, achievement scores have been improving.

Under the firm, at times somewhat autocratic, leadership of Schools Chancellor Fernandez (himself a New Yorker of Puerto Rican descent) the chance arose for some important improvements in the schools and their management. But the challenges only became more burdensome. Schools' budgets were drastically reduced just when added funding support was most needed.

Average class size in many of the most congested community schools in the inner city is already at twenty-eight students per teacher and threatening to go well beyond that in too many schools. No single indicator of educational quality is as telling as class size. All parents want their children to get the teacher's attention. Suburban schools typically pride themselves on low student-teacher ratios. Inside New York City, there is a dire shortage of teacher attention due, in part, to the increasing number of immigrant children in the schools and to the staff cuts the schools have also experienced. The 1990 census informs us that there are 1.78 million children in New York under the age of eighteen years, 24.3 percent of the total city population. Thirty percent of these children live in families officially classified as poor. Over 50 percent reside in single-parent households. So many children in the city's poor communities come from homes where adult attention is in short supply that incidents of acting out and levels of misbehavior are well above what one expects for children who have more adequate care at home and more opportunities for attention in home and school. These have long been serious problems of inner-city education where so many of the students come from poor households and where parents and guardians have few educational advantages to share with the children. Now the city's educators are struggling with the added burden imposed by children and parents who need immediate language attention if they are ever to be able to master the increasing demands of the school curriculum.

Conservatives in and outside the Bush administration continually promoted family education vouchers as the single and sovereign response to the nation's educational problems. The scheme has the beauty of fitting quite well into a television sound bite. One claimed the scheme would work and in the same breath blamed the opposition for not voting it in. Families would be granted some annual sum in the form of chits they could use to pay for any type of school they wish. This would include religious schools and highly innovative (yet somehow profit-making) schools supposedly to be created in the private sector. Public schools would also compete for these vouchers, for the theory is that, faced with competition for their students, they would be forced to become more innovative and efficient.

I have never met a school person who works in the poor or in the lower-middle-class communities of New York City who supports the voucher plan. Although most teachers and administrators support educational reform of various kinds, they are convinced that a voucher system would "cream off" the best students, especially those whose families can afford to supplement whatever meager funding the federal vouchers would supply. The great fear is that competition would leave the public schools inside the cities in an even worse state than they are in now.

Well before the current fad in thinking about individual solutions to the problems of schooling, and following its long history of urban innovations, New York began developing a system of "alternative public schools." Parents are encouraged to "shop around" for the schools that fit their educational requirements, that offer the kind of programs and qualities they are looking for. Educators, for their part, are encouraged through special leaves and grant programs to work with like-minded colleagues in developing smaller schools based on an innovative educational model. Often these schools are housed together in an older school building. Elsewhere they share space with other institutions. At first they were most commonly found in Manhattan, where middle-class parents had long been clamoring for alternatives to the antiquated public schools. But increasingly these alternative schools within the public system are springing up in the outer boroughs as well. The demonstrated success of this model of choice within the public sector has received national attention. New York educators like Deborah Meier, the founder of a number of successful alternative public schools, are in demand all over the United States and especially in cities where the multiple needs of immigrant and poor children are growing in severity.

Defending New York's Public Housing

Census figures also show that 20 percent of the city's children live in federally sponsored "public housing" projects, almost all of them built in the 1960s or earlier. On the housing front the greatest volume of erroneous received wisdom and self-serving policy tends to be directed at this same public housing, a creature of the New Deal and liberal Republican administrations. In New York City, there are about 520,000 people living in federally funded public housing, almost all of it built before the 1970s. In addition to this official population, there are an estimated one hundred thousand or more people "doubled up" with kin or friends in the apartments.

Were it not for this precious stock of low-rent flats, New York's rate of homelessness would be even worse than it is. Yet American intellectuals almost invariably think of public housing as an abject failure of the hypertrophied welfare state. Public housing is said to be a cradle of the dependent underclass. Reagan and Bush followers liked to call it "federal slum housing." As usual the truth is mainly elsewhere.

In 1988, the U.S. Department of Housing and Urban Development commissioned a major inventory of the entire U.S. stock of public housing—a paltry 1.5 million housing units where reside some 3.5 million residents. In France, with one-fifth the U.S. population, there are about 12.5 million residents of public housing. Motivated by the hope that it would reveal how sordid conditions are in the nation's public housing, the Reagan administration study of U.S. housing projects found that only 15 percent of the projects were stereotypical slum housing such as one sees in the worst Chicago projects. New York's public housing was singled out as the best big-city federal housing in the nation. And why not; in none of the city's 360 or so housing projects does one find such burned-out apartments or semiabandoned buildings as one sees in the notorious public housing projects which command all the media attention. In any case, the report's findings must have been buried with a deep anger, for they had no influence whatsoever on later public pronouncements.

The Bush administration continued to lend its support to ill-conceived plans to sell the housing. A feature of the Kemp wing of the Bush administration was to allow "qualified" tenants in public housing projects the opportunity to buy their flats and become property owners "with a real foothold in the American Dream of home ownership." (Do people who get to buy their council flats realize the British Dream of home ownership?) Before the Los Angeles riots, the president had actually never embraced this proposal from his housing secretary and sometime political competitor, Jack Kemp. Bush's closest advisors warned him, with good reason, that while the Kemp "New Paradigm" proposals sounded as if they were addressing social problems without committing massive public funds, in fact if they were to be accomplished nationwide they would cost money and would lead to the trap of meeting the liberals on their own social policy turf. After the riots, however, the administration wanted desperately to appear to take some action on behalf of the central cities. President Bush began calling for more forceful legislation to speed the sale of the public housing to tenants. In fact this idea, and the promise of small business loans and the creation of "enterprise zones" in the ghettos, were the only proposals advanced, other than the usual exhortations to lock up the evildoers and renew the strength of the family.

If there were as large a stock of public housing in the United States as there is in England or France, or even if the minimal stock of U.S. public housing were expanding, however slowly, it would make sense to offer flats for sale to tenants under some conditions and in some areas. But there were almost no additions to the nation's already inadequate federal public housing inventory after the Reagan years began. To sell the limited supply off, while thousands of families are demanding a chance to move from their decaying tenements into the subsidized flats, and when there has been no growth of low-cost housing in the public sector for well over fifteen years, seems merely another cruel joke on the poor. Everyone involved in actually seeking housing for the poor in New York City, or those who have responsibilities for administering the existing housing projects, or those who seek to find shelter for the city's growing number of homeless families, agree that the Kemp housing legislation did not come close to addressing the need to build more low-cost housing. The city's community of housing advocates is not locked in to older formulas for federally subsidized housing. They want a far wider array of public support for low-cost housing than has ever existed before, but their voices have still to be heeded.

Housing activists in New York City (as in other major cities) often advocate a form of satellite public housing. Public housing funds under this system are used to rehabilitate abandoned or blighted apartment houses near the larger projects. Tenants of the large projects who can afford payments on a modest loan are then offered the opportunity to buy a remodeled apartment in the new buildings, thereby freeing up a flat in the federal housing project for a family on the waiting list (which in New York includes over two hundred thousand families). New York City and State have conducted some exemplary demonstrations of this strategy. Without considerable renewal of federal funding for housing rehabilitation and public housing construction, however, little easing of the serious housing emergency for the inner-city poor is likely.

New York's public housing projects are not always the most desirable places to live, but after more than a decade of disinvestment in the housing needs of the poor, they offer some of the most dependable and secure low-cost housing available anywhere in the city. Their tenants' councils are among the city's most active grass-roots organizations. This has been true in many instances for decades. Public housing in the United States was pioneered in New York, where the needle trades unions and civic voluntary associations built models of what would later become the system for federal subsidies of low-cost housing. Many in New York and elsewhere, who know the vital role this housing has come to play in the life of the city, are itching for a chance to finally begin some serious housing construction and rehabilitation with help from the federal government. Block after block of abandoned housing in the city's poor communities, in the Bronx and Central Brooklyn and Northern Manhattan and parts of Queens, await this vital stimulus to community development.

NEW YORK COMMUNITIES IN AN ERA OF FEDERAL NEGLECT

For Americans who do not live in or near New York City, the magical looming presence of Manhattan fully encompasses their perception of New York. Many Europeans also hold such a Manhattan-centric view, as well they might since within Manhattan there are not only the spires of commerce and the great cultural institutions of the city but well-known and complex communities like Greenwich Village, Harlem, the Lower East Side, the Upper East Side gilded ghetto, the Upper West Side (that somewhat zany cradle of the city's progressive politics), Chinatown, SoHo, and others. But who has heard of Elmhurst, New Dorp, Maspeth, Jackson Heights, Hunts Point, Crotona, Far Rockaway, Tottenville, or East New York? These and scores of other communities in the city's hinterland are usually terra incognita to non–New Yorkers, as they are to many natives. Communities like Howard

Beach or Bensonhurst or neighborhoods of the South Bronx that are featured in sensational news stories and films may become "known" worldwide (in a warped sense) for a brutal event or a condition of racial and ethnic tension or a great heist. This does not mean one actually knows much about how daily life continued after the bad events occurred in those places. And for the native New Yorker, especially one who did not grow up in Manhattan and does not live there now, the city's political boundaries are increasingly arbitrary. Communities in Nassau County on Long Island or those on the PATH Train across the Hudson in New Jersey, or the heavily minority communities north of the Bronx, in Westchester, are thought of as part of the city in a social and cultural sense because one has friends and relatives and workmates there. In mentioning these communities to friends from England, the fact that they are a few minutes over the political boundary becomes insignificant. Unfortunately for the inner city's tax revenues, the political and economic separation of these older suburban communities is of major fiscal importance. And these are not small neighborhoods either but residential and commercial areas with thousands upon thousands of residents, such that the sum of their populations added to that of the city's communities yields the fifteen or twenty million residents of the New York metropolitan area (depending on how imperiously one defines the region).

These communities throughout the greater city all have their ethnic and racial characteristics and their particular class composition. Some are among the most densely populated urban places in the world; others are mainly row houses and detached homes and have become the older, inner suburbs of the region. Many of the communities on the edge of the city had their most rapid growth after World War II but are already receiving their second or third wave of new residents. The immigration and migration to the city is occurring with such speed and at such a magnitude that there is hardly any community which is not touched in important ways by it. Since the 1960s, the city proper has "exported" about two million white residents, most of whom have been replaced with new immigrants from all parts of the world. New Yorkers like to use metaphors of melting pots or rainbows or tossed salads to describe the mixing of groups and cultures in the city, but these meteorological or kitchen images mask the tensions and conflict such rapid change brings with it in many of these communities.

The city's far-flung communities are among its greatest strengths, but they also pose obstacles to progress on citywide problems like homelessness and drug addiction. Most of the communities, especially those outside Manhattan, are fairly undistinguished; they make the city mundane, rather like any other urban place in America. The communities shelter their residents from many of the shocks of New York life. When there is a water main disaster or a subway fire and hundreds are evacuated with some injuries and deaths, New Yorkers shake their heads in dismay at how bad things are getting. But in the warm company of the tavern mates or the parish friends or the ladies on game night—neighbors and street-corner acquaintances who cluck in sympathy—one feels less afraid and alone, and so the memory of the disaster or most recent outrage fades, to be replaced immediately with a fresh one. Yet each outrage closes New Yorkers a bit more into their communities. They use less of the entire city with each great shock or feel just slightly more ill at ease on the subway. They become more urgently dependent on the safety of their community and more inclined against any new housing or residential drug treatment programs or other measures that would address the larger needs. "Not in my back yard," they shout at public meetings. And these declines in their feeling toward the city itself, the greater city outside their own community, become a fact reflected in the opinion polls and the studies of what people do with their time.

When *Time* reported in its "Rotting Big Apple" cover story (September 17, 1990) that 59 percent of New Yorkers interviewed said they would choose to live somewhere else rather than stay in New York, this seemed to many commentators a shockingly high figure. An earlier CBS–*New York Times* poll (June 17, 1990), however, had similarly found that 59 percent hoped to live somewhere other than the city. The CBS–*Times* polls also produced evidence of trends in this disaffection: at the end of 1981, 48 percent hoped to live somewhere else; by 1985, with its financial and real estate sectors heated by foreign investment, economic conditions were improved and the disaffected had dropped to 42 percent. These differences show that opinions about the city are highly sensitive, as one would expect, to changes in the regional economy, and a serious recession like the one the city's working class and poor began experiencing some time ago is reflected in these negative opinions about the city. But when interviewers from the Center for Social Research at the City University of New York Graduate School asked a large sample of New Yorkers about their communities as well as about their opinions of the city, they found that the majority (53 percent) would highly recommend their community to a newcomer while far less than a majority (42 percent) would be likely to recommend the city of New York to a prospective newcomer. And as one might expect, the more affluent the respondent, the more likely she or he was to recommend both the community and the city.

When the sensational episode of teenage "wilding" occurred in Central Park in April 1990 (including the infamous jogger rape), followed by the equally sensational killing of a young African American, Yusef Hawkins, in Bensonhurst, Brooklyn, the feeling in New York communities that race relations were taking a major turn for the worse increased in the polls from 60 percent to 72 percent (CBS-*Times*, June 20, 1990). Shortly after the violence, however, a Center for Social Research study of people who go to Central Park showed that a majority of park users continued to believe the park was becoming a safer place due to the city's anticrime efforts there. But this research also noted a rather sharp decrease in use of Central Park by people from the communities outside Manhattan, another piece of evidence to show that people can feel their own community and its amenities are not so bad even when others are frightened away by television and newspaper stories of violence. Of course, a sadder consequence of the violence is that the city becomes steadily more fragmented into communities where residents feel defended and somewhat secure. Meanwhile the great public spaces—Times Square, Central Park, the subways—these places or public systems that embody the aspirations of the entire city become more feared.

Former Mayor David Dinkins's brilliant police commissioner, Lee Brown, attempted to institute a new program of community policing which would draw on some of the strengths of the city's communities. A program which might seem routine to an English or continental city, the "daring" plan in New York was to require police officers to decrease their automobile patrols in favor of more labor-intensive street duty. It is not easy to entice any Americans out of their cars, and the police have made their patrol vehicles into personal forts. To increase the beat walking and the reliable presence of police officers where they are most needed can be an important step toward more effective responses to the kind of teenage violence that eventuated in the Central Park "wilding" episode or the Bensonhurst killing (some would say lynching). It might also provide part (but just part) of the answer to the epidemic of drug-related killings and random shootings of the past few years.

The crack epidemic peaked in New York City sometime in 1988, at least as measured by the volume of users and street drug sales. The escalating violence now associated with street drug markets is due in great measure to the presence of a large number of street drug hustlers (many of whom are also addicts themselves) who are chasing a dwindling number of potential buyers. This market competition is aggravated by increased police pressure on the retail dealers and by the easy availability of devastating firepower. New York City and New York State can pass all the gun control legislation they might wish, but the failure of any national leadership on this issue will continue to make local and state laws ridiculous. Presidents and Congress have been simply too afraid of the gun lobby to act appropriately on this issue.

In the communities, however, there is hope that a new spirit of cooperation among city officials, police, and local leaders can improve conditions even without a breakthrough on gun control. But however brilliant the police commissioner and however avid the police officers are to try a new program of community policing, the sad truth is that such innovations require more officers, which in turn requires more funds. Since far more individual tax dollars in the United States flow to the federal government than to city or state, it is reasonable to ask what one can expect in the way of help on this problem from the national level.

Americans feel well protected against sudden attack from Canada or Mexico, but what about some help battling the greater threat from violence in the city streets? A very quick look at some simple budget facts is instructive in this matter. From every $100.00 the U.S. government in Washington collects in taxes, it spends about $26.00 on national defense, $28.00 on Social Security, $13.00 on income security (federal pensions, unemployment insurance, food and nutrition assistance, Aid to Families with Dependent Children, etc.), and $18.00 on debt interest. Of the remaining $13.00, it spends about $1.00 to run the federal government, $4.00 on health care services and research (not including Medicare), $3.00 on transportation (especially highways for the sacred automobile), and $0.02 on criminal justice assistance to the states and cities. One need not be a sophisticated political theorist, nor would it take a great deal of formal training in social theory of any variety, to present these facts to New Yorkers or other Americans. But it is rare to hear sensible discussion of how our public funds are spent. For too long, we have heard "single and sovereign" solutions to complex issues and exhortation to better behavior. Finally and rather desperately, Republicans attempted to appropriate the idea of empowerment as a seemingly noncost item in what some hoped would become a conservative-populist "New Paradigm." But when it is suggested that two dollars per hundred be shifted from national defense to community law enforcement assistance—with community leaders guaranteed a say in how the funds should be spent—well, that is labeled the return of the "Old Paradigm" (spend-and-increase bureaucracies).

Similar sad tales can be told about prospects in the United States for improved primary and secondary education or for increased low-cost housing to address the shameful problem of homelessness. The federal government in 1992 gave communities back seventy-six cents on every hundred dollars of tax income for help in educating their children. This sum has decreased steadily over the last thirteen years. By far the greatest share of the cost of education is paid for by real estate taxes, so levels of funding for schools in U.S. cities vary widely from one community to another. As I indicated earlier in this essay, the poor communities of New York, lacking the independent tax base of the more affluent communities outside the city proper and unable to command the political influence to improve their schools, suffer the most loss in mean times like these.

As I have attempted to show in these brief excursions into the city's communities, its schools, and its public housing, New York is no newcomer to coping with hard times and social stress. It has long-standing traditions of social democratic approaches to housing, job creation, intervention in violence, educational change in the public sector, and much more. One need only think of the importance of its cultural institutions, its museums and performance institutions like Lincoln Center, to remember some of the city's outstanding collective achievements that extend far beyond the scope of this essay. But all its achievements as a city are always had with less support from the national society than is generally the case for other great cities. After all, unlike other world cities New York is not a national capital. The growth of its institutions depends on local talents drawn from all its social classes. Of course, the current of thinking in the United States has not favored such communal solutions. Much of what the city has achieved in the past has been denigrated as if it were a failure across the board.

New Yorkers do not believe this. They have a lively grass-roots democracy; they take pride in their social institutions, their schools, their public housing, even in their city government, and, of course, in their central cultural institutions. But as we have seen in numerous examples, they have not received anything like a fair shake from the national government. In fact, they have been penalized in a real sense for their past successes. But in the United States, this is also true for Chicago, Los Angeles, Miami, and all the major cities whose primary products these days are educated, sophisticated people who leave for better opportunities elsewhere. There is at last growing discontent about these inequalities. It began to become evident well before the Los Angeles riots; it is accelerating and is likely to produce some fundamental realignments in the way wealth is distributed in the United States in the next century. There is an excellent chance that the era of community development and local democracy is about to begin, at least in the most tenacious and innovative cities like New York.

3

Soup Kitchen Blues: Postindustrial Poverty in Brooklyn

William DiFazio

White man. Forty years old. Middle class. Warehouse manager with twenty years of experience. Hasn't worked in a year.

> You should see the people I have to compete with. I'm waiting for a job interview in a moving company. Beautiful operation. They liked me but they said they didn't want to train me. It's not because I'm obese. At least not this time. It's a computerized operation, and I would have to be trained on the computer. But I'm sitting waiting for the interview, the other guy waiting to be interviewed is an MBA, also my age. Knows how to use computer. Laid off from Wall Street, $80,000-a-year job. He's competing with me. I told him that I just applied for a warehouse job at Busch Terminal. He asks me for the information and if I mind that he'll apply for the job. I give him the address. He's more desperate than I am. How am I going to get a job, I have all on-the-job experience and only a two-year college degree. How can I compete for warehouse jobs with MBAs? And it happens all the time.

Hossein, the director of the Bread and Life Soup Kitchen at Saint John the Baptist Church in Bedford-Stuyvesant, is trying to get him a job. They have five job counselors, and they can't find him a job.

Black man. Forty years old. Homeless. Begging on the G train in Queens.

> You look at me and you say I should get a job. That I'm a bum. Why am I bothering you. But I just want some change so I can get something to eat, a room for the night. You know that there's people doing drugs, killing each other, raping children, doing all kinds of terrible things. I'm just asking you for some money. And you say that I should get a job. Well let me tell you there aren't any jobs out there. If there were jobs in Brooklyn and Queens there wouldn't be people on this train going to

Manhattan to work. And every time they advertise a job there wouldn't be 150 people waiting for that job. There aren't any jobs out there. It's a lie that there are jobs for everyone. And that's why people are robbing, stealing, doing drugs, murdering. There aren't any jobs out there. So please give me some change. God bless you.

White man. January 20, 1989, President George Bush's Inaugural Address.

It is to make kinder the face of the Nation and gentler the face of the world. My friends, we have work to do. There are homeless, lost and roaming. There are the children who have nothing, no love and no normalcy. There are those who cannot free themselves of enslavement to whatever addiction—drugs, welfare, the demoralization that rules the slums. There is crime to be conquered, the rough crime of the streets. There are young women to be helped who are about to become mothers of children they can't care for and might not love. They need our care, our guidance, though we bless them for choosing life.... I have spoken of a Thousand Points of Light, of all the community organizations that are spread like stars throughout the Nation, doing good. We will work hand in hand, encouraging, sometimes leading, sometimes being led, rewarding. We will work on this in the White House, in the Cabinet agencies. I will go to the people and the programs that are the brighter points of light, and I'll ask every member of my government to become involved. The old ideas are new again because they're not old, they are timeless: duty, sacrifice, commitment, and a patriotism that finds its expression in taking part and pitching in. (Bush 1989, 2)

White man. President Bill Clinton, Economic Address to Joint Session of Congress, February 17, 1993.

Later this year we will offer a plan to end welfare as we know it. I have worked on this issue for the better part of a decade and I know from personal conversations with many people, that no one—no one wants to change the welfare system as badly as those who are trapped in it. I want to offer the people on welfare the education, training, the child care, the health care they need to get back on their feet, but say after two years they must get back to work, in private business if possible, in public service if necessary. We have to end welfare as a way of life and make it a path of independence and dignity. (*New York Times*, February 2, 1993)

White woman. I'm serving juice with Louella at the soup kitchen. Kate walks up for some water and says hello. She is in her thirties but looks older. She has sores on her face. When she first started coming to the kitchen she weighed thirty pounds more than she does now. All the junkies assume they have AIDS. I assume she has AIDS.

"Bill, can I have seconds on the Kool-Aid?" I give her more Kool-Aid and ask her if she has a sore throat.

I have a bad throat. I can't get rid of it. Living on the streets it's cold and you can't get warm. Now I'm living on the subway platform. Sometimes I ride the trains but they chase you. My counselor wants me to go to the shelter in South Harlem. I tell her that if she's so hot on the shelter, why don't you go there. It's not safe. Everyone is always fighting. They fight over sheets, over beds, over food, everyone has a bad attitude. I hate the shelters, everyone is always fighting.

Her coughing is increasing. Not knowing what to say, I tell her that she has to find a way to keep warm.

I won't go to the shelter. The subway's bad but not as bad as the shelter. The other day some kids attacked me on the subway. One of then whacked me in the back with a 2-by-4 [wooden beam]. I thought he broke my back. It's still killing me. They didn't try to rob me or anything. The fucking bastards thought it was funny to whack me with a 2-by-4.

A male friend walks over and says they have to go. She says good-bye and leaves.

A Vocabulary Shift

In American social science and social policy of poverty, social welfare, hunger, and homelessness, there has been a "vocabulary shift" (Rorty 1989, 78; Fraser 1989, 95). For Richard Rorty, vocabularies are contingent rather than true; "a recognition of that contingency leads to a recognition of the contingency of conscience, and . . . both recognitions lead to a picture of intellectual and moral progress as a history of increasingly useful metaphors rather than of increasing understanding of how things really are" (Rorty 1989, 9). In the vocabulary of social policy, the metaphors of the conservatives have become dominant. In the mid-1970s, with the continuous increase in poverty, the recession, the oil crisis, the fiscal crisis, there was a vocabulary shift. "Community control" and "black power" gave way to the language of "benign neglect" and the "failure of social programs." The poor became "pathetic victims," "junkies," "the homeless." Vocabulary shifts signify the political shifts of the 1970s and 1980s. At first, the language of social change became the liberal language of advocacy. The poor could no longer talk for themselves; they were no longer part of dynamic social movements; experts would speak for them. The language of activism first was overturned by the liberal language of advocacy, and then that gave way to the new conservative hegemony. The "language of possibility" faded, and the conservative "language of individual achievement" came to the center. This shift excluded the poor, "a future in which human freedom was entrusted to as yet undreamt-of metaphors, vocabularies unborn" (Rorty 1991, 26).

Though the Reagan administration guaranteed that the "truly needy" would be provided for by the "social safety net," social welfare programs were slashed in the 1980s and by the Bush administration into the 1990s. Poverty, hunger, and homelessness, a level of destitution unknown in the United States since the Great Depression, were the results of these budget cuts. Bush did react to this new poverty, not by redirecting federal money to the poor, but by promising that the private sector would make up the difference through the mobilization of volunteers, "the Thousand Points of Light."

The language of possibility has become the one-dimensional language of the free market, in Rorty's sense, a "final vocabulary." "It is final in the sense that if doubt is cast on the worth of these words, their user has no non-circular argumentative recourse. Those words are as far as he can go with language: beyond them there is only helpless passivity or a resort to force" (Rorty 1989, 73). The key terms in the final vocabulary of conservative social policy are "work," "productivity," "moral," "duty," "responsibility," "sacrifice," "achievement," "free market," "competition," and "patriotism."

Both conservative and liberal social scientists have been transformed by this vocabulary shift. The victory of conservative policy makers is not just that their views have become dominant but that liberal social scientists and their policy experts now speak the language of limitations of the free market. For them economic redistribution through taxation and government intervention to correct the significant increases of homelessness and hunger have been severely restricted by the forced austerity of budget cuts.

Programs for the poor are determined not by needs but by market forces. The new poverty advocates speak the language of accommodation and survival maintenance. This can be seen in two government studies. A Congressional bill, *America 2000 Excellence in Education Act*, proposed to reform education in the United States by creating "New American School Communities" in which federal money would be allocated to these public schools based on standards of excellence (Bill HR 2460, Washington, D.C., May 23, 1991). Schools in poor districts which were already underfunded would have to compete with schools in middle-class and wealthy districts which were already well funded. "The Bush administration argued that the competition for funds would make the poor schools shape up or shut down" (*New York Times*, July 12, 1991).

The second study, *Beyond Rhetoric: A New American Agenda for Children and Families*, by the National Commission on Children, reported on the condition of poor, battered, unhealthy, homeless, and hungry children in the United States. "The National Commission on Children calls on all Americans to work together to change the conditions that jeopardize the health and well being of so many of our youngest citizens and threaten our future as an economic power, a democratic nation and a caring society. Our failure to act today will only defer to the next generation the rising social, moral and financial costs of our neglect. Investment in children is no longer a luxury, but a national imperative" (National Commission on Children 1991, xxxviii).

The Commission proposed "$52 billion to $56 billion in new federal funds in the first year" (ibid., xxxv). This is not feasible in the current austere fiscal condition. It is not cost-effective. It is too costly, and it will increase taxes. It will hinder American competitiveness in the global market. The language of possibility is quickly muted. Liberals must accommodate or become silent. The poor do not have a voice; without a social movement they are spoken for. Advocates, though well meaning, are isolated and impotent. They cannot speak the vocabulary of social change. They "settle for"; they "do the best they can." Without power, they engage in piecemeal struggles. They do not struggle for new housing but for the right of the homeless to have a shanty town in Tompkins Square Park on the Lower East Side of Manhattan. Instead of struggling for the legalization of drugs and of extensive programs for addicts and poor people infected with AIDS, they provide clean needles for junkies to prevent AIDS or soup kitchens in Bedford-Stuyvesant, Brooklyn, to feed endless lines of hungry people. The vocabulary of advocacy is never a transformative vocabulary; instead it rules out social movement, rules out change, rules out possibility. It supports the status quo, and for the poor this means their poverty is permanent.

The first part of this chapter describes the everyday life of poor people at the Bread and Life Soup Kitchen in Brooklyn. The second part summarizes the two main thrusts in poverty policy, one conservative and one liberal. The third part outlines the conditions of the poor in postindustrial America. In this context, I argue that the liberal and conservative policies suffer from the same defect; they both contend that employment is the solution to the problem of poverty.

I contend in this paper that postindustrial poverty is a function of income and not of jobs.

The Soup Kitchen

In the spring of 1989 we are serving lunch to twelve to thirteen hundred hungry men and women (guests) from Monday to Friday. They are served efficiently in a friendly and courteous manner. Saint John's Bread and Life Program is a voluntary soup kitchen in Saint John the Baptist Church in Bedford-Stuyvesant, Brooklyn. Crack and heroin are sold openly in the streets or in the abandoned buildings that surround the church. Crack vials, with their multicolored plastic tops, litter the streets and sometimes find their way into the kitchen. Periodically a guest may smoke some crack inside the kitchen, but this is extremely rare. The majority of soup kitchen guests are not heavy drug users. They are almost all very poor, either working or on public assistance. Most live in public housing projects or tenement buildings. Some live in shelters, in welfare hotels, or on the streets or in subway stations. 1989 is hard times in the largest black neighborhood in Brooklyn.

The Bread and Life Program is run by its director, Hossein Saadat, and the daily operations of the soup kitchen by Sister Bernadette Szymcak. Though the soup kitchen is the largest part of the Bread and Life Program, it also includes job counseling, fund-raising, medical care, drug counseling, and housing and welfare assistance staffed by doctors, social workers, medical assistants, secretaries, and volunteers. Independent of the Bread and Life Program, Saint John the Baptist Church Pastor Fr. Thomas Hynes has housing assistance, a food pantry, and a school, which is also providing training in computer literacy. These are excellent voluntary facilities. They successfully provide service to a community in great need. At the same time, it only serves a small proportion of the community. It cannot do enough. The people of Bedford-Stuyvesant need more help. Federal, state, and city budget cuts have been disastrous for this community, and for people throughout the United States. In the first four years of the Reagan administration alone, health, education, and welfare spending was cut 20 percent. These radical cuts of social programs continued into the Bush administration. Two presidential administrations had declared war on the poor.

These budget cuts occurred in the context of serious wage declines in the United States. From 1973 to 1990, wages either stagnated or declined (Peterson 1991, 29–31). The United States has been the "big job machine" and has continually created jobs since the 1960s. The 1980s seemed to continue the trend, "but nearly three out of five (58 percent) of new jobs created between 1979 and 1984 paid $7,400 or less a year (1984 Dollars). In contrast, less than one in five of the additional jobs generated between 1963 and 1979 had paid such low wages" (Harrison and Bluestone 1984, ix).

With "real incomes" in stagnation or decline because of the decline of American manufacturing, deindustrialization, disinvestment, and severe budget cuts, the poor in American inner cities were ravaged. "By 1988, the share (income) going to the lowest fifth of families had dropped from 5.4 percent in 1975 to 4.6 percent in 1988." In 1988 the lowest fifth earned $7,669 per year, and 50 percent of American families earned $22,389 per year (Peterson 1991, 33).

As the living standards of American poor people declined, so did the poverty rate. As Michael B. Katz tells us in *The Undeserving Poor*, the attempt was to diminish the poor through statistical manipulations; as the budgets were cut midway through the Carter administration, the poverty line was redefined. "In 1960, the poverty line was 48 percent of the median family income for a family of four; by 1980, it had dropped to 34 per cent" (Katz 1989, 168).

As Ruth Sidel in *Women and Children Last* points out, Aid to Families with Dependent Children (AFDC) is the major welfare program in the United States. As needs increased, benefits decreased and the proportion of poor people receiving these reduced benefits declined. "The policies of the Reagan administration resulted in a dramatic drop in the number of poor families receiving AFDC. In 1979, 88 percent of all poor families were receiving AFDC; by 1983, only 62.9 percent were AFDC recipients. If we examine the number of poor children receiving AFDC, the discrepancy is even greater. After a high of 83.6 per cent of poor children receiving AFDC in 1973, by 1983 only 53.3 per cent were recipients" (Sidel 1986, 87).

These changes can be seen at the soup kitchen. In 1982 through 1983, 50 guests per day were served; by April 1989, 1,026 per day were being served. In 1991, it served 700 to 800 guests per day. This decrease was the result not of a decrease in need but of decisions by the Bread and Life staff and Catholic Charities that they could not finance or continue to safely serve over a thousand guests per day.

December 1, 1989. The soup kitchen is getting more and more crowded even though it's check day. It's cold, people huddling together on the line that winds down Willoughby Street. Everyone is waiting for the soup kitchen to open. As I wait on line, a man goes through the line asking, "You want dope, good dope?" Bill, who works at the door, allows some people to wait inside, where it's warm. People are irritable. They begin to yell at Bill to let them in. Richard, a soup kitchen volunteer, is standing next to Bill. A woman on line seeing Richard starts to yell at him, "No wonder the line is moving so slowly, they have the dwarf at the door." The woman has two broad (a quarter-inch wide and three inches long) scars on her face. It is not uncommon for these poor black women to be bruised or have facial scars. Women at the soup kitchen have told me that they are the result of the brutality of their boyfriends or husbands. Recently a black woman in the kitchen told me, "These women say look at how much he loves me and they come in with a broken nose or scars that make their faces look like a road map. That's love? That's not love. A man beats you up is a disgrace.... These men are good for nothing."

Most of the talk on the line is everyday talk. They trade information or anecdotes about social services, or they exchange neighborhood gossip, or they engage in good-natured fooling around, or they complain about the weather. The black man next to me tells me he is feeling sick. "I changed my methadone program because I'm working part-time now. I'm sick but I want to eat. If I don't eat now when am I going to eat. Oh, I just went in yesterday, but my hours are different, I'm all screwed up." He's on a take-home program. He gets three bottles of methadone, one a day. This reduces the amount of time necessary for him to go to the clinic and makes it easier for him to work. "I can't make it, I'm going to the clinic." I ask, "Do you have your bottle?" He answers, "Yeah, yeah, I got to go." He leaves. If he doesn't have his bottle, the nurse doesn't have to medicate him. He'll return to the clinic and give the nurse his bottle, demonstrating that he hasn't sold it. She'll make him drink a bottle in front of her and supply him with bottles until Monday.

Another black man standing next to me is also on methadone.

I haven't worked in years. I could never be on a take-home program. I've got dirty urine. I take Valium, it relieves the pressure, especially since I'm detox now. I hate it. I'm going back on methadone. Since I detoxed I have no energy. I functioned better. When I took methadone I never cheated. I never took other drugs. Except Valium. I was an intravenous drug user for twenty-five years. I can't function without it. I'm too old. The methadone saved my life. I plan to be on methadone for the rest of my life.

We finally get in. Bill asks me what I'm doing on line: "Too lazy to work today?" He laughs. I tell him that I'll work later. I sit down with José. I know that he's a single man on public assistance and that I would like to ask him some questions about welfare. He also jokes with me about not working today. I laugh and ask him to explain check day.

Well, today is SSI [Social Security] check today. You get SSI on the first of the month. That's why there's fewer people here than usually. On Tuesday, it's emergency food stamps. On Thursday, a lot of people will be getting welfare checks and regular food stamps. But it's all different. Even the days are different. But SSI always comes on the first of the month.

I ask him, "What are your benefits?" José responds:

I get $100 every two weeks that's welfare. I don't get SSI. I get $90 once a month, food stamps. And I get a housing check, a rent check. I endorse it and give it to the superintendent, he deposits it. I can't cash it. Only the landlord can cash it. I think the maximum rent that they'll give for a single man is $215. Not much. But different people get different amounts. My buddy here gets $111 in food stamps but no welfare, everyone's different. I try to eat here as much as possible and then save $30 a month of my food stamps. All the bodegas around here will buy them. They give you $7 cash for $10 of food stamps. It gives me some freedom. Yeah, some buy drugs and alcohol, but you don't really make enough and you need necessities. A shirt, cigarettes, go to a movie. I also will use them to go to restaurants. Get bacon and eggs for breakfast. I love that. And then I save them so at the end of the month, I always save at least $30, I can go to the A&P and pig out. Cake and chocolate milk, some luxuries.

Unfinished Business: Report on the Interagency Task Force on Food and Hunger tells us that "13.5 percent of all people living in the United States were poor as compared to 23.2 percent of those living in New York City. The city's poverty rate for children was 37.9 percent as compared to the national average of 20.6 percent.... The effectiveness of federal food stamp programs decreased dramatically between 1980 and 1987. Food stamp participation dropped nationally by almost one million people; during the same period, the number of people in poverty rose by two million. In this same period, the number of soup kitchens and food pantries rose from 30 in 1981 to 603 in 1987. These six hundred programs feed approximately 570,000 people per month" (Grinker 1989, v–vi).

Still too many go hungry, and because of their disadvantaged daily lives they are often forced to sell food stamps for other "luxuries." Only a guaranteed, adequate standard of living for all citizens will prevent the selling of food stamps in the underground economy.

I sit down with Bea. She lives in the projects across the street from the soup kitchen. She's lived there all of her life. Even though there's crime and it's dangerous at night, she says, "Everyone knows me and I feel safe there." In general, the projects are the best housing that the area offers. There are some well-kept and more expensive homes where middle-class and working-class blacks live. Still the projects are better than most of the housing in the neighborhood. Bea says:

We have a five-and-a-half-room apartment in the projects. There are four of us, my sister and her son and my son. I get $48.50 in public assistance every two weeks. My son gets SSI because he's disabled. He's blind. The rent is $217 per month, and we get $196 food stamps per month. That's hard. Things are expensive. I baby-sit and clean house, and I make about $75 more a week [this is not allowed, and technically she is a welfare cheat]. That helps, but what we live on is really nothing.

I ask her about selling food stamps. She answers:

I don't think the system is fair. They don't give you enough to live on. But I think it's wrong to trade them in and not buy food. That's unfair. Food stamps is how I survive. They're like gold to me. I may have no money, but I always have food. Like now, it's the first of the month. I'm going to buy my meat. I buy a case of chicken, a loin of pork chops, big shell steak, chopped meat, rice, and noodles. We'll have enough food for a month, and I'll eat my lunches here at least a few days a week. And I get to see my friends and talk. And Sister Bernadette is just beautiful. But again, I think it's wrong to sell food stamps to buy cigarettes, clothes, crack, or OTB [Off Track Betting]. Even though it's not much money and we don't have much, it's wrong.

Bea is typical of the women who come to the soup kitchen and of poor women who raise children without the aid of men. Female-headed families did not cause poverty but were caused by poverty and race and gender discrimination. Nor were they caused by overgenerous welfare programs as conservatives claim. Female-headed families kept increasing after the budget cuts in social welfare programs in the 1970s and 1980s (Levy 1988, 189). As Ruth Sidel describes:

> Of poor people in the United States today, the vast majority are women and their children. According to the Census Bureau, in 1984, 14.4 percent of all Americans—33.7 million people—lived below the poverty line. From 1980 to 1984, the number of poor people increased by 4½ million. For female headed households in 1984, the poverty rate was 34.5 percent, a rate five times that for married-couple families. The poverty rate for white female-headed families was 27.1 percent, for black female-headed families, 51.7 percent, and for Hispanic families headed by women, 53.4 percent. The poverty rate for the elderly, most of whom are women, was 12.4 percent in 1984. Two out of every three poor adults are women, and the economic status of families headed by women is declining. (Sidel 1986, 3)

It's already 12:15 P.M. when I finally start to serve food. I find an apron and relieve Mary, who has been serving the tomato, rice, and vegetable soup. Because it's check day there is plenty of soup left. I can give out seconds. Bill told me that yesterday there were 984 guests. Sister tells me some good news. United Parcel Service is donating $50,000 to remodel the soup kitchen. It will be in another part of the Parish Center of the church. It will no longer seat 125 but will now seat 105. Even though there is increased need in the neighborhood, we will feed fewer guests.

January 8, 1990. Serving food. Machinelike. Trying to be courteous and friendly to the guests. Bill Baker counts the guests and lets them in the Willoughby Street entrance. The guests are 70 percent black, 20 percent Hispanic, 10 percent white. They pick up trays, and then they pick up their food. The hot food first, followed by bread, dessert, and juice. They sit and eat at tables with eight other guests. They eat, and talk and socialize with their friends.

I hear some talk directed at Bill. "Food's good here. At the shelter all you get is a little food and cold storage. Sleeping at the shelter is cold storage."

Bill and a wide-eyed young man, blond hair and blue eyes and wearing a pea coat, are rating the refugee centers in Reagan-Bush America. They are refugees from market capitalism. They are two men among the 1.7 million people living in poverty (Grinker 1989, 11) and the sixty to one hundred thousand who are homeless in New York City. The extent of the housing crisis was summarized in *City Limits*: "As the 1990's approach, New York City remains mired in a housing and homelessness crisis of unprecedented proportions. More than 250,000 people are homeless, living on the streets, in shelters, doubled or tripled-up in over crowded apartments or in substandard housing. The wait for an apartment in public housing hovers near twenty years. These facts bear witness to the city's mammoth shortage of affordable housing." (Ad hoc coalition on Housing, "Housing New York: A Coalition Platform," *City Limits*, Vol XV, Number 1, January 1990, 22.)

The young man comments, "Port Washington is the worst, though I heard that Harlem 1 and 2 are not bad." I ask him which shelter he's living at. "Atlantic and Bedford, the Armory. A thousand beds lined up, that's the worst. Gangs of guys go around beating up people. Mostly the old and the sickly. They never beat up anybody who can defend themselves." Have you been beaten up? "No, I know how to take care of myself. You never show weakness. They stare at you, you stare right back at them. You give them the look. Tells them that you'll get them if they try to do something to you."

The homeless problem is the dramatic edge of a nationwide housing crisis for low-income families. This crisis is clearly stated in *New York Ascendant* by the Commission on the Year 2000:

> According to the 1984 Housing and Vacancy survey, the poorest fifth of New York households earned 4 percent of the city's income, or $4,300 annually. Median annual income of the city's 1.9 million households in rental apartments was $12,800. Such incomes cannot usually command good housing. As it is, over one-fifth of the city's households pay more than 50 percent of their income for rent, and one-third pay more than 40 percent. Having to spend an excessive proportion of income on rent is most prevalent among those who are poorest and whose numbers will be growing in the future, including blacks, hispanics, female headed households, and the elderly. (Wagner 1987, 131–132)

Shelters for the homeless are terrible places with violence, drugs, AIDS, tuberculosis often running rampant. Still, they have been home for thousands. To shut down shelters and to remove people without finding alternative housing is scandalous. With the election of Mayor David Dinkins, there was great hope on the streets of New York that conditions for the homeless and the hungry would improve, but conditions only got worse. More and more homeless were turned away, and the shelters are in even worse condition. *100 Days of Neglect: Mayor Dinkins and the Homeless*, by the Coalition for the Homeless, reported: "On February 1, 1990, Mayor Dinkins released a financial plan that proposed deep cuts in shelter services, drug treatment, supportive services to families, AIDS case management, information and referral, and permanent housing for the homeless. Since then, the Mayor has announced an additional

$75 million in cuts for the homeless, and $500 million in service cuts. But if preliminary cuts are any indication, we can be sure that New York's neediest will bear undue burden" (Coalition for the Homeless 1990, 19).

January 31, 1990. I go down to the kitchen. It's jumping. Crowded and noisy. Pat Johnson, one of the volunteers, is serving the soup, thick with noodles, vegetables, and meat. Our volunteers are like Pat, poor black women on public assistance who live in a housing project. Pat is a single mother; she has an adult son who has been bedridden since he was a teenager because he was seriously burned in a fire in the housing project. As I enter, a lot of people say hello to me. I start to serve the soup. The line is continuous, endless, and I work like a machine. Bill tells me that last week they had over sixteen hundred guests. As usual everyone is quite friendly.

Sister Bernadette has let me give seconds from the start this morning. Sister Bernadette is both saintly and competent. She wants to feed everyone who is hungry even though she, better than anyone, knows the constraints of the soup kitchen resources. People are coming for seconds, thirds, fourths. We use seven pots in the first hour. We have four pots for the second hour. Bill had come over to me earlier and said to me that Sister is allowing seconds too early. But the soup is thick and people are hungry. Sister gets angry and starts to criticize President Bush. "He says this works (voluntarism), but this doesn't work. He's a jerk, and he says this works." Everyone who works in the soup kitchen knows that we do a good job, that we feed as many people as we can and we feed nutritious meals, but we only feed a small portion of the needy in the neighborhood. We do not do enough, a thousand points of light is not enough, not even the heroic dedication of Sister Bernadette is enough. A tremendous increase in government spending is necessary to overcome the massive problems of hunger, poverty, AIDS, and homelessness. Increased government spending is unlikely in the Reagan-Bush-Clinton years; these are Presidents who were more committed to tax cuts, free market policies, waging war in Iraq and Bosnia, military spending, and bailing out failing savings and loans. The conditions of the poor only got worse in Bush's America and Clinton's policies have proved just as disastrous.

September 13, 1991. Walking down Stuyvesant Avenue. Crumbling buildings, crumbling people. A man collecting bottles. He has a shopping cart with a green lawn-and-leaf bag draped in it. The bag is full of bottles and cans which he can redeem at the supermarket for a nickel apiece. Another example of the Protestant work ethic and free enterprise in Bedford-Stuyvesant. In my own neighborhood, Greenpoint, Brooklyn, the bottle redemption center is next to the Key Food supermarket. Men and women line up with trash bags full of bottles and cans. Hundreds of nickels the fair exchange for their hard work. Many of the men in line live at the Greenpoint Men's Shelter.

This is how they earn a living. They keep the streets clean. They are underpaid.

The director from Catholic Charities says to me, "It's very depressing, the age of these people, they're young. They're not old, disabled—these are physically able people. It's very depressing."

I'm serving cookies. I take a handful and wrap them in a napkin and give them out. I talk to Danny, who works in the kitchen. He's living down the hall from Bill at the Glenwood Hotel on Broadway and Havermeir Street in Williamsburg, Brooklyn. Bill was forced to leave the Greenpoint Shelter because of budget cuts about a year ago. Bill says, "The hotel is a fleabag. It's shit, but it's better than the shelter. It's $6.50 a night and welfare pays."

Dan says, "The hotel is hell, but I couldn't live on the streets. I've been worried about living on the street since my sister-in-law don't want me staying in the basement at their house. She says she wants to rent it and she can get more than I can pay. I'm too old to be in the streets. It would kill me."

Bill interrupts, "We did it, we spent a whole winter in the streets, and then a long time at the shelter."

Dan: "It would really kill me now. I could never do it again." He laughs. "Do you remember, you spent almost the whole winter without a coat. That was our project, to get you a warm coat."

Bill: "I don't know how I survived that whole winter without a coat."

Dan: "We finally got him a coat, but it was February."

Bill: "It's great having Dan down the hall."

Later Dan tells me that he hates living in the hotel. "All kinds of terrible people, but it's better than the shelter or the streets."

All of these poor people are trying to cope, but they are always "between a rock and a hard place." Professor E is a West Indian black man who has taken it upon himself to educate me. I remember what Professor E said to me about President Bush's solution to poverty, the Thousand Points of Light. He said, "If President Bush was serious he would know that a thousand points of light ain't enough. At least a million is necessary."

Two Exemplars of Free Market Social Policy

The Conservative

Charles Murray's *Losing Ground* (1984) is the basic statement of the conservative position on poverty and social welfare. Though the work of George Gilder (1981) and Lawrence Mead (1986) is crucial to understanding the conservative position, Murray's study was the Bible (Katz 1989, 153) of the Reagan administration's war on poverty. Murray's discourse on poverty, enframed in the language of the free market, is the essential vocabulary shift. It becomes clear, signified by substantial scientific evidence, that government social welfare programs are the problem. The behavior of the disadvantaged is independent of social and psychological factors. They are determined by economically motivated rational choices. Social welfare programs create a context in which the rational choices of the disadvantaged are "to not enter the labor force," "to not get an education," and "to not get married." In short, the social welfare programs of the 1960s and 1970s had failed, and they failed because "we made it profitable to be poor." (Murray 1984, 9)

His analysis claimed that poverty increased in spite of the federally funded social programs of the 1960s and 1970s. For Murray, social welfare programs decreased incentives for disadvantaged young blacks to enter the labor force, take available jobs (even at low wages), and continue working. Thus these programs increased black unemployment. They also increased black female-headed families because benefits provided incentives for blacks not to marry. Murray's arguments were based on flimsy data, and critics easily disproved them (Katz 1989, 153; Jencks 1985). His arguments were based on thought experiments, the most important of which was the case of Harold and Phyllis.

Harold and Phyllis have low-income parents, are not generally well educated, and have no special vocational skills, and Phyllis is pregnant. (Murray 1984, 156–57) Harold and Phyllis are the children of Aid for Dependent Children (AFDC), the most extensive public assistance package in the United States. For Murray, it has destroyed the motivation of Harold and Phyllis to form a family and to struggle at low-wage jobs. AFDC has made it more advantageous for Phyllis to live off her welfare package and for Harold to work periodically, only enough to collect unemployment benefits. They live together because if they got married they would lose benefits. For Murray, social welfare programs have made this a norm for poor people. The norm that Phyllis and Harold followed is simply the norm of the rational choice of economic advantage. It is not economically rational to work hard at a low-paid job and get married. Social welfare programs have made the personal dignity of both an economic disadvantage.

> When economic incentives are buttressed by social norms, the effects on behavior are multiplied. But the main point is that social factors are not necessary to explain behavior. There is no "breakdown of the work ethic" in this account of rational choices among alternatives. There is no shiftless irresponsibility. It makes no difference whether Harold is white or black. There is no need to invoke the spectres of cultural pathologies or inferior upbringing. The choices may be seen more simply, much more naturally, as the behavior of people responding to the reality of the world around them and making the decisions—the legal, approved, and even encouraged decisions—that maximize the quality of life. (ibid., 162)

Murray assumes that both Harold and Phyllis could work at low-wage jobs if they wanted to, that they could get married if they wanted to, but social welfare programs have made it easier for them to live off the tolerable misery of public assistance. Especially because from 1965 through the early 1970s subsidies increased, altering the structure of incentives for the poor. As Murray states:

> It was easier to get along without a job. It was easier for a man to have a baby without being responsible for it, for a woman to have a baby without having a husband. It was easier to get away with crime, it was easier to obtain drugs. Because it was easier to get away with crime, it was easier to support a drug habit. Because it was easier to get along without a job, it was easier to ignore education. Because it was easier to get along without a job, it was easier to walk away from a job and thereby accumulate a record as an unreliable employee. (ibid., 175)

All of this was, for Murray, the result of the creation of increasingly generous social welfare programs: AFDC, food stamps, Medicaid, housing subsidies. These programs degrade the poor. If it were not for these programs, Harold and Phyllis would have chosen an alternative path (ibid., 173). Harold and Phyllis would have married. Harold would have worked at a low-paid job, which after years of hard work would have provided them with a decent life. Independent of welfare they would have personal dignity. "Work hard, stick to the job no matter how bad it is, and you will probably climb out of poverty but not very far out" (ibid., 177).

Murray comes to this conclusion based totally on the fictitious case of Harold and Phyllis, thus, "social programs ... tend to produce net harm in dealing with the most difficult problems" (ibid., 218). Thus Murray in his final thought experiment proposes "the scrapping of the entire welfare and income support structure" (ibid., 227). The poor would have to take the available low-wage jobs. This would help to stabilize their family structure. Hard work is the moral solution to poverty. Murray concludes, "Billions for equal opportunity, not one cent for equal outcome—such is the slogan to inscribe on the banner of whatever cause my proposals constitute. Their common theme is to make it possible to get as far as one can go on one's merit, hardly a new idea in American thought" (ibid., 233).

Thus Murray's underlying assumption is that low-wage jobs are available if you are willing to work. Cut social programs severely, and the poor will become motivated to take these jobs.

His solution is a job solution.

The Liberal

William Julius Wilson's *The Truly Disadvantaged* embodies the liberal response to Murray. Wilson asks "why the behavior patterns in the inner city today differ so markedly from those of three decades ago" (Wilson 1987, 7).

For Wilson, the success of social welfare programs of the 1960s and the race-specific programs of the 1970s was to enlarge the size of the black middle class. As this class became more affluent, it moved out of the inner-city ghetto. This increased the concentration of underclass blacks in the ghetto. "150,000 blacks departed these communities during this ten year period (1970–1980) leaving behind a much more concentrated poverty population." (ibid., 50)

The concern of Wilson is that during this period there was an increase of underclass blacks in the inner city. Wilson's use of "underclass" is problematic and controversial. As Bob Blauner proposes, social scientists should stop using the term, because "it suggests a group of people who are permanently outside of the class structure." It also "calls up images of black people who whites find both frightening and morally irredeemable" (Blauner 1990, 17).

Wilson understands the problems with the term and uses "underclass" because he wants to move away from "race" as the dominant concept for the explanation of the continuation and overrepresentation of blacks among the poor. Wilson doesn't deny that blacks are a highly stigmatized group, but he believes that "underclass" is a better term for describing the profound economic and social dislocations of the inner-city ghetto (Wilson 1987, 8).

For Wilson, crucial for understanding these dislocations is the deindustrialization of the American economy and the loss of union jobs. For Wilson, blacks have been disproportionately hurt by these changes. It is with an analysis enframed by these economic transformations that he confronts two of Murray's major contentions: first, that black unemployment is a result of the increase of social welfare programs; and second, that the breakup of poor people's families, as indicated by an increase in female-headed families, is the result of social welfare programs. For Wilson, the problem is not social welfare programs but joblessness.

First, to Murray's contention that the increase in welfare benefits has led Harold and Phyllis to choose welfare over full employment, Wilson argues:

> Real benefits in fact have fallen dramatically since the early 1970's. Danziger and Gottschalk reveal that by 1980 the real value of the AFDC plus food stamps had been reduced by 16 percent from their 1972 levels. By 1984, the combined payments were only 4 percent higher than their 1960 levels and 22 percent less than in 1972. In the words of Greenstein, no other group in American society experienced such a sharp decline in real income since 1970 as did AFDC mothers and their children. (ibid., 94)

Second, black joblessness is not a result of young black men choosing not to work as a rational choice but the result of deindustrialization, which had greater impact on black workers than on white workers because they were more concentrated in inner-city areas.

Between 1947 and 1972, the central cities of the thirty three most populous metropolitan areas... lost 880,000 manufacturing jobs, while manufacturing employment in their suburbs grew by 2.5 million. The same cities lost 867,000 jobs in retail and wholesale trade, at the same time that their suburbs gained millions of such positions, while the black populations of these central cities lost more than 9 million whites and added 5 million blacks. (ibid., 100–101)

Third, the geographical deindustrialization for urban and suburban became national from the mid-1970s through the 1980s. For Wilson, these employment changes had a major impact on family life. Wilson conceptualizes this in terms of what he calls the "male marriageable pool index." By this, he means the men who are available to marry and support a family. He says, because of increased black joblessness caused by urban deindustrialization, "combined with high black mortality and incarceration rates, that there has been a decrease in black men who are available to support families. This has resulted in the increase in black female-headed families." For Wilson, it is not welfare that has caused this situation (ibid., 83).

His solution to these problems is to remedy black joblessness. His "hidden agenda" (ibid., 155) is that race-specific programs suffer because they increase the stigmatization of the target group. He prefers universal programs for increasing employment. His key assumption is that "improving the job prospects of men will strengthen low-income black families" (ibid., 150).

Central to Wilson's concerns are a mixture of public and private programs to increase economic opportunity. The truly disadvantaged "would also benefit disproportionately from a program of balanced economic growth and tight labor market policies because of their greater vulnerability to swings in the business cycle and changes in economic organization, including relocation of plants and use of labor-saving technology" (ibid., 153).

Though Wilson disagrees with Murray's contention that work is available to all who are morally willing to work, though he contends that deindustrialization has reduced greatly the amount of jobs available to inner-city blacks, he shares with Murray a job solution to the problems of American poverty.

Postindustrial Poverty

After the soup kitchen closes for the day, I walk to the subway station with Joe and Professor E.

Joe: "Things just getting worse, and you can't even get treated like a man. If they'd only treat you like a man."

Professor E: "There's no jobs. Oh, there's jobs, but I mean decent-paying jobs—jobs that people could afford housing—and you'd clean up crack. But there aren't any. These young kids know that, and they just get meaner and meaner."

It is clear to these men in their sixties that jobs are scarce. That there will be an increase in good-paying jobs in the future is unlikely. Crack, poverty, crime, and hopelessness run rampant in Bedford-Stuyvesant. Life just gets "meaner and meaner." Cornel West writes of the "nihilism that increasingly pervades black communities.... It is ... the lived experience of coping with a life of horrifying meaninglessness, hopelessness, and (most important) lovelessness." (West 1993, 14)

As poverty spreads, the nihilism spreads, beyond the hundreds of years of oppression of black people. With no alternative vocabulary shift to the conservative hegemony over social policy, the nihilism spreads throughout the lives of all poor people in postindustrial society. There has been no policy shift, no new vocabulary to explain the crucial transformations that relate to poverty in a postindustrial world. In the words of Fred Block and Larry Hirschhorn: "We argue that the most developed societies—both capitalist and state socialist—face a transition from industrial society, organized around the production of goods, to postindustrial society organized around the provision of services and advanced technologies that release labor from direct production" (Block and Hirschhorn 1987, 99–100).

This is the scenario for postindustrial poverty, nihilism with permanently declining occupational opportunities for the lower classes. Neither the full-employment option of liberals nor Murray's conservative option of the poor working at low-wage jobs and struggling their way to dignity is a possible solution. Full employment would mean bad jobs at below-poverty wages unless there is massive federal funding that guarantees good wages. Currently not even liberals speak this language. The conservative solution of cutting social programs to force poor people to work at low-wage jobs would only mean that the conditions of the poor would become even more degraded and that nihilism would spread. Simply put, working your way out of poverty is impossible if there is an insufficient number of above-poverty-wage jobs.

Bad jobs with low wages have increased in all sectors of the economy, including college-trained professionals. In this context, I agree with Wilson that blacks have been disproportionately hurt by these trends. Blacks have suffered more because of deindustrialization. My disagreement is with his implication that through reindustrialization jobs would be created and thus blacks would benefit from this economic growth. They would get a share of the newly created jobs. But this reindustrialization is a myth (Block 1987, 110).

Even if taxpayers were willing to pay for it, it would not produce a sufficient amount of jobs at decent wages in these new highly automated factories.

Instead, postindustrial transformations decrease the production of new jobs in all sectors, hurting the poor disproportionately.

> The sharp declines in employment are no longer restricted to old line manufacturing firms or old blue collar workers. Plant closings, layoffs, and paycuts have swept high technology industries as well. In just the first six months of 1985 . . . employment in the computer and semi-conductor industries—the core of the new technology—shed more than twenty thousand jobs.
> The BLS [Bureau of Labor Statistics] reported that between 1981 and 1986 more than 780,000 managers lost their jobs as a result of plant closings and permanent layoffs. And the pace has increased even as the economy entered its fourth year of recovery. In the drive to make the ranks of management "leaner and meaner," nearly 600,000 middle and upper level executives lost their jobs between 1984 and 1986. Such companies as AT&T, United Technologies, Union Carbide, and Ford are leading the management massacre. (Harrison and Bluestone 1984, 37–38)

In postindustrial society, growth in productivity does not mean job creation. Economic growth does not "trickle" through the whole society. The new forms of organization and new technologies from high-tech expert systems to robotics displace the productive forces of the old industrial society. Postindustrial efficiencies create declines in the production of jobs, especially for the poor.

> The decline of the old productive forces means that the economy cannot provide the millions of unskilled, entry level jobs that are needed to absorb the available labor power. The result is that millions of people, particularly inner-city minority residents, become a surplus population with little prospect for even minimal economic security. But now, with employment declining in many traditional sectors of the economy, "structural unemployment" threatens many industrial workers of all races. (Block 1987, 110)

The final vocabularies of both liberals and conservatives are structured in terms of job solutions to poverty. But jobs are not the solution: income is. Only income solutions would significantly raise the standard of living of poor people. In a postindustrial society in which the new technologies are labor destroying, only solutions whose central focus is on income can possibly work. Even the massive rebuilding of the decaying American infrastructure, which would create jobs, would be insufficient to lift the masses of poor and near poor out of the heavy burdens of poverty. These jobs would have to pay wages which would enable workers to have decent food, housing, education, medical care, etc.

The rebuilding of the infrastructure is needed and would increase American competitiveness in the global marketplace. But with the current fiscal crisis and continuously growing federal deficits, in the range of more than $200 billion a year, these deficits have ruled out the extensive federal spending that is required. Massive public works have been ruled out by a permanent austerity economy (Lichten 1986).

Even if this were funded and created a sufficient amount of decent-paying jobs, there would have to be a guaranteed annual income. All workers who were displaced as new technologies and forms of organization made their work obsolete would have to be guaranteed their wages at their current levels. They would have to be guaranteed through the time that would be required for them to be reeducated and until they could be hired at a new job. This is the type of income-based solution that would be required to guarantee a good life to all. This is not imaginable in the current free market vocabulary of both liberals and conservatives.

Income solutions to poverty would require a major vocabulary shift. Only a social movement with the vision to redefine the relation of work to income to morality could accomplish this goal. This is also not imaginable at this point in American history. The current progressive social movements in the United States, the struggle over AIDS and the struggle over abortion, are both middle class. In the 1990s, there are no poor people's movements in the United States. Since the immense government spending that would be required to finance income solutions to poverty seems unlikely, nor are there poor people's movements against poverty, postindustrial poverty looks set to grow. It seems permanent and without a solution.

References

Blauner, B. 1990. "Black Workers and the Underclass." *New Politics* 2, no. 4 (winter): 12–20.

Block, F., ed. 1987. *Revising State Theory: Essays in Politics and Postindustrialism.* Philadelphia: Temple University Press.

Block, F., and L. Hirschhorn. 1987. "New Productive Forces and Contradictions of Contemporary Capitalism: A Postindustrial Perspective," in F. Block, ed., *Revising State Theory: Essays in Politics and Postindustrialism.* Philadelphia: Temple University Press.

Bush, G. 1990. *Public Papers of the Presidents of the United States: George Bush, 1989*, Book 1, January 20 to June 30, 1989. Washington, D.C.: U.S. Government Printing Office.

Coalition for the Homeless. 1990. *100 Days of Neglect: Mayor Dinkins and the Homeless.* New York: Coalition for the Homeless.

Fraser, N. 1989. *Unruly Practices: Power, Discourse, and Gender in Contemporary Social Theory.* Minneapolis: University of Minnesota Press.

Gilder, G. 1981. *Wealth and Poverty.* New York: Basic Books.

Grinker, W. J. 1989. *Unfinished Business: Report on the Interagency Task Force on Food and Hunger.* New York: Human Resources Administration.

Harrison, B., and B. Bluestone. 1984. *The Great U Turn: Corporate Restructuring and the Polarizing of America.* New York: Basic Books.

Jencks, C. 1985. "How Poor Are the Poor?" *New York Review of Books*, May 9, 41–49.

Katz, M. B. 1989. *The Undeserving Poor.* New York: Pantheon Books.

Levy, F. 1988. *Dollars and Dreams: The Changing American Income Distribution.* New York: W. W. Norton.

Lichten, E. 1986. *Class, Power, and Austerity.* South Hadley: Bergin and Garvey.

Mead, L. 1986. *Beyond Entitlement: The Social Organization of Citizenship.* New York: Free Press.

Murray, C. 1984. *Losing Ground: American Social Policy, 1950–1980.* New York: Basic Books.

National Commission on Children. 1991. *Beyond Rhetoric: A New American Agenda for Children and Families.* Washington, D.C.: U.S. Government Printing Office.

Peterson, W. C. 1991. "The Silent Depression." *Challenges*, July–August.

Rorty, R. 1989. *Contingency, Irony, and Solidarity.* New York: Cambridge University Press.

Rorty, R. 1991. *Essays on Heidegger and Others: Philosophical Papers*, vol. 2. New York: Cambridge University Press.

Sidel, R. 1986. *Women and Children Last.* New York: Viking Penguin.

Wagner, R. F., Jr., chair. 1987. *New York Ascendant: The Commission on the Year 2000.* New York: Commission on the Year 2000, June.

West, C. 1993. *Race Matters.* Boston: Beacon Press.

Wilson, W. J. 1987. *The Truly Disadvantaged.* Chicago: University of Chicago Press.

# 4

Poverty in London

Carey Oppenheim

> Poverty is at the root of powerlessness. Poor people in Urban Priority Areas are at the mercy of fragmented and apparently unresponsive public authorities. They are trapped in housing and environments over which they have little control. They lack the means and opportunity which so many of us take for granted, of making choices in our lives.
>
> (*Faith in the City*, 1985)

Faith in the City, published by the Archbishop of Canterbury's Commission on Urban Priority Areas, created a storm in 1985 when it drew the neglected and forgotten inner cities to the attention of the British public. Six years later, we were faced with newspaper headlines which announced that restaurant owners in London's Strand planned to employ a cleaning firm to flood out, like so much rubbish, homeless young people who had made the pavements their home. Restaurant-goers would no longer have to climb over the sleeping bodies of homeless people.

In the railway and tube stations of London, beggars of all ages and backgrounds have become the norm rather than the exception. These shocking images are the more visible signs of the poverty and inequality of this capital city.

Alongside such deprivation, London also experienced a leap in incomes at the other end of the scale. Conspicuous poverty accompanied the conspicuous consumption of a minority who gained lavish incomes from the boom in the City. Until "Black Monday" in 1987 when the stock market collapsed and the deep recession of 1992 and 1993, the shiny confidence of the new affluent went unpunctured.

Economic restructuring, fragmentation, growing divisions, and decay have characterized life in the inner city over the last decade or so. These changes have been underpinned by a Thatcherite ideology which placed the individual and the market as paramount and relegated the idea of "society" to the scrap heap. The widespread currency of these ideas was inimical to the very notion of a *city* and of welfare for that city, for in some sense the city is the very embodiment of the social and of society.

The impressions of deprivation are borne out by hard facts. In 1983–85, it was estimated that 12 percent of people living in Greater London—635,000—were living in poverty (defined as living below 50 percent of average income); of those, 203,000 were children, 19 percent of all children. Data from the 1981 census showed that the ten most deprived English local authorities were all in London. Even today, some of the Inner London boroughs have unemployment rates which rank with those of Northern Ireland. The latest figures show that it is London and the southeast which are experiencing the sharpest rises in unemployment, as the recession has spread to new areas of employment in the service industries.

The causes of the recent rise in poverty are familiar: sharp rises in unemployment; changes in employment patterns with the growth of casual, temporary, and marginal work, accompanied by the low pay that goes with such jobs; changes in family patterns; and the increasing inability of the social security system to meet today's needs. Each factor is, of course, shaped by social class, "race," and gender. London is no exception to these changes; it does, however, have particular features which mark it out. London has experienced a more drastic revolution in its industrial base than the rest of Britain; it also has a larger share of single-parent families; black people and other ethnic minorities are more likely to live in London; and there are larger inequalities of income in London than in Britain as a whole. This means that London has a number of fault lines which cross over one another, dividing it more sharply than the rest of Britain: divisions between Inner and Outer London; divisions inside the boroughs themselves; divisions between rich and poor; divisions between men and women; and between black people and white people.

This essay aims to look at changes in poverty and inequality in London in recent years. It focuses on recent economic and social changes, indicators of poverty in London, consequences of poverty in London, and conclusions and prospects for the city.

Poverty in Britain

In the United Kingdom, unlike some other countries such as the United States and Australia, there is no official poverty line, no government-sanctioned marker which admits the existence of poverty.

The government has, however, published figures on low income, the Low Income Families statistics (LIF) (1988), now replaced by the innocuously entitled Households Below Average Income (HBAI) (1992). HBAI figures published by the government in 1992 were derived from the Family Expenditure Survey (FES), an annual government survey of around seven thousand private households which monitors both incomes and expenditures. It is important to be aware of the limitations of the FES. It provides no breakdown by ethnic origin or by gender; it also excludes people living in institutions and homeless people. Thus it *underestimates* the extent of poverty in Britain today.

What is the context in which we are looking at the changes in poverty? Since 1979, there have been major economic and social changes in Britain, with deeper roots in the 1970s. They include:

- the tripling of unemployment to a peak of over three million in 1986, followed by a small drop in the later part of 1987, a recent rise to touch three million, and a slight fall once again
- very substantial rises in average incomes in the 1980s before the onset of the recession
- a small rise in the percentage of single parents
- a weakening of the contributory parts of the social security system such as unemployment benefit and retirement pension, leaving many more people to fall back on means-tested benefits
- a change in employment patterns, with part-time labor and the growth of self-employment and temporary jobs playing an increasingly important role in the development of industrial strategy
- the continuation of a substantial shift from manufacturing to service industry
- reductions in income tax bringing bonuses for the average earner but windfalls for the rich
- the deregulation of wages through weakening employment legislation
- a dramatic change in tenure patterns with large rises in the proportion of the population owning their own homes, accompanied by sharp increases in house prices, and by a substantial shrinking of the public rented sector and a rise in homelessness

In short, the persistence of high unemployment coupled with increased average earnings forged a much wider gap between people who were dependent solely on benefits (which generally rise by the level of inflation only) or reliant on low wages and people on average earnings and above.

HBAI enables us to look more closely at the changes which occurred between 1979 and 1988/89. HBAI shows that in 1988/89 12 million people—22 percent of the population—were living below half the average income, doubling the figure in 1979 when 5 million (9 percent) lived at this level of income. The series shows clearly children's vulnerability to poverty: in

1988/89, 3.1 million children (25 percent of all children) were living in families with incomes below half the average, compared to 1.4 million in 1979 (10 percent). Children's higher rate of poverty over this period was due to the greater chance of being in unemployed families and in single-parent families. HBAI also shows the risk of poverty by group. It is unemployed people, single-parent families, and single pensioners who are more at risk of poverty (see Figures 1 and 2).

The *composition* of the poorest groups also changed after 1979. Looking at the poorest 10 percent, pensioners made up a smaller proportion in 1988/89 than in 1979 (down from 31 percent to 14 percent of the bottom 10 percent); couples with children made up a larger proportion (up from 41 percent to 44 percent); and in particular, single people without children leapt from making up 10 percent of the bottom 10 percent in 1979 to 22 percent in 1988/89 (largely due to higher unemployment and changes in benefit rules). Looking at *economic* status, unemployment is directly apparent: in 1979 only 16 percent of the bottom 10 percent were unemployed, but by 1988/89 the figure had risen to 30 percent. Even the proportion of people in full-time work in the bottom 10 percent increased by a few percentage points, despite the fact that average earnings over the period rose substantially.

Official statistics tell us little about women's poverty because they are based either on the "household" or the "family" unit, hiding women's experiences inside the unit. Moreover, statistics about levels of income only capture one aspect of poverty. Studies of poverty which have focused on women have emphasized the importance of three factors: access to income; time taken generating income; and the distribution of resources within families.

Despite the limitations of official data, it is possible to pull together some crude indicators which reveal how women are more exposed to poverty than men. The Child Poverty Action Group (CPAG) estimated that in 1989 approximately 5.1 million women and 3.4 million men were living on or below the income support poverty line (Oppenheim 1993). The reason for this disparity based on gender is that women make up the overwhelming majority of two groups with high risks of poverty: single parents and elderly people, particularly the former. Figures from the Low Pay Unit bear out the same story; in 1991, 65 percent of the total number of people on low wages were women—some 6.53 million (Low Pay Unit 1991/92). Data from the FES show that in 1991 women's incomes (under pension age) were only 82 percent of men's and that they were more reliant on social security payments than men (particularly in retirement). (Central Statistical Office 1991). (See Table 4.1)

The evidence in this section has shown that poverty grew rapidly between 1979 and 1988/89. Around a fifth of the United Kingdom's population were living in poverty in 1988/89. Women are more at risk of poverty than men.

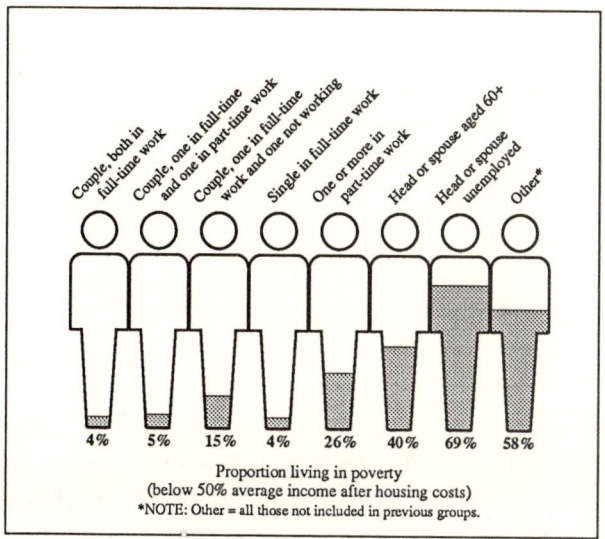

FIGURE 1   The Risk of Poverty by Economic Status in 1988/89

Source: Poverty: The Facts (C. Oppenheim), CPAG Ltd, 1993. Reprinted by permission.

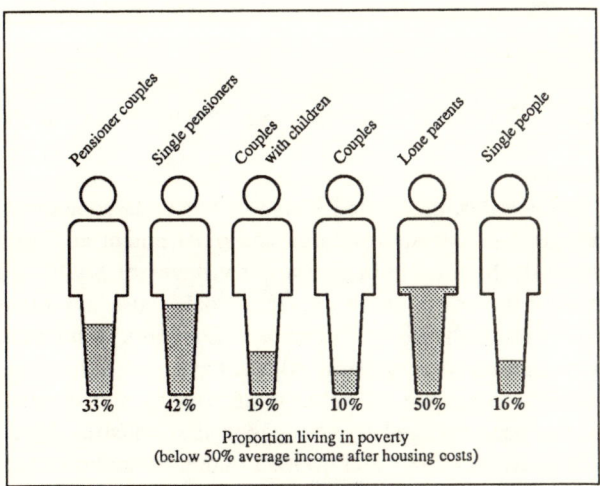

FIGURE 2   The Risk of Poverty by Family Status in 1988/89

Source: Poverty: The Facts (C. Oppenheim), CPAG Ltd, 1993. Reprinted by permission.

TABLE 4.1   Sources of Income, Single-Person Households in 1991

	BELOW PENSION AGE		ABOVE PENSION AGE	
	Men aged under 65	Women aged under 60	Men aged over 65	Women aged over 60
Gross normal weekly income	£263.99	£215.39	£157.72	£121.26
% of income from:				
Wages/salaries	69%	73%	8%	4%
Social security	5%	8%	36%	47%
Other	26%	19%	56%	49%

Source: Central statistical office 1991

The poverty encountered by children is even greater than for society as a whole: around a quarter of children in Britain were in poverty. Above all, it is unemployment which is responsible for the rise in poverty. There have been important changes since 1979 with a fall in the proportion of pensioners in the poorest 10 percent of the population and a rise in the proportion of families with children and single people without children. While the average person has found that his/her real income grew very comfortably, by 30 percent after housing costs, the poorest tenth saw a fall in their real income after housing costs of 6 percent. For the first time since 1949, the poorer half of society saw their share of overall income drop (Atkinson 1990).

RECENT ECONOMIC AND SOCIAL TRENDS IN LONDON

Economic Trends

Over the last two decades, the United Kingdom has undergone drastic changes in its economic and industrial structure. The most potent and familiar symbols of industrial decline are perhaps the pit villages of South Wales or the decimated cities of the north where the steel, coal, and heavy manufacturing industries are now mere shadows of their past. London's own economic problems are only beginning to be acknowledged. Particular aspects of London's economic profile have shaped its patterns of poverty and inequality.

London too has been ravaged by changes in the industrial base of Britain (see Table 4.2). Between 1982 and 1990, London alone accounted for well over a third of the loss in manufacturing jobs in the whole of Britain (DE 1990a, b). Over the same period, the fall in production, construction, and manufacturing sectors has been much sharper in London than in Britain as a whole—a 30 percent fall in London compared to 12 percent in Britain. Con-

TABLE 4.2 Rises and Falls in Employment by Sector between 1982 and 1990 in Greater London, Rest of the Southeast, and Great Britain (000s and % Changes)

	Greater London	Rest of Southeast	Britain
Total employment	+239	+603	+1,790
	(+7%)	(+17%)	(+9%)
Services	+501	+693	+2,732
	(+19%)	(+29%)	(+21%)
Production/construction	−260	−79	−880
	(−31%)	(−7%)	(−12%)
of which:			
Manufacturing	−237	−89	−656
	(37%)	(−9%)	(−11%)

Source: DE 1990a, b.

trary to expectations, the rise in the service sector was not as steep as in the rest of Britain. Despite this, service industries now account for 84 percent of all employment in London, of which the largest sectors are in banking, finance, and insurance (29 percent) and in education and health (25 percent). These are the sectors worst hit by the recent recession.

Comparing London to the affluent southeast region highlights the disadvantage of the capital. Between 1982 and 1990 the rest of the southeast had a fall of only 7 percent in production, construction, and manufacturing, way below the average for Britain, and a rise of 29 percent in services, above the average for Britain (DE 1990a, b). This confirms the well-known trend of new industries locating outside London in the southeast, the southwest, and East Anglia. The Chartered Surveyors, Jones Lang Wootton, reported a record number of companies locating outside central London in 1990–91 (Jones Lang Wootton 1991). Part of the change is explained by the rise in employment in the London Docklands, but, interestingly, it is the public sector which is moving substantial numbers of jobs outside London's heartland.

A number of reports highlighted the effects of the recession on London. The London Chamber of Commerce documented the first fall in London's service sector since it first kept records from 1985 (LCCI 1990). The Henley Centre forecast a growth of only 1.5 percent per year in London over the first five years of the 1990s—among the lowest in the United Kingdom (ALA 1991).

There has been a substantial change not only in the types of industry but also in the forms of employment (see Table 4.3) (DE 1990a, b). Male employment has fallen, and female employment and self-employment have risen.

TABLE 4.3   Changes in Employment Patterns between 1982 and 1990 in Greater London, Rest of the Southeast, and Great Britain (000s and % Changes)

	GREATER LONDON		%	SOUTHEAST		%	GREAT BRITAIN		%
	1982	1990		1982	1990		1982	1990	
Total employment	3,506	3,745	+7%	3,640	4,243	+17%	20,916	22,706	+9%
Male	2,028	1,957	−4%	2,025	2,133	+5%	11,930	11,720	−2%
Female (all) of which	1,477	1,788	+21%	1,617	2,110	+31%	8,985	10,986	+22%
Part-time	497	555	+12%	749	943	+26%	3,783	4,640	+23%
Full-time	980	1,233	+26%	868	1,167	+35%	5,202	6,346	+22%

Source: DE 1990 a, b.

While London exhibits similar patterns to the rest of Britain, there are some differences: between 1982 and 1990 there was a sharper fall in male employment in London (4 percent compared to 2 percent for Britain); and a greater proportion of women's employment is full time—69 percent in London compared to 57 percent in Britain as a whole. The rest of the southeast showed a different rend: there was a rise of 5 percent in male employment and much higher rises in female employment than the average for the country in this period.

Social Trends

> Migration has been selectively reversed, and the inner city is increasingly the territory of those left behind in the scramble for comfortable survival.
>
> *(Faith in the City*, 1985)

POPULATION.   As in other inner-city areas, there has been a fall in the population of Greater London, especially of Inner London. However, this exodus of population to the suburban areas has dropped in intensity, and in the 1990s the population of London is projected to rise slightly (especially for the very old and very young) (London Research Centre 1990). According to the London Research Centre, between 1971 and 1981 the population of Inner London dropped by 18 percent and Outer London by 5 percent. But between 1981 and 1989, the population of Inner London fell by only 2 percent and by 0.1 percent in Outer London.

ETHNIC MINORITIES.   Two-fifths of black people and other ethnic minorities in Britain live in Greater London—numbering around one million people.

The London Research Centre estimates that 300,000 are Caribbean or Guyanese, 300,000 Irish, 230,000 of Indian origin, 64,000 Pakistanis, 61,000 Africans, 40,000 Chinese, and 28,000 of Arab origin. Over the period 1981 to 1986, the number of people over retirement age from black and other ethnic minorities increased by 41 percent; this upward trend has continued as people from ethnic minority communities have grown older. Most black people and other ethnic minorities live in Inner London, but also in some Outer London boroughs including Newham, Ealing, Brent, and Haringey. The London Research Centre has estimated that migrants and travelers number anything between 76,000 and 340,000. They also show how the number of refugees has been rising: in 1989, 15,500 people applied for asylum, three times the number in 1985–86; 90 percent of new refugees in Britain live in London (London Research Centre 1990).

ONE-PARENT FAMILIES. There has been a rise in the number of single-parent families in recent years: in 1971, 8 percent of families with children were single-parent families; by 1979, this had risen to 12 percent; and by 1987 to 14 percent (Kiernan and Wicks 1990). Nine out of ten of these families are headed by a woman. Again, single parents are more likely to live in London: the 1981 census showed that 27 percent of all single parents lived in Inner London (NCOPF 1985).

Indicators of Poverty in London

The drastic changes in the industrial landscape of London have created areas of high unemployment alongside highly paid employment in some of the business services which expanded so rapidly during the 1980s. The higher proportions of black people and other ethnic minorities living in London found themselves exposed to very high rates of unemployment. Many single parents, largely women, in London found themselves squeezed out of the labor market and dependent on social security benefits for long periods of time. These patterns provide the backdrop to the changes in the character of poverty and inequality in London.

There are no official figures which look at low income in London. The Low Income Families statistics (LIF) and Households below Average Income (HBAI) contain no regional breakdown. Instead, we have to piece together a jigsaw from a number of sources.

The Numbers on Supplementary Benefit/Income Support

In 1988–89, around 607,800 people—about 10 percent of Londoners—*claimed* income support (the means-tested benefit for people who are not in full-time work) (London Research Centre 1989). This figure takes no account of the numbers of partners and children supported by income support. Using the same ratio for London as for Britain, roughly one million Londoners (15 percent) were supported by income support. A higher proportion of people supported by income support are women, because of the larger proportion of women pensioners and lone mothers on income support. The national figures show that 62 percent of people on income support are women (Oppenheim 1990). Table 4.4 shows the slow rise in the proportion of the Greater London population claiming supplementary benefit/income support between 1971 and 1979 (5.0 percent to 5.8 percent) and the sharp rise after 1979 when the proportion on benefit almost doubled from 5.8 percent to 10.3 percent (London Research Centre 1989). However, there was a slowing down of the rise between 1986 and 1988 which was a reflection of both the drop in unemployment and the change in the social security system in that year, which excluded some groups from claiming income support, such as sixteen- and seventeen-year-olds. The Unemployment Unit estimates that some 86,000 unemployed sixteen- and seventeen-year-olds would now be included in the unemployment count but are excluded because they are not entitled to benefit. With the onslaught of the recession, the numbers on income support have risen again.

In 1989–90 over 10 percent of Londoners aged sixteen and over claimed income support. The proportion of all Londoners claiming income support increased by three-quarters between 1979 and 1986, from 5.8 percent to 10.2 percent.

Free School Meals

A useful measure of poverty among children is the proportion of children who receive free school meals. Until April 1988, all children in families receiving one of two benefits—income support and family income supplement (a wage top-up for families with children in low-paid work)—were entitled to free school meals. Children in families on low incomes but not receiving these benefits were also eligible for free meals at the discretion of the local education authority. After the social security changes in 1988, only children in families on income support were entitled to free meals.

Table 4.5 shows the rise in the proportion of children getting free meals until 1988 and then the sharp fall-off after the change in social security policy. In 1987, nearly two-fifths of children in Inner London Education Authorities (ILEA) were receiving free school meals on the grounds of poverty and low income compared to 12 percent in Outer London and 18 percent in England as a whole. The higher level of children getting free school meals in ILEA is the outcome of higher unemployment, single parenthood, and poverty but also indicates more generous policies by ILEA, which used its discretionary powers to provide free meals to a larger number of children. After 1988, the sharp drop indicates the impact of changes in social security policy. All the figures underestimate the extent of deprivation among

TABLE 4.4 Numbers and Proportion of Greater London on Supplementary Benefit/Income Support between 1971 and 1989/90

	1971	1979	1986	1988/9	1989/90
Numbers of supplementary benefit/income support claimants	378,000	396,400	691,200	607,800	581,200
Proportion of population in Greater London	5.0%	5.8%	10.2%	11.2%	10.7%

Source: London Research Centre 1989 and Office of Population Censuses and Surveys 1990.
Note: Proportions are expressed as a percentage of the total population of London up to and including 1986 but as a percentage of Londoners aged sixteen and over for 1988–89 and 1989–90.

TABLE 4.5 Proportion of All School Children Receiving Free School Meals between 1979 and 1990

	ILEA	OUTER LONDON	ENGLAND
1979	23%	9.2%	12%
1980	22%	8%	10%
1981	25%	8%	12%
1982	28%	10%	14%
1983	31%	11%	16%
1984	34%	11%	17%
1985		no survey	
1986	36%	–	18%
1987	38%	12%	18%
1988	27%	9%	12%
1989	28%	10%	11%
1990	27%	10%	11%

Source: Department of Education and Science 1979–1990.
Note: There is some discontinuity: figures before 1989 show the number of children taking free school meals as a proportion of children in attendance; figures after 1989 show the number of children taking free school meals as a proportion of children on the school roll.

children because of the inadequate take-up of means-tested benefits. Family income supplement had a rate of take-up of 50 percent, and supplementary benefit had a take-up rate of around 84 percent at the latest date available (DSS 1989).

Households below Average Income

A regional analysis of HBAI by the Institute for Fiscal Studies gives us some data for Greater London (SSC 1990). Their figures are for two periods,

TABLE 4.6 Number and Proportion of Individuals and Children Living in Poverty (Below 50 Percent of Average Income) by Region in 1980–82 and 1983–85

	1980–82		1983–85	
	INDIVIDUALS	CHILDREN	INDIVIDUALS	CHILDREN
Greater London	538,000	161,000	635,000	203,000
	9%	12%	12%	19%
Southeast	791,000	290,000	710,000	245,000
	8%	12%	7%	10%
United Kingdom	6,300	2,200	7,090	2,480
	12%	16%	13%	19%

Source: SSC 1990.

1980–82 and 1983–85. (The figures are pooled for two years because of the small sample.) They show that in 1983–85, 12 percent of people and 19 percent of children in Greater London were living below half of the average income (see Table 4.6). This rate of poverty was below the average for the United Kingdom as a whole but above the rate for the southeast region. The overall figures for the United Kingdom show a sharp rise in the numbers living below 50 percent of average income between 1985 and 1988/89, so it is likely that these figures are much higher today.

Unemployment

We have already identified unemployment as a principal cause of poverty. In Greater London, it has soared in recent years to levels found in the early 1980s, after falling in the later years of the 1980s. In 1966, in Greater London, unemployment was just 0.6 percent; by June 1976, it had risen to 3.8 percent and by June 1986, to 10.2 percent. Unemployment in Greater London was 7.6 percent in March 1991 (DE 1990b). However, yet again the rate of unemployment varies substantially between parts of London (the difference in the proportion on income support partly reflects this). Table 4.7 shows the concentration of high unemployment in Inner London, particularly in the east.

Unemployment also varies greatly according to class, "race," and ethnic origin. The unemployment rate is six times higher for general laborers (14.9 percent) than for people with professional/managerial posts (2.4 percent) (DE 1990c). Despite higher levels of qualifications, black people and other ethnic minorities have had double the rate of unemployment in Britain as a whole. This high level of unemployment is the outcome of discrimination, working in occupations which have faced the brunt of the recession and

TABLE 4.7 Unemployment Rates of London Boroughs in May 1991 (Percentages)

	DEPT. OF EMPLOYMENT INDEX	UNEMPLOYMENT UNIT INDEX
Barking and Dagenham	9.0	13.0
Barnet	6.4	9.3
Bexley	6.4	9.4
Brent	11.0	18.1
Bromley	5.4	7.8
Camden	11.0	15.2
Ealing	8.0	11.5
Enfield	8.3	12.0
Greenwich	11.0	16.0
Hackney	18.6	27.1
Hammersmith and Fulham	11.7	16.3
Haringey	16.2	23.6
Harrow	5.1	7.4
Havering	5.8	8.4
Hillingdon	5.3	7.9
Hounslow	7.1	10.3
Islington	14.9	21.2
Kensington and Chelsea	7.8	10.8
Kingston	4.7	6.6
Lambeth	14.8	21.6
Lewisham	12.6	18.6
Merton	7.0	10.0
Newham	14.9	21.6
Redbridge	6.8	9.8
Richmond	5.0	7.0
Southwark	15.1	22.0
Sutton	5.3	7.5
Tower Hamlets	18.1	26.1
Waltham Forest	11.1	15.7
Wandsworth	9.7	14.0
Westminster	7.9	11.0
United Kingdom	7.9	11.3

Source: Unemployment Unit 1991.

change in industrial structure, and living in areas where manufacturing has declined substantially.

Ethnic minorities in London also had twice the unemployment rate of white people in 1984 and in 1989 (see Table 4.8) (*Hansard*, November 13, 1990, col. 123). However, some groups such as people from Pakistan and Bangladesh have unemployment rates of well over three times those of white people and, significantly, unlike all other groups have barely seen their unemployment rate fall since 1984. They were entirely excluded from any

TABLE 4.8 Unemployment Rates by Ethnic Origin in Greater London (Aged 16 and Over)

	1984	1989
All	9.9%	6.7%
White	8.7%	5.8%
Nonwhite	17.5%	11.9%
Caribbean/Guyanese	20.0%	13.5%
Indian	11.5%	8.9%
Pakistani/Bangladeshi	28.1%	27.3%
Other ethnic origins	19.3%	9.1%

Source: House of Commons 1990.

improvement in the economy. Well over a quarter of the Pakistani/Bangladeshi population in London seem to be permanently excluded from work. This may be due to a combination of factors such as greater discrimination, language difficulties, and living in areas of London such as Tower Hamlets with very high unemployment levels.

Women's experience of unemployment remains hidden both in terms of statistics and in terms of their identity and experiences. The rates of unemployment for women are hard to measure because of the way that unemployment statistics have been compiled in Britain since 1982. Unemployment is defined as people without work *and* claiming benefit as unemployed, i.e., it is the claimant count. This excludes large numbers of women who do not claim social security benefits because they would not be entitled to benefit in their own right. The Unemployment Unit compared the official estimate of unemployment (the claimant count) and the International Labor Organization/Organization for Economic Cooperation and Development (ILO/OECD) estimate, which takes a different definition of unemployment which is not based on benefit status. It found that (see Table 4.9), using the official estimate, women accounted for 26 percent of all unemployed people; on the ILO/OECD estimate, women accounted for 41 percent of the unemployed: If the ILO/OECD definition is used in addition to those who wanted work, were available, but had not looked for work in the previous four weeks, women made up 50 percent of the unemployed.

Disparity in Incomes

London has a far wider divergence of income than anywhere else in the country. The London Research Centre found that in 1988 the wealthiest 10 percent had an average income of £687.39 a week, more than twelve times as much as the lowest 10 percent, whose average income was £56.97. (In

TABLE 4.9   U.K. Unemployment in Spring 1990

	MEN	% OF ALL	WOMEN	% OF ALL	ALL
CLAIMANT COUNT	1,194,000	74%	423,000	26%	1,617,000
(1) Unemployed by ILO/ OECD definition	1,147,000	59%	802,000	41%	1,949,000
(2) Want work, available, but not looked in four weeks (or not stated)	330,000	32%	694,000	68%	1,024,000
(1) + (2)	1,477,000	50%	1,496,000	50%	2,973,000

Source: Unemployment Unit 1990.

the United Kingdom the ratio is nine times.) This disparity has grown: in 1980 the richest 10 percent of households had seven times as much on average as the poorest 10 percent (London Research Centre 1990).

GENDER, ETHNICITY, AND POVERTY

The rise in poverty and inequality has become much steeper since the late seventies, bringing larger disparities between Inner and Outer London and within London boroughs. Certain groups were particularly vulnerable, such as children, women, and black people and other ethnic minorities.

We have looked at broad indicators of poverty in London. There have been a number of small-scale studies of poverty in London which allow us to look more specifically at the issues of gender and "race." We pick out just two here. The first is *Islington: Poverty in the 1980s*, published by Islington Council (1990), and the second is an analysis of the London Living Standards Survey by Irene Bruegel which looks specifically at women and "race" (Bruegel 1989).

The Islington study commissioned Market Opinion and Research International under the guidance of Professor Peter Townsend to undertake a survey of living standards in the London borough of Islington. Using seventy-seven indicators of deprivation (devised by Townsend et al.), the survey examined the patterns of income and material and social deprivation in 1987 (Gordon and Townsend 1989). Material deprivation covered diet, clothing, housing, home facilities, local facilities, and working conditions. Social deprivation covered lack of rights in employment, family activities, lack of integration in the community, political participation, recreation, and education. The survey showed higher levels of deprivation among certain groups such as black people and ethnic minorities, women, the elderly, and so on. Table 4.10

TABLE 4.10 Proportions of Different Groups Experiencing High Material and Social Deprivation

	High Material Deprivation	Severe Social Deprivation
All groups	33%	33%
Women	35%	31%
Men	31%	37%
Very old (75+)	46%	70%
Retired	51%	61%
Employed (f-t)	16%	11%
Unemployed	65%	67%
People with home responsibilities	50%	52%
Couples with 2 children	31%	25%
Couples with 3 children +	39%	42%
One-parent families	64%	54%

Source: Islington Council 1990.

shows the proportion of different groups vulnerable to high levels of material and social deprivation. Unemployed people, single parents, the retired, and people coping with home responsibilities all have high levels of social and material deprivation.

The survey also found a strong correlation between deprivation and income. For example, it found high levels of deprivation for people living on social security benefits (income support/unemployment benefit): they had twice the level of deprivation of people who were not on benefits. People living on benefit thought they needed higher benefits in order to cope; the average amount was 78 percent above the then supplementary benefit rates.

The Islington survey also revealed important findings on race and poverty. Not surprisingly, ethnic minorities were more likely to have low incomes and to experience high material and social deprivation. White people had more than half again as much disposable income as any of the four minorities: Afro-Caribbean, Asian, Irish, and Cypriot. They found that 30 percent of the total population of Islington were living in or close to poverty (up to 140 percent of the supplementary benefit income level). Two-fifths of people from ethnic minorities were living in or close to poverty levels and below, compared to a quarter of the white population. While the income data were clear cut, the survey also showed that there is not always a clear link between income and material and social deprivation. Table 4.11 shows income and material and social deprivation by ethnic group.

The Irish community were the most materially and socially deprived and had the highest proportion of people on low incomes. Afro-Caribbeans also had high levels of deprivation. A smaller proportion of Asian people than

TABLE 4.11   Income and Material and Social Deprivation by Ethnic Group in Islington in 1987

	PROPORTION WITH INCOME LESS THAN £3,900	HIGH DEPRIVATION	
		MATERIAL	SOCIAL
Afro-Caribbean	39%	37%	36%
Asian	25%	35%	34%
Irish	38%	47%	42%
Cypriot	35%	24%	50%
Other	32%	39%	34%
White	29%	33%	34%

Source: Islington 1990.

white people had low incomes, and their levels of deprivation are also similar (although a bit higher for material deprivation). Cypriots have low levels of material deprivation but high levels of social deprivation. This may be due to the fact that the Cypriot community has the smallest proportion of elderly people living alone and a high level of owner occupation. The survey also looked at income and deprivation together; it found that at the lowest level of income (under £3,900), white people and Irish people had higher levels of material and social deprivation than people from ethnic minorities. A number of factors may explain this: family patterns, religious and cultural patterns, tenure, working conditions, and so on.

The second report, by Irene Bruegel, is drawn from the London Living Standards Survey, a major study of the living standards of Londoners. She focuses on the position of black women in the labor market. Her analysis reveals important findings both about London and about black women's employment more generally.

A number of studies, in particular the Policy Studies Institute survey *Black and White Britain* by Colin Brown (1984), have found that the disparity between black women and white women is not as large as expected, that Afro-Caribbean women had higher earnings than white women, and that the wage differential between black men and women is not as great as between white men and women. Bruegel challenges this, showing that this does not allow for the longer hours that black women work, the special London effect (51 percent of economically active black women work in London), and the younger age profile of black women. If these factors are allowed for, then Bruegel finds different results from those of the Policy Studies Institute: white women earned 23 percent more per hour than black women; black women earned only 63 percent of the average black men's weekly earnings, compared to white women earning 72 percent of white men's weekly wage.

TABLE 4.12 Weekly Earnings for Men and Women in 1986 in London by "Race"

	WEEKLY PAY
White men	£195
Black men	£165
White women	£133
Black women	£109

Source: Bruegel 1989.

TABLE 4.13 Benefits of Full-Time Workers by "Race" in 1986 in London

% WITH:	BLACK	WHITE
Training	36%	44%
Paid holiday	80%	84%
Two weeks notice	70%	76%
Sick pay	64%	73%
Union coverage	45%	50%

Source: Bruegel 1989.

The results from the London Living Standards Survey reinforced the evidence of the poorer pay and working conditions that black women face (see Tables 4.12 and 4.13). (Bruegel uses a definition of black which is based on self-assessment; it includes Asian and Afro-Caribbean women.)

Many of the traditional surveys such as the Labour Force Survey miss the more hidden aspects of the labor market, such as homeworking, family employment in shops, and paid child care—all of which are more associated with black people's work. Moreover, the occupational groupings for women do not reveal very much about the distribution of women inside, say, nursing, or clerical workers, i.e., there may be considerable disparity within nonmanual jobs. This is borne out by the London survey which found that the average pay for black women within nonmanual jobs in London was only £137 a week, £31 less than white women working in nonmanual jobs.

Bruegel also stresses the importance of looking at full-time work patterns to highlight the position of black women. She found that in London black women full-time workers were three times more likely to be manual workers than white women and thus have lower pay and poorer working conditions. Looking at both full-time and part-time work, the ratio is smaller: three black women were manual workers compared to two white women.

The Islington Survey showed high levels of poverty in an Inner London borough, with a third of its population experiencing severe material and social deprivation. It was important in exploring the links between income and deprivation, in particular the importance of looking at minority groups separately to reflect an accurate picture of their situation. Bruegel's analysis of the London Living Standards Survey showed that black women in London were at the bottom of the pile.

THE CONSEQUENCES OF POVERTY

We know that poverty brings hardship, both physical and social. There is a wealth of evidence which shows how difficult it is to manage on state benefits: people living on supplementary benefit went short of food, clothing, ordinary recreational activities. Perhaps the strongest indicators of the impact of poverty are morbidity and mortality data. I shall focus on two areas: the broad data that are now available about perinatal mortality rates in London and some specific evidence on childhood illness in Hackney and Tower Hamlets.

Perinatal Mortality Rates

In 1988, in Greater London, the perinatal mortality rate stood at 8.8 per thousand, slightly down from the figure for the year before of 9.1 per thousand. In 1981, the perinatal rate for Greater London was 11.4 per thousand, so there has been a decline since that date. However, the decline was much more rapid between 1971 and 1981—from 21.3 per thousand to 11.4. There is a small difference between Inner and Outer London: in 1988 the perinatal mortality rate was 9.6 per thousand in Inner London and 8.4 in Outer London. The patterns of change over time are also different in Inner and Outer London. Inner London shows a slight increase in perinatal mortality rates: in 1985, it stood at 9.6 per thousand, falling to 8.9 in 1986 and then up again to 9.6 the following year where it has stayed. Outer London has continued its slow decline.

However, some boroughs show different patterns (though patterns are so varied that it is difficult to generalize). Hounslow, Kingston-upon-Thames, Lewisham, Merton, Redbridge, and Southwark all show slow rises in their perinatal mortality rates since 1986. What is abundantly clear is the disparity in rates between different boroughs. It ranges from 11.5 per thousand in Tower Hamlets, followed by 11.3 per thousand in Hounslow and Lambeth and by 11.2 in Lewisham, to 5.3 per thousand in Kensington and Chelsea, 5.5 in Camden, and 5.9 in Bromley.

Admission to Hospital

A study of 593 children admitted to hospital in East London showed the link between material deprivation and coming in to hospital for care. It concluded that "adverse socio-economic conditions have a deleterious effect on the health of children of all ages and result in their admission to hospital with various illnesses which may have been prevented had they lived in better circumstances" (Carter et al. 1990, 186).

The study also revealed the following information:

- In 50 percent of cases neither parent of the child admitted was in employment (the average rate of unemployment for Hackney and Tower Hamlets was 22 percent).
- 59 percent of families were living in overcrowded conditions and 30 percent in severely overcrowded conditions (the average rate of overcrowding was 9 percent in Hackney and 10 percent in Tower Hamlets).
- 28 percent had inadequate water supply or sanitation.
- 24 percent reported significant damp.
- 28 percent said their heating was inadequate.
- 48 percent came from families whose head of household was Asian, African, or Afro-Caribbean (they make up 18 percent of the population in Hackney and 11 percent in Tower Hamlets).

The authors concluded:

> Despite the rapid advances in medical technology in the twentieth century and the current economic growth of Britain, the majority of children admitted to an inner city hospital are suffering from infectious diseases such as respiratory tract infections and gastroenteritis. Prevention of such conditions is more likely to be facilitated by improving housing conditions and poverty than by improving hospital and medical services. (Carter et al. 1990, 185)

The 1980 Black Report is perhaps the best known recent exposition of the impact of poverty on poor health and premature death (Townsend and Davidson 1982). It was updated in 1987 by *The Health Divide*, which showed the persistence of health inequalities (Whitehead 1987). The *British Medical Journal* has shown that this gap is still widening and likely to become even more pronounced in the future:

> The notion of the dispossessed and feckless underclass that imposes costs on the rest of society and is to blame for most social ills is becoming popular. Such an idea has obvious consequences for social policy, yet it sits uneasily with the evidence from studies of differential mortality, which reiterate the fact that British society is stratified to a fine grain from top to bottom. (Davy Smith, Bartley, and Blane 1990, 377)

CONCLUSIONS AND PROSPECTS

In 1988/89, over a fifth of the population of the United Kingdom was living in poverty, as were around a quarter of its children. Between 1979 and 1988/89, inequality grew substantially. For the first time since the Second World War, the share of income of the poorer sections of society is shrinking. In London, about one in seven of the population was living on means-tested income support. The faster rise in poverty and inequality began in the mid-seventies but galloped after 1979.

The principal causes of this increase in poverty are both access to the labor market and the extra costs of sickness, children, old age, and so on, which are inadequately supported by social security payments or welfare agencies. The rapid industrial changes—more rapid in London over recent years than in other parts of the country—brought widespread unemployment, often long-term. Alongside, employment structures changed radically, exposing a growing proportion of people to low-paid and insecure jobs. Changing family patterns, in particular the rise in the number of lone mothers, have also pushed a growing group into poverty and long-term reliance on social security. Each of these factors is of course shaped by class, "race," gender, and region. As we have seen, in London, the Pakistani and Bangladeshi population received none of the benefits of the decline in unemployment that happened for a few years after 1986–87, and they remain in the recession-hit 1990s apparently firmly excluded from employment.

The consequences of such poverty are well known. Poverty means going short materially, socially, and emotionally. It means spending less on food, on heating, and on clothing than someone on an average income. But it is not what is spent that matters, but what isn't. Poverty means staying at home, often being bored, not seeing friends, not going to the cinema, not going out for a drink, and not being able to take the children out for a trip or a treat or a holiday. It means coping with the stresses of managing on very little money, often for months or even years. It means having to withstand the onslaught of society's pressure to consume. It impinges on relationships with others. Above all, poverty takes away the tools to build the blocks for the future—your "life chances." It steals away the opportunity to have a life unmarked by sickness, a decent education, a secure home, and a long retirement. It stops people being able to plan ahead. It stops people being able to take control of their lives. So poverty widens the gap between reality and potential.

The figures we have looked at mainly stop in the late 1980s. They take no account of a number of more recent changes. When challenged with the stark evidence of inequality and poverty derived from their own figures, the Conservative government's confident response is that these findings are out of date. They argue that they take no account of the changes in employment patterns or social security reforms. The situation, they say, is getting better. But how sustainable is such a view?

Ministers now admit that we have experienced the effects of a deep recession. The Gross Domestic Product was predicted to grow by just 0.7 percent in 1991–92, a fall of 3 percent from the average rise for each year over the previous ten years. Unemployment rose to touch three million in 1993. Recent rises have hit the southeast more than other regions. Industrial surveys are gloomy, and the figures show manufacturing output is at its lowest level since the bottom of the recession of 1980.

Income distribution has been further skewed in the direction of the more affluent. The 1988 budget brought in further income tax cuts for those on average incomes, but also especially for the rich. The introduction of flatrate poll tax would have hit not only the most vulnerable but also the near-poor and given a generous bonanza to people on high incomes. While the pattern of tax reform moved resources toward the top of the income scale, social security policies toward the poor were stringently controlled.

The most radical overhaul of social security was fully implemented in April 1988. On the government's own figures, 43 percent stood to lose, 37 percent to gain, and 20 percent to experience no change in their incomes as a result of the changes (DHSS 1987). All the evidence indicates that poverty is as entrenched as ever and that some claimants have experienced real falls in their standard of living. For some people, the experience of poverty may be even more acute, as they have to meet repayment of social fund loans and cover all their water rates from their basic benefit. Further changes to VAT announced in the 1993 budget hit the poor hardest, especially the imposition of VAT on domestic fuel. In the future, the picture may well be worse.

London carries many different tensions and contradictions. As one of the leading international financial centers, it draws the very richest. But it is a magnet for the dispossessed and displaced and those who come in search of the "streets paved with gold." There is no London-wide authority, and many Inner London local authorities are barely able to cope with their responsibilities. This is both the result of enormous financial pressure and also a product of the problems of how large bureaucracies function. The legacy of high unemployment, low wages, and sharp polarization between wealth and poverty, white and black, Inner and Outer London and divisions within authorities themselves make the task of evolving a London-wide strategy particularly difficult.

Alongside the grim prospect on the national economic front, the mood among people in general may be changing. The British Social Attitudes Surveys show a substantial rise in the proportion of people who are prepared to finance greater social spending from increased taxes—a rise from a third to well over a half since 1983 (Jowell et al. 1990). It is on this foundation that we have to develop policies for change that can mitigate and shape the economic and social factors which will otherwise continue to expose a substantial minority of people living in London to poverty and exclusion.

References

Association of London Authorities (ALA). 1991. *The London Economy: The Recession and After.*
Atkinson, A. B. 1990. *Report on Households below Average Income, 1981–1987.* Paper for Social Services Select Committee.
Brown, C. 1984. *Black and White Britain.* Policy Studies Institute, Gower.
Bruegel, I. 1989. "Sex and Race in the Labour Market." *Feminist Review.*
Carter, E. P., et al. 1990. "Material Deprivation and Its Association with Childhood Hospital Admission in the East End of London." *Community Medicine* 15, no. 6 (June): 183–187.
Central Statistical Office. 1991. *Family Spending, A Report on the 1991 Family Expenditure Survey,* HMSO.
Department of Education and Science. 1979–1990. School Meals Census.
Department of Employment (DE). 1990a. *Historical Supplement, Employment Census 1989.*
Department of Employment (DE). 1990b. *Department of Employment Gazette,* November.
Department of Employment (DE). 1990c. "The Characteristics of the Unemployed." *Department of Employment Gazette,* May.
Department of Health and Social Security (DHSS). 1987. *The Impact of the Reformed Structure of Income Related Reforms.*
Department of Social Security (DSS). 1988. *Low Income Families Statistics.*
Department of Social Security (DSS). 1989. *Take-Up of Family Income Supplement, Housing Benefit, and Supplementary Benefit, Technical Notes.*
Department of Social Security (DSS). 1992. *Households below Average Income, A Statistical Analysis 1979–1988/89.*
General Synod of the Church of England. 1985. *Faith in the City, A Call for Action by Church and Nation. The Report of the Archbishop of Canterbury's Commission on Urban Priority Areas.* Church House Publishing.
Gordon, D., and P. Townsend. 1989. *Memorandum of Evidence to the House of Commons Social Security Committee.*
House of Commons. 1990. *Hansard,* November 13, col. 123.
Islington Council. 1990. *Islington Council's Anti-Poverty Strategy, Briefing No. 3, Islington: Poverty in the 1980s.*
Jones Lang Wootton. 1991. *The Decentralisation of Offices from Central London.*
Jowell, R., et al. 1992. *British Social Attitudes, the 9th Report,* 1992/3 Edition, Dartmouth.
Kiernan, K., and M. Wicks. 1990. *Family Change and Future Policy.* Family Policy Studies Centre and Rowntree Memorial Trust.
London Chamber of Commerce and Industry (LCCI). 1990. *London Economic Report and Survey.* October.
London Research Centre. 1989. *Annual Abstract of Greater London Statistics, 1987–88.*

London Research Centre. 1990. *Review of London's Needs*, 5th Ed., *1990–91*.
Low Pay Unit. 1990. "Low Pay in Great Britain and the Regions." Parliamentary Briefing no. 1.
Millar, J., and C. Glendinning. 1989. "Gender and Poverty: a Survey Article." *Journal of Social Policy* 18, pt. 3 (July): 363–381.
National Council for One-Parent Families (NCOPF). 1985. *One-Parent Families in Great Britain*. Information sheet.
Office of Population Censuses and Surveys. 1990. Population Trends, HMSO.
Oppenheim, C. 1993. *Poverty: The Facts*. CPAG.
Smith, G. D., M. Bartley, and D. Blane. 1990. "The Black Report on Socioeconomic Inequalities in Health: Ten Years On." *British Medical Journal* 301, August 18–25: 373–377.
Social Services Committee (SSC). 1990. *Households below Average Income: A Regional Analysis*. HMSO.
Townsend, P., and N. Davidson. 1982. *Inequalities in Health: The Black Report*. Pelican.
Unemployment Unit. May 1991. Unemployment: Totals and Rates in Parliamentary Constituencies.
Unemployment Unit. 1990. Working Brief.
Whitehead, M. 1987. *The Health Divide*. Health Education Council.

5

City of Darkness, City of Light: Crime, Drugs, and Disorder in London and New York

Geoffrey Pearson

Some time ago an American friend, with whom I had been discussing the "underclass" debate, passed on a joke to the effect that the only way to understand New York was that it was being developed as a "theme park" for Charles Dickens's London. The London made known to us by Dickens was a place where glittering wealth lived cheek by jowl against alarming poverty. A fog-bound sprawling city in which crime and violence lurked in every shadow. A place where homeless beggars littered the streets, and where the working poor lived in maggot numbers in their squalid dwellings. It was also the London of Frederick Engels, who reckoned that Manchester was even worse, and of Henry Mayhew. It was a city which was repeatedly described by these and their contemporaries as a "swamp" and a "wen." Its working-class quarter of the East End was judged so remote as to be seen as an "undiscovered country" and a "foreign country," its inhabitants as belonging to a different "tribe" or "race." Drunkenness and depravity issued from every pore of its social being, although one might have even wondered (the Victorians certainly did) whether this was a truly "human" life form or merely a soulless animality. Sanitary metaphors were repeatedly and obsessively applied to these "foul wretches" and "human vermin": a "moral sewerage" which breathed the "miasma of vice" in the "cess-pits," "plague spots," and "sinks of iniquity" which served as their ghetto homes (Pearson 1975). By comparison, Shelley was being almost matter-of-fact when in 1819 he wrote that "Hell is a city much like London."

It must be admitted, nevertheless, that the often alarmist social commentary on mid-nineteenth-century London does an admirable job as metaphor (or joke) for late twentieth-century New York: the tangible fears of the respectable classes about the "dangerous classes" and the "underclass"; the actualities of crime and violence in the streets, together with the associated perceptions that crime is growing and criminals becoming younger, and that lawlessness (like diseases such as cholera and AIDS) is creeping out of the poor neighborhoods into those of the more affluent; the intensified focus on depravity as a consequence of the gin shop, the beer shop, and now the crack house; the untidy proximity of ostentatious wealth and the public squalor of homelessness and begging in the streets. It is an extraordinary set of resemblances, although having "unpacked" the content of this joking metaphor what stands revealed is plainly not a laughing matter.

Forgotten History: Contrasting Visions of Civility and Modernity

Whatever else these historical comparisons might tell us, it seems clear that the "underclass" is not a new phenomenon. It was known at different times in London's history as that of the "dangerous classes," the "residuum," or the "submerged tenth" (Stedman Jones 1971; Himmelfarb 1985). The underclass debate, therefore, should be recognized for what it is: a new engagement with an old problem. One, nevertheless, which has the habit of dressing itself up in new clothes as an "unprecedented" and "unparalleled" development.

Without wishing to diminish the problems of poverty, unemployment, and homelessness in any way, a further recognition is necessary that the social preoccupation with crime and disorder also has its own connected history of complaint against what are imagined to be unparalleled difficulties. Indeed, our understanding of the criminal question is itself so often diminished by the tendency to view crime as if it had suddenly appeared from nowhere. Crime is commonly discussed in narrowly defined generational terms as if it were something which had arisen as a result of the moral weakness of the present day (Pearson 1983). It is then linked to a sense of the artificiality and hollowness of contemporary values by the use of evocative historical reference points such as "twenty or thirty years ago" or "since the war." We know the pattern of the complaint well enough:

> That's the way we're going nowadays. Everything slick and stream-lined, everything made out of something else. Celluloid, rubber, chromium-steel everywhere ... radios all playing the same tune, no vegetation left, everything cemented over.... There's something that's gone out of us in these twenty years since the war.

Or again:

> The passing of parental authority, defiance of pre-war conventions, the absence of restraint, the wildness of extremes, the confusion of unrelated

liberties, the wholesale drift away from churches, are but a few characteristics of after-war conditions.

But here, immediately, is the difficulty. Because these familiar "postwar" complaints come from *before* the war. The first is George Orwell in his prewar novel *Coming Up for Air* (1939). The second is a Christian youth worker, James Butterworth, writing in 1932 about his work and achievements in the South London slum neighborhood of the Elephant and Castle, amidst the sweeping changes of the "postwar" years. It is merely one further historical irony that it was from this same area of working-class London that the "Teddy Boy" youth culture first appeared in the 1950s, amidst ringing accusations that the Teds were symptomatic of the "Americanizing" influences of postwar mass culture signified in the advent of rock-and-roll.

The steadiness of the complaint in this "postwar blues" is merely part of a large historical canvas. The tendency to describe crime and immorality as a recent, unprecedented interruption in our affairs can be traced back through and beyond the nineteenth century, whereby, in a connected history, successive generations have lamented the moral devastation which surrounds them and looked back to a fondly remembered "Golden Age" of tranquility (Pearson 1983). The historical constancy of crime thereby appears through some kind of magician's trick as perpetual novelty: a tendency which is deeply symptomatic of the way in which we talk (indeed, the way in which we feel) about crime.

If one were to trace the cultural and economic trajectories of New York and London, and the way in which each city has succumbed to periods of social apprehension about crime and violence, significant differences would no doubt be revealed. Each city would have its own versions of nostalgia with which to contrast its current state of disrepair. A key element in these differences would be contrasting responses to the experience of modernity—of which the "postwar blues" is a popular version.

If, to follow Raymond Williams (1989, 34) in his account of cultural modernity, New York is *the* city of exiled artists and emigrés, then it is also a city of exiles and emigrés of every kind. New York cannot be thought of except as a city of immigrants—it has no other history—reflecting in an intensified form wider experience of the United States as a nation of immigrants. On one reading of events, the dominant culture of the United States has distanced itself from this turmoil of cultures and peoples—embracing in its place a mythic culture of "sameness" whereas New York remained a "centre of 'difference'" (Bender 1989). Accordingly, in the context of New York's current and prolonged moment of decline, one vital aspect of the nostalgia which laps at its shores is that which remembers a rich pluralism (a "mosaic," as Mayor Dinkins once described it) which once held together peoples and cultures of many different origins. Now, to follow this sorry narrative, all that has fallen apart into warring ethnic factions, suburban discontents, and "white flight" from the embrace of pluralism (Sleeper 1989). The story line is, of course, not unique to New York: it is one that has already been told by Richard Sennett (1970) in his lament for the "good old days" of Chicago.

London is, of course, a much older city than New York. What this means, at least according to some versions of events, is that London has been falling apart for much longer. Henry Fielding in his *Enquiry into the Causes of the Late Increase of Robbers* (1751) had already glimpsed the awful future whereby the anonymous concealments of city life offered a sanctuary for lawlessness:

> I make no Doubt, but that the Streets of this Town, and the Roads Leading to it, will shortly be impassable without—the utmost Hazard.... Whoever indeed considers the Cities of *London* and *Westminster*, with the late vast Addition of their Suburbs—the great Irregularity of their Buildings, the immense Number of Lanes, Alleys, Courts and Bye-Places, must think, that, had they been intended for the very Purpose of Concealment, they could scarce have been better contrived. Upon such a View, the whole appears as Vast Wood or forest, in which a Thief may harbour with as great Security, as wild Beasts do in the Deserts of *Africa* or *Arabia*. (Fielding 1751, 76)

In spite of the "unmodernized" language, this is an immediately familiar complaint against the dense folds of the city within which civilization has begun to unravel into a novel form of savagery, physically embodied in the "concrete jungle." From an English point of view, perhaps the only oddity is that Fielding looked to "Africa" and "Arabia" for his alien reference points, rather than discerning the portents of the future in some dreadful process of "Americanization." That would come later.

English fears of "Americanization" can offer a useful point of entry in terms of comparison between the myths and traditions of civility in London and New York. The complaint is by no means new. Matthew Arnold, author of *Culture and Anarchy*, which was profoundly influential in defining the assumed character of English civility, had in 1848 already warned of "a wave of ... American *vulgarity*, moral, intellectual and social, preparing to break over us" (O'Connell 1950, 68). Again, in 1861, he was to be found brooding over how one might "prevent the English people from becoming 'Americanised,'" which was, he thought, "to use a short and significant modern expression which everyone understands" (Super 1962, 16). As documented by Martin Wiener (1981) in *English Culture and the Decline of the Industrial Spirit*, a profound counterrevolution took place among the English middle class from the mid-nineteenth century onwards, whereby the home of the first Industrial Revolution turned its back on industry, modernization, and urbanism as its defining characteristics and embraced a nostalgic vision of ruralism as the organizing principle of the "English way of life." It was a tradition of Englishness which was "both idyllic and drenched in anxiety about change" (Wiener 1981, 53). A central element of this structure of feeling concerned what Wiener calls the "American spectre" which, for both conservatives and socialists, came to stand for vulgarity, mechanization, excessive individualism, materialism... and crime.

In a somewhat trivialized version of the complaint, "America" was to come to represent what the future held in store: the adoption of the term "mugging" to describe street crime in the early 1970s, together with more recent warnings of an impending crack explosion in Britain offer specific instances of this kind of thinking. But the general preoccupation with the threat of "Americanization" has been informed and consolidated by a long and connected history. One form of opposition was reflected in a steady downpour of accusation in the twentieth century against the American cinema and popular culture, which was seen by highbrow critics such as F. R. Leavis and lowbrow headline writers alike to be both criminogenic and to be undermining the "English way of life" (Pearson 1983, 1984; Wiener 1981). Writing in 1930, Leavis summed up the general temper of these complaints against modernity which were understood to be indelibly associated with America:

> The automobile (to take one instance) has, in a few years, radically affected religion, broken up the family, and revolutionised social custom. Change has been so catastrophic that the generations find it hard to adjust themselves to each other, and parents are helpless to deal with their children. It is a breach of continuity that threatens. It is commonplace that we are being Americanised. (Leavis 1930, 6–7)

One significant effect of Leavis's complaint is the way in which it links "Americanisation" as a symbol of modernity with the question of generational conflicts, reflecting the way in which "youth" and "modernity" also often appear as twinned concepts within these troubled discourses. Moreover, in view of the fact that both in criminological theory and in commonsense reasoning it is a basic assumption that crime is a consequence of "modernity"—through the loosening of custom and tradition—and taking into account that "youth" and "crime" are also regarded as synonomous, we arrive at a whole cluster of potential discontents whereby the youth-crime-modernity connection is aligned with the process of "Americanization."

The prewar anxieties of Leavis and others (which they would, of course, have understood as an expression of a "postwar" malaise) would continue in the years following the Second World War in an intensified form around the "youth question." For Richard Hoggart, writing in the 1950s, the "Jukebox Boys" and "Teddy Boys" were deeply symptomatic of the weakening influences of "affluence" and "admass" within the English working class: "boys between fifteen and twenty, with drape suits, picture ties, and an American slouch" (Hoggart 1958, 248). Elsewhere, the accusation was carried to excess, as in the exclamations of the Tory *Daily Mail* newspaper directed against the arrival of rock-and-roll music. At a time when "Teddy Boys" were attracting widespread publicity as a result of cinema riots—tearing up the seats and dancing in the aisles as a means of welcoming films such as Bill Haley's *Rock around the Clock*—rock-and-roll was described as a "music of delinquents" and a "communicable disease."

> It is deplorable. It is tribal. And it is from America. It follows rag-time, blues, dixie, jazz, hot cha-cha and the boogie-woogie, which surely originated in the jungle. We sometimes wonder whether this is the negro's revenge. (*Daily Mail*, September 5, 1956)

Here we have all the components of the structure of feeling: a youthful, criminogenic symptom of modernity, imported from America and impregnated with "alien" inspirations. Against this backcloth of a general aversion to what is taken as "American," we can point to more specific points of opposition in the historical trajectories and myths of civility in London and New York. Where London is concerned, we need to contrast the city's actual history as against its mythic history. London's actual history, as for many years the world's largest port, is that of a teeming cosmopolitan center (Braudel 1984; George 1966). Unlike New York's, however, its remembered history—history, that is, as myth—is quite different. Not only is it a much older city, thereby both dignified and burdened by the traditions (real and imagined) of the past. It is also the seat of national government (the "Mother of Parliaments") and of what had been taken for a unified and homogeneous ethnicity—namely "Englishness." So that, whereas in the case of New York, the turmoil of ethnic pluralism and modernity could be taken as one and the same thing, for London the modernizing impact of the city was grasped as an internalized breakup within a supposedly unified ethnicity.

At the dawn of the twentieth century, faced with what was seen as a "new race" of city dwellers, numerous social commentators had been baffled by what they understood as the "fickle excitability" of London's urban population. There was "a characteristic physical type of town dweller," Charles Masterman (1902, 7–8) thought in *The Heart of the Empire*, "stunted, narrow-chested, easily wearied; yet voluble, excitable, with little ballast, stamina or endurance." "A new race has sprung up, a street people," wrote Jack London (1902, 137) in *The People of the Abyss*. "The traditional silent and reserved Englishman has passed away. The pavement folk are noisy, voluble, high-strung, excitable." There was a repetitious familiarity in these complaints. Reginald Bray (1907, 145–46) in *The Town Child* agreed that

> a deliberate slowness in action was once the characteristic of the Englishman. He would look around a situation before he leapt into it.... This quality has of late years been less in evidence.... The most remarkable effect of an urban environment is to be sought in the disappearance of the habit of self-control.

Whereas for Baden-Powell, in the first edition of his *Scouting for Boys*, the sight of the "hysterical" urban mob at a football stadium summoned up a characteristic Edwardian English swan song on the decline of the "race" and the lessons of the fall of the Roman Empire:

> They paid men to play their games for them, so that they could look on without the fag of playing, just as we are doing in football now.... Thousands of boys and young men, pale, narrow-chested, hunched up, miserable specimens, smoking endless cigarettes, numbers of them betting, all of them learning to be hysterical as they groan or cheer in panic unison with their neighbours.... One wonders whether this can be the same nation which had gained for itself the reputation of being a stolid, pipe-sucking manhood, unmoved by panic or excitement, and reliable in the tightest of places. (Baden-Powell 1908, 314, 338)

Within the selected tradition of what it is to be English, notions of "fair play," the "stiff upper lip," and sangfroid are thus dominant. Crime and violence are understood to be utterly foreign to these traditions. So that whereas a history of New York would be unimaginable without reference to the rougher side of its street life—reflecting the wider glorification of rugged individualism in the mythic history of the American Wild West—London, like England more generally, suffers from a profound amnesia where any hint of disorder in the past might be concerned. The image of the unarmed "British bobby," personified by the unhurried stride of Dixon of Dock Green, aptly sums up this idea of a city once at peace with itself.

As myth, the idea of crime-free streets in a preexisting era of tranquility is powerfully evocative within English culture. As actuality, however, it is instantly refutable. There is, for example, abundant evidence that in late Victorian London and the earlier decades of the twentieth century, policemen attempting to make arrests in the open street were frequently assaulted, sometimes by large crowds intent on rescuing the prisoner (Pearson 1983; White 1979, 1983, 1986). The extent of hostility to the police was such that in the late 1890s and early 1900s, one in four of London's uniformed policemen were assaulted each year in the course of their duty, of whom one in ten would be on the sick list for a fortnight or more (Parliamentary Papers 1900,

1908). These traditions of resistance to arrest remained active into the interwar years—although they are overlaid and obscured, once again, by historical amnesia and myth.

The actualities of crime and disorder in the past not only insist upon a reassessment of London's criminal history and street life. More particularly, accusations such as these against the breakdown of family life require a reconsideration of the actual character of "Victorian values." Quite apart from the many material injustices which might be placed at the door of Mrs. Thatcher during her period of government, there was also an ideological emphasis which elevated the Victorian era to one of a gold standard of moral worth. "Victorian values" became an emblem of defiance to the supposedly weakening influences of "permissiveness," a Medusa's Head which could freeze and immobilize all reasonable opposition to the Iron Lady's attempts to dismantle the welfare state and to impose the virtues of self-help and the free market upon the nation. "Victorian values" would guarantee that Great Britain was great again. They would reassert parental authority, revitalize the rule of law, and rid us of the "worm within" of crime.

It is a matter of no satisfaction whatsoever to report that recorded crime doubled during Mrs. Thatcher's years in office. It is, however, a matter of some historical satisfaction that it was in the twilight years of Queen Victoria's long reign that a decisive word entered into common English usage: "Hooligan." The precipitating events in the late summer of 1898 involved an excessively violent August Bank Holiday celebration in London (Pearson 1983, 1989). There were numerous reports in the press of gangs of youths fighting pitched battles in the street, jostling and pushing down innocent bystanders, and hurling themselves at policemen attempting arrests in the open street with cries of "Rescue! Rescue!" and "Boot 'im!" Some of the gangs were reported to be armed with pistols and revolvers. More commonly, they fought with a conventional armory of iron-toed boots, leather belts with metal buckles, sticks and knives, and powerful catapults. They were organized by street, neighborhood, or public house, and there must have been many overlapping bonds of kinship. Moreover, the original Hooligans had adopted a uniform dress-style: bell-bottom trousers cut tight at the knee, with a tasty buttoned vent in the leg; a rakish neckscarf and a jaunty peaked cap; and heavy belts adorned with metal-stud designs. There was also a characteristic Hooligan hairstyle: the "donkey fringe" in which the hair was cut very short on the scalp with a fringe at the forehead.

The newly named "Hooliganism" provided a crystallizing focus not only for rampant fears of "racial degeneration" at the turn of the century but, more particularly, for the supposed deterioration of the morals and habits of the young. Reginald Bray (1911, 102), an otherwise careful observer on the youth question, took the view that "the city-bred youth is growing up in a state of unrestrained liberty." The complaint was widespread. Young people were said to "have tasted too much freedom" (Braithwaite 1904, 189) and to "have emancipated themselves from all home influence and restraints" (Gorst 1901, 213). Evidence placed before the Inter-Departmental Committee on Physical Deterioration described how young people "throw off all parental responsibility . . . get to congregating about the street corners at night . . . become what we call 'corner boys,' and get drunken habits" (Parliamentary Papers 1904, 2107). Another government enquiry of the period went so far as to assert that "the gamins of our large towns . . . live a bandit life away from their homes, free of all control" (Parliamentary Papers 1910, xxviii).

The origins of the word "Hooligan" remain obscure (and dictionaries are of little help), but the word probably emerged from the London music hall culture of the early 1890s. Indeed, initially the words "Hooligan" and "Hooliganism" were applied specifically to London street life. Gang formations such as these had, however, been known and feared in Manchester since the 1880s, where they were called "Scuttlers" and their gang fights "Scuttling." "Ikes" or "Ikey Lads" had been another common Manchester expression, whereas, in Birmingham, gangs with the same fighting habits and the same taste in clothes were known as "Peaky Blinders." From Manchester, Charles Russell's *Manchester Boys* (1905) provided detailed observations on the Scuttler and his habits. And it was also from Manchester that we have the following description of the ornamental designs which adorned the belts worn by the gangs, which together with the "puncher's cap" and "narrow-go-wide" trousers were said to be the main features of the Scuttler's dress-style.

> Many of these belts are very curious, bearing remarkable designs upon them. These are made by the insertion of a large number of pins, which are used to form a design the whole length of the belt. The pins are inserted into the leather, then broken off, and filed down to a level with the leather. These designs include figures of serpents, a heart pierced with an arrow (this appears to be a favourite design), Prince of Wales' feathers, clogs, animals, stars, etc., and often either the name of the wearer of the belt or that of some woman. (Devine 1890, 2)

If this is reminiscent of more recent dress-styles in which young people create metal-stud designs on leather belts and jackets, there were other points of similarity. One way-out young man who appeared before a London magistrates' court amidst the August disturbances of 1898 had adopted an exaggerated version of the Hooligan "donkey fringe" in a manner which prefigured the haircare of later Skinheads or Mohican fashions: "His hair had been clipped as closely as possible to the scalp, with the exception of a small patch on the crown of the head, which was pulled down over the forehead to form a fringe" (*Daily Graphic*, August 6, 1898). We were told that "the appearance of the witness caused some amusement in court." And with good reason. What these late Victorian Londoners were looking at, although they did not know it, was the visible manifestation of a "youth culture:" supposedly the distinctively modern stamp of youthful "freedom" in the postwar "permissive" generation. Plus ça change.

Not Poverty, but "Wickedness": Crime and Disorder in the Thatcher Years

I have dwelt upon the "amnesiac" qualities of English responses to crime and violence because of the way in which they set a context for the events of the 1980s—the Thatcher years. The "Iron Lady" had been elected on a law-and-order ticket and never made any secret of the fact that she was contemptuous of any way of thinking about crime other than as "wickedness." The idea that crime might be linked to socioeconomic conditions was repeatedly shouted down by both Mrs. Thatcher and her ministers, to the point where the Church of England was accused of "Marxism" when the report of the Archbishop of Canterbury's working party *Faith in the City* (1985) was published and, among its other arguments, pointed to the roots of crime and disorder in the impoverished inner city (*Guardian*, December 2, 1985). And this is certainly not the only time that the Conservative government has found itself on a collision course with the Church on questions of crime and poverty (*Guardian*, November 19, 1984, February 11, 1988, September 20, 1991; *Daily Telegraph*, September 21, 1991).

In spite of the law-and-order rhetoric of the Thatcher governments, recorded crime advanced rapidly in the 1980s, which also witnessed sporadic outbreaks of serious rioting and looting in a number of Britain's cities—London, Liverpool, Manchester, Birmingham, Bristol, and elsewhere (Benyon and Solomos 1987; Solomos 1988). Areas of England and Scotland also experienced a major heroin epidemic during the 1980s, which settled with particular severity in areas of high unemployment, social deprivation, and housing decay (Pearson, Gilman, and McIver 1986; Pearson 1987a, 1987b; Pearson and Gilman 1994; Burr 1987; Parker, Bakx, and Newcombe 1988). As the British Crime Survey conducted by the Home Office Research and Planning Unit confirmed, crime and the fear of crime were also concentrated in the poorest neighborhoods (Hough and Mayhew 1985). In some areas of Inner London, local crime surveys such as the Islington Crime Survey suggested that as many as one-third of all women avoided going out after dark, which was said to amount to "a virtual curfew of the female population" (Jones, MacLean, and Young 1986, 201).

As one consequence of the impact of crime and the fear of crime in working-class neighborhoods of London and elsewhere during the 1980s, we have not only the conventional brand of law-and-order enthusiasts from the ranks of the Conservative party—urging tougher penalties and a return to "traditional" values—but also a new kind of "left realism," which has attracted support from some sections of the Labour party. Largely associated with the work of Jock Young, this left-realist position argues that we must "take crime seriously" and is highly critical of earlier left and radical responses which organized their understanding of law-and-order politics around the concept of the "moral panic" and orchestrated mass media sensationalism (Young 1986).

Another significant departure is the left-realist critique of earlier victim surveys which had identified a paradox whereby the highest levels of the fear of crime had been found among women and the elderly—social groups which had been found to be the lowest in terms of actual victimization levels (Hough and Mayhew 1983; Gottfredson 1984; Maxfield 1984; Walmsley 1986). Crime surveys had tended to indicate that in Britain the social groups with the highest levels of victimization by personal violence, for example, were young men under the age of twenty-nine years and particularly those who went out drinking regularly. However, as the Islington Crime Survey argues following feminist theorists and researchers such as Jalna Hanmer and Elisabeth Stanko, this "paradox" neglects violence in the private sphere: specifically crimes against women, such as wife battering ("domestic violence") and sexual assaults (including marital rape) among intimates and acquaintances (Hanmer and Saunders 1984; Stanko 1987). When "domestic violence" is counted in the picture, as in the Islington survey, then women's apparently exaggerated fear of crime emerges as a more rational response to actual levels of victimization and harassment; according to the findings of the Islington Crime Survey, women suffer more personal violence than men. Moreover, some age groups and ethnic groups (young Asian women, for example) suffer unusually high levels of victimization in the public sphere, such as snatch thefts.

Unfortunately, the Islington Crime Survey remains silent on the victimization of the elderly, and there are other crucial weaknesses in its approach to crime and policing. For example, it remains trapped within its own version of historical amnesia, ignoring the careful documentation by White (1979, 1983, 1986) of Islington's sometimes turbulent street life in the interwar years. Its authors are also entangled in a complex local antagonism on their attitude toward "race" and crime (Gilroy 1987a, 1987b; Gilroy and Sim 1987; Sim, Scraton, and Gordon 1987). On even the most generous reading, left realism treads a fine line on this matter. In a nutshell, if "taking crime seriously" means offering a privileged epistemological status to popular conceptions and fears of crime—the pulse of anxiety quickened and given shape by explicitly racialist stereotypes in the popular press and elsewhere—

then the definition of "crime" which emerges is one deeply impregnated with racialist meanings.

Even so, although a variety of research has provided abundant (if often complex) evidence of discriminatory practices against black people by both the London police and the courts (Smith and Gray 1985; Institute of Race Relations 1987; Walker 1988, 1989; Pearson et al. 1989; Cashmore and McLaughlin 1991), we know surprisingly little in any formal sense about patterns of crime and victimization within Britain's black communities. Unlike New York, where there is a tradition of rich and often sensitive portrayals of the intersections of crime and ethnicity (Joselit 1983; Courtwright, Joseph, and Des Jarlais 1989; T. Williams 1989; Bourgois 1989; Short 1991; Chin 1990), this is a silent chapter in British social research, to be contrasted with the noisy excitements of the mass media. Moreover, we do not find that particular emphasis which is quite commonly found in North American research whereby certain types of crime—typically the provision of illicit goods and services such as illegal gambling, prostitution, and drugs—are understood as a means by which minority groups who are discriminated against and disadvantaged in formal labor markets can stake out an economic niche for themselves (Williams and Kornblum 1985; Reuter, MacCoun, and Murphy 1990). There are hints of such an approach, but it is rarely well developed (Samuel 1981; Dench 1991; Dixon 1991). What we have, by contrast, is reflected in some of the most compelling criminological research in recent years, which has focused on how similar concerns can illuminate the activities of white "villains" in working-class neighorhoods of the East End and South London (Hobbs 1988; Foster 1990). It is clear from this that the "traditional" working-class pursuits of "ducking and diving" and "bobbing and weaving"—whereby entrepreneurial working-class skills are interwoven between the formal and informal, licit and illicit economies—remain an active source of London's criminality.

The question of "race" has nevertheless been propelled into the center of British public discourses on crime, drugs, and disorder. The early 1970s' moral panic concerning "mugging," which was subjected to extensive theoretical analysis by Stuart Hall and his colleagues in *Policing the Crisis*, was a means by which the authoritarian social movement which subsequently came to be known as "Thatcherism" flexed its muscles and achieved a cultural and political hegemony (Hall et al. 1978). Evidence produced by the Metropolitan Police (1974) in the Brixton area of South London had suggested that whereas 85 percent of street robberies ("violent thefts" or "muggings") were committed by blacks, a similar proportion of victims were white: a statistic which was quickly latched on to by the National Front as part of its racist political propaganda. Subsequently, a comparison of police statistics in Brixton and other parts of London identified a marked tendency for street thefts to be more likely to be categorized as "violent" in the Brixton area: a process of "up-criming" which helped to fuel a self-fulfilling prophecy of hostility and counterhostility between the police and significant sections of the black community (Blom-Cooper and Drabble 1982).

The "race" issue was given a sharp twist in the tail by outbreaks of rioting (or "uprisings") which visited a number of British cities, including Brixton and other parts of London, in the early 1980s. These invariably took place in "multiracial" areas: Brixton and Tottenham in London; St. Paul's in Bristol; Moss Side in Manchester; Toxteth in Liverpool; Handsworth in Birmingham. But these were not "race riots." Rather, they were "antipolice" riots, and it is not in serious dispute that both black and white youths were involved in most, if not all, of these disturbances which resulted in widespread looting, violent engagements with the police, and the petrol-bombing of houses and shops.

The 1981 Brixton riots occurred in two waves, in April and July. The July disturbances were followed by widespread rioting in other parts of the country which were described as "copycat" riots by the press, although in each case they were informed by long-standing grievances between the police and the African-Caribbean community which can be traced back to the early 1970s (Parliamentary Papers 1977; Pearson et al. 1989). Piecing together a complex and sometimes obscure pattern of evidence, it would appear that the London police had often pursued a low-key response toward potential street disorder in black neighborhoods in the early 1970s, preferring to retreat from moments of high tension and resistance to arrest rather than risk an escalation into full-blown violent confrontation (Metropolitan Police 1974). However, this placed the police in a contradictory position. A specific source of discontent within black communities had focused around active campaigns, which eventually received Parliamentary approval and endorsement, against the antiquated "Sus" law which derived from the 1824 Vagrancy Act and which legitimated the discriminatory use of stop-and-search powers by the police (Home Affairs Committee 1980). It is, then, a matter of tragic commentary that the immediate flashpoint for the Brixton riots was a massive stop-and-search street policing operation known by the Metropolitan Police as "Operation Swamp" which had targeted street crime (and hence young black men) in the area. It goes without saying, given English historical amnesia, that street robbery ("mugging") was widely understood as an entirely novel development which was utterly foreign to the English national character.

The public response to the summer riots of 1981 (principally in Brixton and other parts of London, Liverpool, and Manchester) was, thus, entirely predictable. For Mrs. Thatcher in the House of Commons, "the violence in Liverpool had nothing to do with the city's problems of pay, housing and unemployment. It was a spree of naked greed" (*Times*, July 10, 1981). Under the headline "Unemployment is NOT to Blame," it then fell to Mr. Peregrine Worsthorne, doyen of the *Sunday Telegraph* (July 12, 1981), to offer a characteristically forgetful history lesson to give emphasis to the point: "There was no rioting in the 1930s, when material conditions were far worse."

Mr. Worsthorne's contribution to the litany of historical irony could, in fact, hardly have been better timed: this was the fiftieth anniversary of a wave of political violence in 1931 when more than thirty towns and cities were visited by serious clashes between the police and unemployed who were protesting against dole cuts (Hannington 1973; Stevenson and Cook 1979; Pearson 1987c). It would, of course, be improper to suggest that Mr. Worsthorne might have been reading National Front literature, although some years earlier, in a little pamphlet giving advice to schoolchildren on *How to Spot a Red Teacher* (1977), the National Front had offered its own pennyworth of historical wisdom: "Tell the Red Teacher the poor whites during the Great Slump didn't commit muggings on defenceless old ladies." In fact, Mr. Worsthorne was himself not slow to play the race card: "Brixton is the iceberg tip of a crisis of ethnic criminality which is not Britain's fault, except in the sense that her rulers quite unnecessarily imported it" (*Sunday Telegraph*, November 20, 1981).

In her first response to the Brixton riot, Mrs. Thatcher had admittedly dithered on the question of social deprivation. "It may well be that unemployment is a factor," she had said in the House of Commons, "but I do not believe it is the principal factor" (*Daily Telegraph*, July 7, 1981). As her government learned that it was possible to survive electorally in spite of rapidly increasing unemployment, in the early 1980s, after Mr. Geoffrey Howe's "monetarist" budget of 1981 had crashed the economy, there were to be few further concessions to the idea that social and economic policies were linked to inner-city problems of crime and violence.

There was a particularly blunt expression of this kind of view by Mr. Douglas Hurd, newly appointed as Home Secretary, in response to the devastating riot in the rundown Birmingham district of Handsworth in September 1985. Mr. Hurd had visited the scene of the riot for a photo opportunity, chatting with distressed residents in the burned-out streets. He had arrived in an upmarket Daimler motorcar but had found it necessary to make a hurried exit in the back of a police van after he had been stoned by an angry crowd. The rioting, he said later, was "not a social phenomenon but crimes" (*Guardian*, September 11, 1985). Stressing his view that it was a matter of human "wickedness," he was also quoted as saying that "it is not a case history for sociologists to pore over, but a case for the police" (*Guardian*, September 23, 1985).

Indeed, to an overwhelming extent the events of 1981 and 1985 were understood not as a problem to be confronted in terms of the socioeconomic difficulties of impoverished inner-city communities but as a question of police tactics and strategy. The tragic circumstances which accompanied and provoked the renewed rioting in London only days after the Handsworth disturbances—when, in Brixton, an innocent black woman, Mrs. Sherry Groce, had been accidentally shot and seriously wounded by the police; and, on the Broadwater Farm estate in Tottenham, an elderly black woman, Mrs. Cynthia Jarrett, had collapsed and died during a police raid at her home on a trumped-up charge against her son—necessarily justify a detailed scrutiny of police procedures. Nevertheless, such tragic events do not in themselves "cause" riots. Serious disorders such as those which set many parts of Britain's cities ablaze in 1981 and 1985 draw upon much more deeply rooted grievances, grievances which were submerged in the emphasis on "law-and-order" tactics and the need to "regain control" of the inner cities. So that, if we adopt Neil Smelser's (1962) formulation of an understanding of "collective violence," the focus of official attention was on the "precipitating factors" of the riots rather than the "underlying structural strain."

Admittedly, in 1981, there had been some feeble attempts by members of the Labour party to set the events in the context of unemployment and social deprivation. However, it was really only in Lord Scarman's report on the Brixton disorders that questions of housing, education, and employment were centrally positioned in his discussions of the social frustrations with which policing under such socioeconomic circumstances must contend: "Unless the police adjust their policies and operations so as to handle these difficulties with imagination as well as firmness, they will fail, and disorder will become a disease endemic in our society" (Scarman 1982, 15). One can question the weakness of Scarman's analysis of racial disadvantage and racism (Hall 1982). His ideas on community policing were not always well received by chief police officers (Reiner 1991). Nor were they flavor of the month with the boys on the beat, and there is no reason to believe that the "canteen culture" of the policeman in London and elsewhere, documented by Reiner (1985) and Holdaway (1983) among others, is not still an active force which reproduces and intensifies racist and sexist mentalities and approaches to the tasks of policing and contacts with the public (Smith and Gray 1985; Sampson et al. 1991; Pearson et al. 1989). Nevertheless, Lord Scarman's openness to the likelihood that "where deprivation and frustration exist on the scale to be found among the young black people of Brixton, the probability of disorder must be strong" (Scarman 1982, 36) was something of a beacon-light amidst an otherwise shabby official response.

As the complex events leading up to the Broadwater Farm riot indicate, when a community policeman, Mr. Keith Blakelock, was brutally murdered, long-standing grievances, mingled with new controversies such as drug dealing on the estate and a substantial police presence in the area, combined to provide a "flashpoint" (Gifford 1986). Tension had been raised on the "Farm" by a police operation directed against a suspected drug-dealing network. On October 5, a young black man, Floyd Jarrett, was stopped while driving his car on suspicion of having stolen the car. In an ensuing argument, he was charged with assaulting a police officer, a charge which was subsequently thrown out by the court, with Mr. Jarrett being awarded £350 costs against the police. While he was being detained by the police, however, police officers used his keys to enter his mother's home, whereupon she collapsed. Within hours of Mrs. Jarrett's death, the estate had become a tumult of rumor and activity. On the police side, these rumors included the bizarre idea that the largely disused underground car parks to high-rise flats had been flooded with "lakes of petrol," intended as a trap for policemen lured into the estate in the aftermath of the Broadwater Farm disturbance. Moreover, police enquiries merely reproduced and intensified such discontents. After a truly massive roundup of suspects in connection with PC Blakelock's death—he had been stabbed more than forty times in the chest and neck, and there were rumors that it was intended to carry his head around on a pole, but in all likelihood all that we will ever know in the way of truth is that he had been run over by a mob while attempting to give protection to a fire-fighting team—most of these charges were rejected on procedural grounds by the courts, but three men were charged and found guilty of his murder. Five years later, however, in November 1991, all three men were cleared on appeal in view of the fact that there had been scandalous abuses of police powers in the manufacture of evidence. Each of them had been convicted solely on the basis of uncorroborated "confessions," leading to widespread calls for a revision of the English system of justice in terms of evidence and procedure.

Quite apart from weighty points of constitutional detail, however, the Broadwater Farm disturbance had brought together all necessary elements in the tangled history of the riots of the early 1980s: an area of social deprivation and unemployment; a long-standing history of tension between the black community and the police; the discriminatory use of stop-and-search powers; the death of a black matriarch as the result of a police raid; a rapid and sustained period of rioting and looting; clear evidence of police malpractice in the collection of evidence and the bringing of cases against the accused; and a drugs angle. All this was already known to the black community. The one novel and tragic detail was the death of a police officer. It is a sad epitaph for Keith Blakelock, but his death might yet eventually trigger something more agreeable than an inner-city riot: a revision of English law (unnecessary in Scotland, where trials have to be arranged more promptly and where uncorroborated confessions are not accepted) which will serve all the people, black and white.

SMACK NOT CRACK:
THE 1980s HEROIN EPIDEMIC

There had also been a drugs angle in the Handsworth riot, where police action against cannabis dealing in a public house had been one of the precipitating factors. The official mention of an explicit drugs factor in the Handsworth and Tottenham disorders has suggested to some commentators that this is merely a further means by which to distance public responses from socioeconomic considerations (Solomos and Rackett 1991). Nevertheless, by the mid-1980s, it had become clear that a truly unprecedented illicit drug problem had emerged in many parts of Britain in the form of a heroin epidemic (Pearson, Gilman, and McIver 1986; Dorn and South 1987).

Britain had been something of a late developer in terms of drug problems. In spite of a Victorian legacy of widespread opium use, throughout the first half of the twentieth century, illicit drug use remained virtually unknown in the British Isles (Berridge and Edwards 1981; Spear 1969). In the late 1960s, London had experienced a miniepidemic of heroin misuse which, although it involved some severe local difficulties, has been widely misunderstood among otherwise well informed observers in the United States as resulting in the entire downfall of the health-oriented British drug control policy (Stimson and Oppenheimer 1982; Pearson 1991, 1992). It was, to all extents and purposes, a storm in a teacup. The real trouble brewed up from 1979, or thereabouts, when heroin started to become available in cheap and plentiful supply from the southwest Asian region of Iran, Afghanistan, and Pakistan (Lewis et al. 1985).

The 1980s heroin epidemic was initially associated with the novel practice of "Chasing the Dragon"—an expression adopted by some obscure process of linguistic diffusion from the Cantonese Hong Kong dialect, *júi lung*—which involved heating the drug on metal foil and inhaling the fumes. By circumventing the profound cultural taboo against self-injection, the habit spread like wildfire in many parts of England and Scotland where heroin had been previously quite unknown—Merseyside, Manchester, Glasgow, Edinburgh. Even so, there were huge local and regional variations in the spread of the problem, whether in terms of its severity or the extent to which the preferred mode of administration was intravenous drug use, or "chasing" (Pearson and Gilman 1994). The contours of the "smack" or "skag" culture in some areas of South London in the early 1980s have been well charted by Angela Burr (1987, 1989). In Glasgow, Jason Ditton had been the first to note the sudden upturn in the new heroin problem (Ditton and Speirits 1982; Haw 1985). In the north of England, and particularly in the northwest, the emerging difficulty was perhaps first noticeable in 1983 (Pearson, Gilman, and McIver 1985, 1986; Pearson 1987a; Parker, Bakx, and Newcombe 1988).

Whatever else might be said about the phoney novelty of Britain's problems of crime and disorder—the "foreign" importation of street crime; the "unprecedented" nature of hooliganism; the "sudden" interruption of rioting into an otherwise tranquil century—the heroin problem was new, and it was also seriously bad news, not only for drug users themselves but also for the communities in which they lived (Gilman and Pearson 1991). The difficulty soon adopted the form of a relentless drift toward self-injection, with the attendant risks of HIV infection. It was also a problem which was experienced with the utmost severity in already embattled and downtrodden working-class communities (Pearson 1987a, 1987b; Pearson and Gilman 1994).

A style of life emerged around the new heroin problem which would be immediately recognizable in New York, as the metronomic routines and hustles of "taking care of business" described by Ed Preble and James Casey (1969) came to the streets of Manchester, Liverpool, working-class London, and elsewhere. Here are just two examples (cf. Pearson 1987a, 134) of how young people described a typical day:

> "Like you get up, you've gotta go out, get your money, get your smack, come back, use it.... You're alright for ten minutes, go back out again, get money.... You're turkeying after a couple of hours, can't get nothin', whatever, back out again." (Colin, 23 years, Manchester)
>
> "What was your typical day, like?"
>
> "You just, get your gear, smoke it, and then... wonder where you'll get your next bag from and watch a bit of telly, well that's it.... That just makes you realise and you start thinking, 'God, what am I gonna do for tonight now?'... So, like, you try and go out and get more money, and that like, so your whole day's just taken up.... Go and do whatever you do for your money, buy your gear, get back, by then like... you smoke it... then tea-time comes around." (Sharon, 21 years, Merseyside)

The expression "tea-time" speaks volumes to the nature of the heroin epidemic of the 1980s. Young people from otherwise conventional working-class backgrounds and families were drawn into the wildfire epidemic, unlike the 1960s miniepidemic in London, which had often involved quasi-bohemian sections of hedonistic "freaks" and "deviants" (Stimson and Oppenheimer 1982). This is a characteristic pattern of serious drug epidemics, reminiscent of the way in which the rapid escalation of cocaine use in the United States in the late 1970s transformed and generalized both the image and actuality of the "typical" cocaine user (Waldorf, Reinarman, and Murphy 1991).

Where the British heroin epidemic differs markedly, however, from the U.S. experience of drug problems—sometimes to the astonishment of North American observers—is that black people were noticeable by their absence from the new heroin problem of the 1980s. In the face of this, we prosecute the necessary arguments as to why and whether black people are absent (or merely invisible) within the observable dimensions of the problem. Black heroin users certainly exist (Awiah, Butt, and Dorn 1990, 1992; Mirza, Pearson, and Phillips 1991). But they are considerably underrepresented in known populations of problem drug users. Is it that there are forms of cultural opposition to heroin use within the African-Caribbean community, for example, against what is seen as a "dirty white man's drug"? Or is it that black people are deterred from making contact with the available services either because of their perceived unresponsiveness and inaccessibility, or their actual discriminatory policies and practices? The truth of the matter is that we do not know.

Cocaine and crack use is another area of considerable uncertainty in Britain, and where the British experience again departs significantly from that of North America. Cocaine use is not unknown in Britain, and, during the miniepidemic of drug misuse in London in the 1960s, drug injectors would sometimes use a "speedball" cocktail of heroin and cocaine. Freebasing cocaine has also been a known technique among some sections of drug users for some years, although it was not commonly encountered. Indeed, where stimulant drugs are concerned, the use of amphetamines (known colloquially as "speed" or "whizz") has been a more traditional pursuit in Britain, although somewhat surprisingly it has been subject to little scrutiny by social researchers. Amphetamines are also much cheaper than cocaine, which still retains an image in Britain as a "champagne drug" rather than a "street drug" although there are some signs that this is beginning to change (Green et al. 1994).

When it comes to crack use, where local subcultural terminology will often refer to "rock" or "wash," although it is again not entirely unknown, it has failed to make any significant impact on the general character of British drug problems. Indeed, cocaine's marginality within patterns of illicit drug use in Britain is further underlined by the recent new wave of recreational drug use involving MDMA, or Ecstasy, which since the late 1980s has become increasingly popular among young people attending all-night dance venues, or "raves" (Pearson et al. 1991a, 1991b).

Nevertheless, there are reasons to remain extremely cautious about assessing the nature and scale of cocaine misuse in Britain. There is no doubt, for example, that a large amount of cocaine has been washing around the shores of Europe in recent years. Cocaine seizures in Britain as a whole have tended to outstrip those for heroin since 1987, although yearly figures have sometimes been distorted by single seizures of unusually large amounts of cocaine (National Drugs Intelligence Unit 1990). Even so, unless the interception rate for cocaine is higher than that for heroin for whatever reason, these high seizure levels would seem to stand in a contradictory relationship to the relative lack of evidence of large scale cocaine misuse and its associated problems in the British Isles.

Some clarity can be introduced into this otherwise confused picture on the basis of a survey of patterns of known drug use in an inner-city area of South London (Mirza, Pearson, and Phillips 1991). The London borough of Lewisham, in which the survey was conducted, has a population of one-quarter of a million people, of whom approximately 20 percent are black and largely of African-Caribbean descent. In its northern district of Deptford, which borders on the river Thames, Lewisham contains some of London's most serious poverty and social deprivation: an "urban wasteland" of high-rise housing estates where the borough's black population is also more densely concentrated (Hyde, Balloch, and Ainley 1989). In 1989 and 1990, a number of police raids had been directed against drug-dealing networks in this area, where quantities of crack and cocaine had been seized. Indeed, some sections of the press had dubbed one of Deptford's public housing estates "Crack City" as a direct consequence of these police operations (Pearson, Mirza, and Phillips 1993). This neighborhood of London therefore offered a useful testing ground for the widely assumed connection between the threatened crack problem and black people. Because, as the Metropolitan Police had confidently asserted in evidence to the Home Affairs Committee (1989, 51), "at the moment, crack is almost exclusively in the province of the black, mostly Jamaican, areas."

The Lewisham survey identified more than one thousand problem drug users known to a variety of agencies, including specialist drug agencies, the probation service, social services departments, and the police. Of these, little more than 5 percent were primarily cocaine users. By contrast, heroin and opiate use accounted for almost one-half of the total sample. One-third of all known cases concerned cannabis use, almost entirely as a result of police arrests for the unlawful possession of cannabis. The remaining 10 percent involved other drugs such as amphetamines, tranquilizers, and hallucinogens such as LSD.

There were, however, striking disparities between the kinds of drug users known to different kinds of agencies. Where drug agencies were concerned, for example, heroin and other opiates were identified as the central difficulty in 85 percent of known cases, whereas heroin accounted for only 5 percent of police arrests. Cannabis, on the other hand, accounted for 80 percent of police work but only 1 percent of the reasons for referral to a drug agency. Where cocaine and crack were concerned, they accounted for no more than 3 percent of agency work and 12 percent of police arrests for drug offences. But perhaps the most striking variation between drug agencies and the police was to be found in the racial composition of the sample: whereas little more than 5 percent of drug users known to agencies were black, almost 50 percent of police arrests involved black people.

A more detailed scrutiny of cocaine use within the Lewisham survey also highlighted major differences between the routine work loads of helping agencies and the profile of police arrests (Pearson, Mirza, and Phillips 1993). Although only tiny numbers of drug users known to agencies were using cocaine as their main drug, one-fifth or more of their clientele were using either cocaine or crack within a pattern of poly-drug use where the main drug used was most commonly heroin. Indeed, approximately 30 percent of white heroin users known to drug agencies were also using cocaine and/or crack, of whom more than two-thirds were intravenous drug users. This finding is consistent with the monitoring of cocaine use in a neighboring area of South London by the Community Drug Team at the Maudsley Hospital between 1987 and 1989, where it was found that only 1 percent of the clinic's patients identified cocaine use as their main drug, as against 92 percent who were opiate users. However, almost one-fifth of the Maudsley sample had used cocaine in the month prior to their assessment (Strang, Griffiths, and Gossop 1990).

Finally, what can this survey evidence say about the supposed connections between cocaine and crack use and the black community? In both the Maudsley and Lewisham surveys, 75 to 80 percent of drug users who were using cocaine or crack were white. Primarily, as already indicated, these were heroin users, and it is clear that the major drug problem in London and Britain as a whole remains the legacy of the 1980s heroin epidemic. Police statistics in the Lewisham survey, however, painted a very different picture. Overall, 75 percent of arrests for cocaine or crack offenses involved black people. And where crack was concerned, whereas 95 percent of police arrests involved black people, 85 percent of crack users known to helping agencies were white. The incidence of cocaine and crack use known to these agencies, moreover, was four times greater than that reflected in police work.

One can state with a degree of confidence, therefore, that although cocaine and crack misuse have not assumed a level of serious difficulty in this part of London, where cocaine use is known it is overwhelmingly found within a pattern of poly-drug use by white opiate injectors. This stands in sharp contrast to media images which have depicted the cocaine/crack problem, such as it is, as a black problem. In its evidence to the Home Affairs Committee on *Drug Trafficking and Related Serious Crime*, the Metropolitan Police was also utterly explicit in this regard:

> This Force has also identified links between Jamaican organised criminals, "the so-called Yardies", and drug trafficking. Their common factors are the ethnic origins of those involved and the use of drugs. These individuals are primarily concerned with the production and distribution of crack and cocaine in inner city areas where policing is already difficult. Many of those involved are Jamaican illegal immigrants who have no fixed addresses but who are bound by their Jamaican origin and reggae

culture and who travel from one location to another with regularity. Such is their nomadic lifestyle that serious offences, for example murders have been, and will continue to be committed wherever the cultural bandwagon happens to stop. (Home Affairs Committee 1989, 47)

Here is such a fearful combination of culturally explosive images—a rootless black "mafia" of nomadic illegal immigrants, orchestrating drug dealing and violence in dangerous enclaves of the inner city—that one might excuse oneself for believing that it was an attack of the gout from the sensationalist tabloid press. Nevertheless, it accurately reflects the view which has gained ground and which has been actively promoted by the U.S. Drug Enforcement Agency—that Britain's streets were soon to be engulfed by a U.S.-style crack explosion. Mr. Bob Stutman of the DEA, for example, has offered his "personal guarantee" that "the UK would be swamped by crack" (*Sunday Times*, April 1, 1990). We are familiar with the common English metaphor which employs "America" as a harbinger of the (usually dreaded) future. The Metropolitan Police view would seem to have succumbed to that wider tradition of future-gazing, offering a presentation of the crack problem as if the nightmare of New York had already arrived on the streets of London.

Conclusion: From Metaphor to Real Time

I began with a joking metaphor whereby Charles Dickens's nineteenth-century London might be thought of as a prefiguration of New York's late twentieth-century underclass. However, New York and the urban American experience more generally have more often been deployed as a signifier for the imagined future of London within the complex fabric of stereotyped English fears of "Americanization."

Reversals such as these abound in human responses to urbanism and modernity. Cities, everywhere, seem to have attracted the same vocabulary of discontents and celebrations. This potential for reversal involving radically opposed assumptions about the costs and benefits of urban life, as described by Raymond Williams in *The Country and the City*, is a variant of the traditions of pastoral. More usually to be found contrasting rural idyll with urban hell, there is a degree of internal complexity within pastoral:

> On the actual settlements, which in the real history have been astonishingly varied, powerful feelings have gathered and have been generalised. On the country has gathered the idea of a natural way of life: of peace, innocence, and simple virtue. On the city have gathered the idea of an achieved centre of learning, communication, light. Powerful hostile associations have also developed: on the city as a place of noise, worldliness and ambition; on the country as a place of backwardness, ignorance and limitation. (Williams 1975, 9)

As we have seen, London had already attracted a reputation as a boisterous and dangerous city at the moment of its spectacular growth in the eighteenth century—unprecedented in world history—whereby it became the home of one million people. As London settled itself into a reconstructed and selected tradition of English civility—the world's largest port and commercial center, a "city of light" at the heart of an empire on which the sun never set—New York would experience an even more phenomenal period of growth in the forty-year period from the 1880s. By the 1920s, by which time New York's population was roughly approximate to that of London's four million souls, New York had overtaken London in many respects in terms of world trade and cultural innovation. Principally through the medium of the "moving pictures," urban America had also come to establish a commanding presence within the English imagination as the "city of darkness": a center of corruption, vice, and lawlessness.

But what happens if we move from joke and metaphor to an attempt to contrast the circumstances of these two cities in contemporary "real time"? Certainly, we can assemble statistics and compare and contrast the directions and velocities of the social changes which these might reveal. Even so, where crime and drugs are concerned, such comparisons invite incredulity. In 1989, for example, there were more than twenty-two hundred homicides in New York State as against fewer than six hundred in the whole of England and Wales (U.S. Department of Justice 1991; Home Office 1991). Where drugs are concerned, reliable estimates suggest that there were some two hundred thousand narcotics abusers in New York in the mid-1980s, which is ten times the number of addicts known to the Home Office in the entire United Kingdom in the late 1980s (Johnson et al. 1985; Pearson 1991). The extent and severity of drug misuse in New York (and other U.S. cities) are given further emphasis by the National Institute of Justice's Drug Use Forecasting program, which employs urine-analysis techniques in order to monitor drug use among persons arrested for a wide variety of offenses— including nondrug crimes. Although there are no comparable data for the United Kingdom, in the light of what has already been said about the marginality of cocaine misuse, it is simply astonishing to find that in 1990 no fewer than 65 percent of arrestees in Manhattan tested positive for cocaine (National Institute of Justice 1991).

While one might wish to draw helpful parallels between these two cities of comparable size, it must be acknowledged (even by way of conclusion) that the gulf between our two cities is often experienced as of such magnitude as to inhibit and obscure the possibilities of dialogue. It is not that London does not have its comparable problems. Quite apart from its recent spasms of riot and disorder, Londoners have become increasingly accustomed to the public spectacle of begging in the streets and subways, cardboard city replicas of homes for the homeless, and a Dickensian system of transport and sewerage. In New York, however, problems such as crack misuse have grafted themselves onto a much more profound process of social and economic destabilization (Fagan and Chin 1991). The territorial divisions between ethnic groups have become so intense, the acreage of devastated buildings in the wastelands of the Bronx so vast, and the problem of homelessness has spilled out onto the streets to such an extent, that these difficulties become essentially inaccessible to an English imagination. Hence, perhaps, the constant resort to metaphor in the baffled attempts to bring the destinies of these two major metropolitan centers of the twentieth century into a common focus: Dickens's London as New York today; New York today as London tomorrow. If Brett Easton Ellis's *American Psycho* had been written in London, it would have been instantly recognized as fiction; whereas in the context of New York, it has the uncanny ring of fact. Charles Dickens would have understood the problem.

References

Archbishop of Canterbury's Commission. 1985. *Faith in the City: Report of the Archbishop of Canterbury's Commission on Urban Priority Areas*. London: Church House Publishing.
Arnold, M. 1960. *Culture and Anarchy*. Cambridge: Cambridge University Press.
Awiah, J., S. Butt, and N. Dorn. 1990. "'The Last Place I Would Go': Black People and Drug Services in Britain." *Druglink* 5, no. 5: 14–15.
Awiah, J., S. Butt, and N. Dorn. 1992. *Race, Gender and Drug Services*. London: Institute for the Study of Drug Dependence.
Baden-Powell, R. 1908. *Scouting for Boys*. London: Horace Cox.
Bender, T. 1989. "New York as a Centre of 'Difference': How America's Metropolis Counters American Myth," in J. Sleeper, ed., *In Search of New York*. New Brunswick, N.J.: Transaction.
Benyon, J., and J. Solomos, eds. 1987. *The Roots of Urban Unrest*. Oxford: Pergamon.
Berridge, V., and G. Edwards. 1981. *Opium Use in Nineteenth-Century England*. London: Allen Lane.
Blom-Cooper, L., and R. Drabble. 1982. "Police Perceptions of Crime." *British Journal of Criminology* 22, no. 1: 184–87.
Bourgois, P. 1989. "Crack in Spanish Harlem: Culture and Economy in the Inner City." *Anthropology Today* 5, no. 4: 6–11.
Braithwaite, A. J. 1904. "Boys' Clubs," in E. J. Urwick, ed., *Studies of Boy Life in Our Cities*. London: Dent.
Braudel, F. 1984. *Civilisation and Capitalism 15th–18th Century*, vol. 3, *The Perspective of the World*. London: Collins.
Bray, R. A. 1907. *The Town Child*. London: Fisher Unwin.
Bray, R. A. 1911. *Boy Labour and Apprenticeship*. London: Constable.
Burr, A. 1987. "Chasing the Dragon: Heroin Misuse, Delinquency, and Crime in the Context of South London Culture." *British Journal of Criminology* 27, no. 4: 333–57.

Burr, A. 1989. "An Inner-City Community Response to Heroin Use," in S. MacGregor, ed., *Drugs and British Society*. London: Routledge.
Butterworth, J. 1932. *Clubland*. London: Epworth.
Cashmore, E., and E. McLaughlin, eds. 1991. *Out of Order? Policing Black People*. London: Routledge.
Chin, K. L. 1990. *Chinese Subculture and Criminality: Non-Traditional Crime Groups in America*. New York: Greenwood.
Courtwright, D., H. Joseph, and D. Des Jarlais. 1989. *Addicts Who Survived: An Oral History of Narcotic Users in America, 1912–1965*. Knoxville: University of Tennessee Press.
Dench, G. 1991. *Crime in a Minority Situation: The Maltese Case*. London: Institute of Community Studies.
Devine, A. A. 1890. *Scuttlers and Scuttling*. Manchester: Guardian Printing Works.
Ditton, J., and K. Speirits. 1982. *The Rapid Increase in Heroin Addiction in Glasgow during 1981*. Background Paper no. 2. Department of Sociology, University of Glasgow.
Dixon, D. 1991. *From Prohibition to Regulation: Bookmaking, Anti-Gambling, and the Law*. Oxford: Oxford University Press.
Dorn, N., and N. South, eds. 1987. *A Land Fit for Heroin? Drug Policies, Prevention, and Practice*. London: Macmillan.
Easton Ellis, B. 1991. *American Psycho*. London: Picador.
Fagan, J., and K. L. Chin. 1991. "Social Processes of Initiation into Crack." *Journal of Drug Issues* 21, no. 2: 313–43.
Fielding, H. 1751. *An Enquiry into the Causes of the Late Increase of Robbers*. London: Millar.
Foster, J. 1990. *Villains: Crime and Community in the Inner City*. London: Routledge.
George, M. D. 1966. *London Life in the Eighteenth Century*. Harmondsworth: Penguin.
Gifford, Lord. 1986. *The Broadwater Farm Inquiry*. London: Karia Press.
Gilman, M., and G. Pearson. 1991. "Lifestyles and Law Enforcement," in P. Bean and D. K. Whynes, eds., *Policing and Prescribing: The British System of Drug Control*. London: Macmillan.
Gilroy, P. 1987a. *"There Ain't No Black in the Union Jack": The Cultural Politics of Race and Nation*. London: Hutchinson.
Gilroy, P. 1987b. "The Myth of Black Criminality," in P. Scraton, ed., *Law, Order, and the Authoritarian State*. Milton Keynes: Open University Press.
Gilroy, P., and J. Sim. 1987. "Law, Order, and the State of the Left," in P. Scraton, ed., *Law, Order, and the Authoritarian State*. Milton Keynes: Open University Press.
Gorst, J. 1901. *The Children of the Nation*. London: Methuen.
Gottfredson, M. R. 1984. *Victims of Crime: The Dimensions of Risk*. Home Office Research Study no. 81. London: HMSO.
Green, A., R. Foster, H. Pickering, R. Power, and G. V. Stimson. 1994. "Who Uses Cocaine? Social Profiles of Cocaine Users." *Addiction Research*, in press.
Hall, S. 1982. "The Lessons of Lord Scarman." *Critical Social Policy* 2, no. 2: 66–72.
Hall, S., C. Critcher, T. Jefferson, J. Clarke, and B. Roberts. 1978. *Policing the Crisis: Mugging, the State, and Law and Order*. London: Macmillan.
Hanmer, J., and S. Saunders. 1984. *Well-Founded Fear: A Community Study of Violence to Women*. London: Hutchinson.
Hannington, W. 1973. *Unemployed Struggles, 1919–1936*. Wakefield: EP Publishing.

Haw, S. 1985. *Drug Problems in Greater Glasgow*. London: SCODA.
Himmelfarb, G. 1984. *The Idea of Poverty: England in the Early Industrial Age*. London: Faber and Faber.
Hobbs, D. 1988. *Doing the Business: Entrepreneurship, the Working Class, and Detectives in East London*. Oxford: Oxford University Press.
Hoggart, B. 1958. *The Uses of Literacy*. Harmondsworth: Penguin.
Holdaway, S. 1983. *Inside the British Police*. Oxford: Blackwell.
Home Affairs Committee. 1980. *Race Relations and the "Sus" Law*. Second Report from the Home Affairs Committee, Session 1979–80, HC 559. London: HMSO.
Home Affairs Committee. 1989. *Drug Trafficking and Related Serious Crime*, vol. 2, *Minutes of Evidence and Appendices*. HC 370-2. London: HMSO.
Home Office. 1990. *Criminal Statistics, England and Wales, 1989*. Cm. 1322. London: HMSO.
Hough, M., and P. Mayhew. 1983. *The British Crime Survey: First Report*. Home Office Research Study no. 76. London: HMSO.
Hough, M., and P. Mayhew. 1985. *Taking Account of Crime: Key Findings from the 1984 British Crime Survey*. Home Office Research Study no. 85. London: HMSO.
Hyde, S., S. Balloch, and P. Ainley. 1989. *A Social Atlas of Poverty in Lewisham*. London: Centre for Inner City Studies, Goldsmiths' College, University of London.
Institute of Race Relations. 1987. *Policing against Black People*. London: Institute of Race Relations.
Johnson, B. D., P. L. Goldstein, E. Preele, J. Schmeidler, D. J. Lipton, B. Spunt, and T. Miller. 1985. *Taking Care of Business: The Economics of Crime by Heroin Abusers*. Lexington, Mass.: Lexington Books.
Jones, T., B. MacLean, and J. Young. 1986. *The Islington Crime Survey*. Aldershot: Gower.
Joselit, J. W. 1983. *Our Gang: Jewish Crime and the New York Jewish Community, 1890–1940*. Bloomington: Indiana University Press.
Leavis, F. R. 1930. *Mass Civilisation and Minority Culture*. Cambridge: Minority Press.
Lewis, R., R. Hartnoll, S. Bryer, E. Daviaud, and M. Mitcheson. 1985. "Scoring Smack: The Illicit Heroin Market in London, 1980–1983." *British Journal of Addiction* 80: 281–90.
London, J. 1902. *The People of the Abyss*. London: Arco, 1963 ed.
Maher, L., and R. Curtis. 1992. "Women on the Edge of Crime: Crack Cocaine and the Changing Contexts of Street-Level Sex Work in New York City." *Crime, Law and Social Change* 18: 221–58.
Masterman, C. 1902. *The Heart of the Empire*. London: Fisher Unwin.
Maxfield, M. G. 1984. *Fear of Crime in England and Wales*. Home Office Research Study no. 78. London: HMSO.
Metropolitan Police. 1974. *Footpad Crime in Lambeth*. London: Community Relations Branch, New Scotland Yard.
Mirza, H. S., G. Pearson, and S. Phillips. 1991. *Drugs, People, and Services in Lewisham: Final Report of the Drug Information Project*. London: Goldsmiths' College, University of London.
National Drugs Intelligence Unit. 1990. *Drug Seizure Statistics 1990*. London: NDIU, New Scotland Yard.
National Front. 1977. *How to Spot a Red Teacher*. National Front.
National Institute of Justice. 1991. *Drug Use Forecasting: Drugs and Crime. 1990 Annual Report*. Washington, D.C.: U.S. Department of Justice.

O'Connell, W. F. 1950. *The Educational Thought and Influence of Matthew Arnold.* London: Routledge and Kegan Paul.
Orwell, G. 1939. *Coming Up for Air.* Harmondsworth: Penguin, 1962 ed.
Parker, H., K. Bakx, and R. Newcombe. 1988. *Living with Heroin: The Impact of a Drugs "Epidemic" on an English Community.* Milton Keynes: Open University Press.
Parliamentary Papers. 1900. *Report of the Commissioner of Police of the Metropolis, 1899.* Cd. 399. London: HMSO.
Parliamentary Papers. 1904. *Report of the Inter-Department Committee on Physical Deterioration,* vol. 2. Cd. 2210. London: HMSO.
Parliamentary Papers. 1908. *Royal Commission on the Duties of the Metropolitan Police,* vol. 2. Cd. 4260. London: HMSO.
Parliamentary Papers. 1910. *Report of the Departmental Committee on the Employment of Children Act, 1903.* Cd. 5229. London: HMSO.
Parliamentary Papers. 1977. *The West Indian Community: Report of the Select Committee on Race Relations and Immigration,* 3 vols. HC 180 1, 2, and 3. London: HMSO.
Pearson, G. 1975. *The Deviant Imagination.* London: Macmillan.
Pearson, G. 1983. *Hooligan: A History of Respectable Fears.* London: Macmillan.
Pearson, G. 1984. "Falling Standards: A Short, Sharp History of Moral Decline," in M. Barker, ed., *The Video Nasties.* London: Pluto.
Pearson, G. 1985. "Lawlessness, Modernity, and Social Change." *Theory, Culture, and Society* 2, no. 3: 15–35.
Pearson, G. 1987a. *The New Heroin Users.* Oxford: Basil Blackwell.
Pearson, G. 1987b. "Social Deprivation, Unemployment, and Patterns of Heroin Use," in N. Dorn and N. South, eds., *A Land Fit for Heroin? Drug Policies, Prevention, and Practice.* London: Macmillan.
Pearson, G. 1987c. "Short Memories: Street Violence in the Past and the Present," in E. Moonman, ed., *The Violent Society.* London: Frank Cass.
Pearson, G. 1989. "'A Jekyll in the Classroom, a Hyde in the Street': Queen Victoria's Hooligans," in D. Downes, ed., *Crime and the City: Essays in Memory of John Barron Mays.* London: Macmillan.
Pearson, G. 1991. "Drug Control Policies in Britain," in M. Tonry, ed., *Crime and Justice: A Review,* vol. 14. Chicago: University of Chicago Press.
Pearson, G. 1992. "Drug Problems and Criminal Justice Policy in Britain." *Contemporary Drug Problems* 19, no. 2: 279–301.
Pearson, G., J. Ditton, R. Newcombe, and M. Gilman. 1991a. "'Everything Starts with an *E*': An Introduction to Ecstasy Use by Young People in Britain." *Druglink* 6, no. 6: 10–11.
Pearson, G., J. Ditton, R. Newcombe, and M. Gilman. 1991b. "MDMA/Ecstasy: New Wave of Drug Use," in Institute for the Study of Drug Dependence, *Drug Misuse in Britain, 1991: National Audit of Drug Misuse Statistics.* London: ISDD.
Pearson, G., and M. Gilman. 1994. "Local and Regional Variations in Drug Misuse: The British Heroin Epidemic of the 1980s," in J. Strang and M. Gossop, eds., *Heroin Addiction and Drug Policy: The British System.* Oxford: Oxford University Press.
Pearson, G., M. Gilman, and S. McIver. 1985. "Heroin Use in the North of England." *Health Education Journal* 45, no. 3: 186–89.
Pearson, G., M. Gilman, and S. McIver. 1986. *Young People and Heroin: An Examination of Heroin Use in the North of England.* London: Health Education Council. 2d ed. Aldershot: Gower, 1987.

Pearson, G., H. S. Mirza, and S. Phillips. 1993. "Cocaine in Context: Findings from a South London Inner-City Drug Survey," in P. Bean, ed., *Cocaine and Crack: Supply and Use*. London: Macmillan.

Pearson, G., A. Sampson, H. Blagg, P. Stubbs, and D. Smith. 1989. "Policing Racism," in R. Morgan and D. J. Smith, eds., *Coming to Terms with Policing: Perspectives on Policy*. London: Routledge.

Preble, E., and J. J. Casey. 1969. "Taking Care of Business: The Heroin User's Life on the Street." *International Journal of the Addictions* 4, no. 1: 1–24.

Reiner, R. 1985. *The Politics of the Police*. Brighton: Harvester.

Reiner, R. 1991. *Chief Constables: Bobbies, Bosses, or Bureaucrats?* Oxford: Oxford University Press.

Reuter, P., R. MacCoun, and P. Murphy. 1990. *Money from Crime: A Study of the Economics of Drug Dealing in Washington, D.C.* Santa Monica, Calif.: RAND Corporation.

Russell, C. E. B. 1905. *Manchester Boys*. Manchester: Manchester University Press.

Sampson, A., D. Smith, G. Pearson, H. Blagg, and P. Stubbs. 1991. "Gender Issues in Inter-Agency Relations: Police, Probation, and Social Services," in P. Abbott and C. Wallace, eds., *Gender, Power, and Sexuality*. London: Macmillan.

Samuel, R. 1981. *East End Underworld: Chapters in the Life of Arthur Harding*. London: Routledge and Kegan Paul.

Scarman, Lord. 1982. *The Scarman Report: The Brixton Disorder, 10–12 April 1981*. Harmondsworth: Penguin.

Sennett, R. 1970. *Families against the City*. Cambridge: Harvard University Press.

Short, J. F. 1991. "Poverty, Ethnicity, and Crime: Change and Continuity in U.S. Cities." *Journal of Research in Crime and Delinquency* 28, no. 4: 501–18.

Sim, J., P. Scraton, and P. Gordon. 1987. "Introduction: Crime, the State, and Critical Analysis," in P. Scraton, ed., *Law, Order, and the Authoritarian State*. Milton Keynes: Open University Press.

Sleeper, J., ed. 1989. *In Search of New York*. New Brunswick, N.J.: Transaction.

Smelser, N. J. 1962. *Theory of Collective Behaviour*. London: Routledge and Kegan Paul.

Smith, D. J., and S. Gray. 1985. *Police and People in London: The PSI Report*. Aldershot: Gower.

Solomos, J. 1988. *Black Youth, Racism, and the State*. Cambridge: Cambridge University Press.

Solomos, J., and T. Rackett. 1991. "Policing and Urban Unrest: Problem Constitution and Policy Response," in E. Cashmore and E. McLaughlin, eds., *Out of Order? Policing Black People*. London: Routledge.

Spear, H. B. 1969. "The Growth of Heroin Addiction in the U.K." *British Journal of Addiction* 64: 245–55.

Stanko, E. A. 1987. "Typical Violence, Normal Precaution: Men, Women, and Interpersonal Violence in England, Wales, Scotland, and the U.S.A.," in J. Hanmer and M. Maynard, eds., *Women, Violence, and Social Control*. London: Macmillan.

Stedman Jones, G. 1971. *Outcast London*. Oxford: Oxford University Press.

Stevenson, J., and C. Cook. 1979. *The Slump*. London: Quartet.

Stimson, G. V., and E. Oppenheimer. 1982. *Heroin Addiction: Treatment and Control in Britain*. London: Tavistock.

Strang, J., P. Griffiths, and M. Gossop. 1990. "Crack and Cocaine Use in South London Drug Addicts: 1987–1989." *British Journal of Addiction* 85: 193–96.

Super, R. H., ed. 1962. *The Complete Prose Works of Matthew Arnold*, vol. 2,

Democratic Education. Ann Arbor: University of Michigan.
U.S. Department of Justice. 1991. *Sourcebook of Criminal Justice Statistics, 1990*. Washington, D.C.: U.S. Government Printing Office.
Waldorf, D., C. Reinarman, and S. Murphy. 1991. *Cocaine Changes: The Experience of Using and Quitting*. Philadelphia: Temple University Press.
Walker, M. A. 1988. "The Court Disposal of Young Males, by Race, in London in 1983." *British Journal of Criminology* 28, no. 4: 441–60.
Walker, M. A. 1989. "The Court Disposal and Remands of White, Afro-Caribbean, and Asian Men (London, 1983)." *British Journal of Criminology* 29, no. 4: 353–67.
Walmsley, R. 1986. *Personal Violence*. Home Office Research Study no. 89. London: HMSO.
White, J. 1979. "Campbell Bunk: A Lumpen Community in London between the Wars." *History Workshop* 8: 1–49.
White, J. 1983. "Police and People in London in the 1930's." *Oral History* 11, no. 2: 34–41.
White, J. 1986. *The Worst Street in North London: Campbell Bunk, Islington, between the Wars*. London: Routledge and Kegan Paul.
Wiener, M. J. 1981. *English Culture and the Decline of the Industrial Spirit (1850–1980)*. Cambridge: Cambridge University Press.
Williams, R. 1975. *The Country and the City*. London: Paladin.
Williams, R. 1989. *The Politics of Modernism*. London: Verso.
Williams, T. 1989. *The Cocaine Kids*. New York: Addison-Wesley.
Williams, T., and W. Kornblum. 1985. *Growing Up Poor*. Lexington, Mass.: Lexington Books.
Young, J. 1986. "The Failure of Criminology: The Need for a Radical Realism," in R. Matthews and J. Young, eds., *Confronting Crime*. London: Sage.

6

Inner-City Crisis and Drug Dealing: Portrait of a New York Drug Dealer and His Household

Eloise Dunlap

Current examination of American society indicates that a wide range of social forces at the macro level—poverty, discrimination, unemployment, education, health, and crime—create conditions that lead to stressful situations in inner-city family life. During the past thirty years, the U.S. economy has shifted from a manufacturing to a technological, information and services economy. For inner-city residents, typical employment in factories and small businesses became rare (Larson 1988). Industrial shifts to other sectors and regions, especially the South and Southwest (Jayne and Williams 1989), left inner-city residents confronting structural changes that had a profound impact on their communities and lives. Unemployment rates for black blue-collar workers grew. Between 1970 and 1980, cities became blacker and poorer with blacks falling deeper into poverty while whites rose from it at the same rate (*New York Times* 1987). *Time* magazine (1987) listed the jobless rate for black teenagers as 40 percent. In 1973, 12 percent of all black male high school dropouts in their early twenties reported earning no money whatsoever; in 1985, this had risen to 43 percent (*Time* 1987).

The larger structural economic changes have had a negative impact on inner-city communities and the lives of those who live there. Lack of financial resources is a major barrier to medical care (Davis and Rowland 1983; Jackson 1981, 1985). Blacks with hypertension of all social classes experience more difficulties in getting into the health care system and have greater dissatisfaction with medical care services than do similarly afflicted whites (Jayne and Williams 1989). There are wide gaps in the mortality and morbidity of blacks compared to whites at all ages except for individuals eighty-five and older. The odds that a black baby will die shortly after birth are consistently twice as high as those for a white baby (Madhubuti 1990). Further, urban residential segregation of blacks is greater than that of any other racial or ethnic group. Whatever the status of blacks, they are not free to live where they want to live. Many are concentrated in areas with high percentages of economically poor and poorly educated families (Jayne and Williams 1989). The same picture can be seen in the educational sphere, where segregation and differential treatment of blacks continue to be widespread in the elementary and secondary school levels (Madhubuti 1990). There has also been a marked decline in college entry levels among black high school graduates since 1977 (Jayne and Williams 1989).

Macrolevel "social forces" create conditions which lead to stressful situations and conflicts at the household level. This is considered in this essay to be *a state of crisis*. Crisis is identified and associated with the attributes of modern mass society and the impact of special events and circumstances, e.g., larger social forces. A conceptualization of crisis, with perceptual, behavioral, and structural dimensions as related to drug dealing, is provided in this essay and serves as a point of departure for further research, analysis, and policy speculation.

Criteria and elements that define crisis require some discussion. In sociological terms, crisis is a turning point, often brought about by a convergence of events which creates new circumstances. It is characterized by pressures, tensions, and uncertainties (Robinson 1968; Habermas 1975). An examination of sociological usage indicates that the term has been applied to situations enduring over a considerable period of time and involves both a subjective and an objective dimension (Habermas 1975). The term "crisis" may be applied in a wide range of contexts (Lyman 1975; Friedricks 1980). In this paper, "crisis" is a term applicable to a social situation in which dramatic changes, conflicts, and tensions exist and active responses are called for.

In particular, I focus here on the role of crisis among inner-city residents. Current economic prospects are not good for many blacks. Adverse changes in labor market opportunities and family conditions—falling real wages and employment, one-parent families with one or no working adults—have made conditions especially difficult for inner-city residents. Individuals and families confront structural changes that have had a negative impact on their living situation. These larger social forces create conditions for inner-city families which call for active responses, but appropriate resources are not available. Many of these responses involve forms of deviant behavior, and these behaviors create other crises in household and interpersonal relations.

A large amount of research literature in the drug abuse field documents multiple crises in the lives of inner-city residents. Many individuals responding to these larger macrolevel forces are principally those committing criminal acts. Robert Coles in *Children of Crisis* (1967) and Oscar Lewis in *La Vida* (1966) document crises occurring in the 1960s. This case study is an example of what happened to the children of the families studied at that time. The children of that era are now adults, and many have families of their own. At that time it was the heroin epidemic. Since that time, economic, social, and political factors have undergone changes that have further affected these people's lives. In the 1950s and 1960s, the concern was not so much about housing as it is today. Additionally, welfare and other support systems were more adequate than those available now. So, for the children of the late 1960s and 1970s, it was the heroin epidemic. For the children of the 1980s and 1990s, it is the crack epidemic and larger social forces which present crisis situations to which they must respond. This essay depicts what has happened in the intervening years, between the two generations, with those who are now adults and their parents. The individual in this case study is one of the children of the heroin epidemic years, now grown up, and his progeny.

METHODOLOGY

The information provided in this paper is derived from an ongoing study funded by the National Institute on Drug Abuse, "The Natural History of Crack Distribution." This research is an ethnographic study of the structure, functioning, and economic aspects of cocaine and crack distribution in New York City (primarily in low-income, minority communities).

I contacted and interviewed dealers representing a range of economic statuses, from street-corner crack sellers to cocaine/crack weight distributors. For almost a year, I have kept close relations with some of them and their families. I have conducted both group and one-on-one interviewing. Of the individuals I have talked to, males are overrepresented. The ages range from about 23 to 38. Two-thirds of the dealers were African American, and one-third were Dominicans.

The volume of material is abundant. There are hundreds of pages of transcribed recorded material and field notes. As I read through much of the material, I began to realize the constant theme of crisis and how many times minor occurrences triggered responses that were symbolic of larger forces acting upon people's lives. An example: Norman was "put out" of the household for eating "one too much sausages." Norman was a "drug baby" who had been raised in foster care and institutional settings. When he "aged" out of state mandated care at 17, he came to live with the only aunt who had a residence. Unable to find employment, he began working for his cousin, Ross, selling crack. He was arrested, placed on probation, and was therefore unable to continue to sell drugs. His presence in the house began to create tension. One evening he was accused of eating too much sausage and was expelled from the household. This made Norman homeless at 18 years old. Three months later, he was arrested for robbery and is now in prison. As this example only suggests, larger forces and chronic privation create crisis situations requiring responses, which in turn create other crisis situations.

Drug use/sale is a response to "larger social/economic/political/historical forces" and these crisis situations. The family-kin responses typically re-create subsequent crisis; drug distribution brings about related ramifications. Certain recurrent crises in family life experiences affect the continued use/sale of drugs. Here I shall demonstrate how these "larger social forces" are played out in an individual's life—and in turn contribute to larger social problems, e.g., overcrowding of prisons/jails or homelessness. Other implications from this study are that policy makers must begin to address the educational, employment, housing, and health needs of inner-city residents. The continuing failure to address these broader forces contributes to the recurrent family-kin crisis situations, to which drug use/sale is only one response.

OVERVIEW OF FAMILY

Ross

Ross is a 32-year-old African American male who was raised in a single-parent household most of his life. At the present time he lives with his mother and sister. He is a major contributor to the economic well-being of his family of orientation. He is presently separated from his wife and has three children by a former girlfriend. While he is important to the economic life of his family of orientation, he is marginally involved with the economic life of his children. He is a high school dropout who held one low-paying legal job for three months ten years ago. His career in drug dealing started while he was still a teenager and has ranged from selling angel dust to heroin and crack. He is a free-lance crack dealer who has close connections with several other free-lance drug dealers in his area. They consider themselves a "family" and attempt to operate on a family basis, but with independent suppliers. He and his comrades are independent dealers who join together for purposes of protection from robberies and police crackdowns and to protect their territory rights. He has been seriously injured during his drug distribution career and this has left him unable to walk.

Mother

Island is a 62-year-old single parent who is dedicated to the survival of her offspring and wider family kin-network. Her household is the stable center of her family kin-network. Island was born in the West Indies but grew up in America. Her father died before she was born. There were six children in her family of orientation, all from different fathers. Most of Island's siblings are heavy alcohol users, but Island is a moderate drinker and does not use drugs. She worked for a short time as a home attendant when her children were young but began to receive welfare stipends due to her insufficient earnings. At the present time, she baby-sits some of her neighbors' children during working hours and has been awarded four of her relatives' children (foster care) by the courts. Island is bisexual and has been with her present "girlfriend" for over fifteen years. This relationship is sometimes a stimulus for stress in family relations. Conflict between the two involves the entire household.

Mary Jane

Mary Jane is Island's girlfriend and is 56 years old. She has been involved in drug use and sale for many years. She is an ex-heroin addict who smokes crack. Mary Jane was a foster child who was put in a mental institution from the age of ten to seventeen due to a rape she experienced as a child. This rape experience by her foster parents' friend caused her to become uncontrollable at home and in school. From this point in her life she began to feel unwanted and began to lash out at the world around her. Her foster parents turned her back over to the state, who in turn placed her in a mental institution. Upon her release from the mental institution, at seventeen, she worked for a short time as a nurse's aid. Through friends, she was introduced to heroin and shortly afterwards became a heroin addict. The habit for the drug encouraged her to sell it in order to supply her addiction. She was arrested for dealing and served time in prison. Mary Jane's main hustle now is prostitution as well as off-and-on drug dealing.

Sonya

Sonya, 35 years old, is Ross's sister. At the present time, she is a prostitute who smokes crack. She is an ex-heroin addict. She started using heroin at the age of 18. Sonya too is bisexual and has a girlfriend and boyfriend who compete with one another when the boyfriend comes to New York. The boyfriend is also a drug dealer in the South and comes to New York to acquire large supplies. When he is in town much conflict arises in the household due to the conflict between her two lovers.

Lisa

Lisa is Ross's cousin. Her father is Ross's mother's brother. She is 36 years old and is also an ex-heroin addict. She now smokes crack and prostitutes to support her habit. She started drinking and smoking marijuana at an early age. At 14, she had her first child, dropped out of school, and began to use various drugs until she became a heroin addict. At the present time, she and her daughter prostitute in the same park together. Lisa has three children, two of which are males. The two sons are in the criminal justice system serving time in jail and prison on drug charges.

Barbara

Barbara, Lisa's daughter, is 22 years old and is also a crack user. She lives with a male friend who is 54 years old. She depends on him for much of her crack. She prostitutes during the day to help support her habit. Generally, while the friend is at work she is out smoking and looking for ways to get crack. Barbara is a very sad young lady. She relates a distressing story about her childhood. As a child she remembers peeking through the bathroom keyhole and watching her parents "shoot up." It was at this point that she began to hate heroin. She would wait until her parents left the household to go to the place in which they kept their "fix" and look at the needle and other works. She was eventually taken from her parents and raised in a foster care institution. She vows she would never take heroin—but sees crack and other drugs as different. Barbara too had a child while a teenager. The child was eventually taken from her, and at this point she became heavily involved in cocaine, angel dust, and other such drugs.

CRISIS IN HOUSEHOLD ARRANGEMENT

Patricia Sexton found in 1965 that, as today, there was a severe shortage of decent housing in Harlem. Almost one in three households were overcrowded. She related this to the presence of "acute stress syndrome" which Dr. Hudson Hoagland found in his experiments. Dr. Hoagland, an experimental biologist, found that "overcrowding in animal society can produce stress-induced maladies—liver disease, heart trouble, sexual deviation.... When crowded, animals die off despite adequate food; rats show abnormal sexual and social behavior. It is part of the 'acute stress syndrome'" (Sexton 1965, 23). The speculation is that humans living in crowded conditions may be reacting in the same physiological way as the biologist's animals. People need and want privacy. A room of one's own to escape from family demands, noise, and conflict serves as a buffer to people's emotional life. Crowding alone produces much stress (Sexton 1965). Over thirty years later, we find similar circumstances. Decent affordable housing is scarce. Thus a livable apartment can become a valuable commodity. Ross's household is an example of the continuation of the crisis of housing and what happens in people's lives because of this.

Inner cities in 1969 housed 48 percent of all poor blacks. By 1976, central cities housed over 55 percent of all poor blacks. An expanding black population put a strain on housing that still exists today in central cities (Bullard 1984). Large families have problems finding apartments to rent. Black families face exclusionary policies which place them at a disadvantage in the open market for housing. Numerous surveys have been conducted in recent years that document the continued exclusionary and discriminatory practices against black families (Bullard 1984). It is estimated that nonwhites pay 5 percent to 20 percent more than whites for comparable living quarters (Kain 1972).

In Ross's household, we see how these larger social forces and their crises are played out. The main members of the household are Island, Ross, and Sonya. All other household members shift and change over time depending on different circumstances. The apartment is an example of a commodity in a scarce residential market. The apartment is in the mother's name. She acquired it many years ago, and with ever-decreasing adequate housing over the years it has become the family's valued possession. It is a three-bedroom apartment and is situated in a convenient location. It is positioned near subway, bus, and the expressway. The upkeep of the building in which the apartment is located is fairly good compared to many buildings in the area. Because an apartment in New York is difficult to find, the main family members may move out of it at various times but always keep the apartment in the family. It is also the main shelter for family members and kin-network. When I met the family, Island was living at her girlfriend's house. Shortly after I began to come to the house, Island moved back into the apartment.

The inability to find employment and the use/sale of drugs disrupt the household and create crises for family members. At the time I met Ross (November 1989) the household consisted of six cousins: Jim, age 7; Joe, age 10; Mary, age 11; Teddy, age 15; Norman, age 18; and Wilbert, age 23. The three younger children had been placed in custody of Island through court orders due to the parents' drug use. One of the children was a "crack child," and the parents of the other two were heroin users. Teddy had also been a "heroin baby." At the time he was attending a special school and taking medication to enable him to function without too much stress. Norman had also been a "drug baby." He had just been released from foster care and become a member of the household. Off and on Wilbert slept at the apartment; he was mostly homeless.

Too many people in one apartment generated much tension. Many times the tension was a stimulant for creating crisis. Both Norman and Wilbert had problems finding employment. They went through job training programs in which they did not receive employment at the completion of the program. These programs paid small stipends while they were in training. At the end of the program, stipends stopped and they were left without any means of supporting themselves. Unable to find legitimate employment, they began to work dealing crack for Ross. Norman was arrested and put on probation. On probation and still unable to find legitimate employment, he attempted to enlist in the armed forces. He was unsuccessful for two reasons. First, his educational skills were grossly inadequate, as the foster care institution in which he had been raised had neglected his education. Second, his probation status and prior drug charges were not looked upon favorably. His inability to find employment left him unable to contribute income to the household. At this point, tension between the cousin and other family members began to arise. Eating too much food became a major issue. Everything Norman ate was carefully watched by other family members. One evening he was accused of eating more than his share of sausage. This resulted in his being expelled from the household. The household was in a constant state of conflict and change due to "larger forces." At this point, Norman became completely socially unattached. He had no housing, no legal income, no education, and was disaffiliated from the family.

Shortly after Norman was expelled from the household, a friend of Ross was taken in. George was approximately 38 years old. He worked for Ross on and off as a cooker (making up crack). Upon his entrance, he developed close relations with Island. They sat up late at night, playing cards together. He became more or less her comrade. He took sides with her in various skirmishes that continually occurred. Just before George joined the household, Sonya's girlfriend, Gena, had moved in. With these additional individuals in the household, a great deal of emotional strain was constantly present. George and Gena had frequent verbal battles. He would refer to her as a "butch," and she would call him a "fag." Each accused the other of taking advantage of Island. Eventually George was not permitted back into the house when he stole a VCR. Gena was replaced with Sonya's boyfriend/husband, Big Man, who came to New York to pick up his drug supplies. Again problems arose. Big Man used the telephone too much.

Although the members of the household fluctuated, the mother was clearly the head of the household and Ross was a major economic figure. The mother, Ross, and the sister were the main members of the household although at times they would leave and live elsewhere. The continual changes in the household's members were illustrative of the crises in larger social forces. Overcrowding in housing, chronic unemployment, and drug dealing/use were a few of the conditions put into motion by larger forces which were played out in this household.

Crisis in Growing-Up Years

Death looms large in Ross's recollections of his childhood and illustrates two factors. First, larger forces of inadequate health care impact directly on the family. Second, drug use/sale is related to an unusual number of traumatic deaths occurring in critical or transitional stages of the family's developmental cycle and not effectively resolved by its members (Coleman and Stanton 1978). Jaynes and Williams (1989) stipulate that blacks are twice as likely as whites to be without a regular source of medical care or to have no regular source other than a hospital outpatient department or emergency room. Health care in public clinics or in outpatient departments and emergency rooms of general hospitals is often impersonal, dehumanizing, humiliating, and abusive. Negative experiences in these settings frequently are associated with avoidance behavior, lack of trust, and a disinclination to seek care or follow treatment regimens except when in dire need (Reissman 1974). When Ross was very young, his family began to experience the effects of the crisis in health care. Ross's father's family of orientation had sixteen children. Over the years their deaths (stemming from the lack of proper medical care) contributed to a constant state of family crisis.

Ross lost his father at four years old. Island's male "friend" helped to bury the father and began to help the mother support the family. Two years later the mother's friend (Ross's quasi-stepfather) died. Death was a constant crisis element in family life. Ross had to adjust to frequent deaths of family members. When asked about typical problems the family had to face while growing up, his reply was *death*:

> After I lost my father, we were [constantly] going to a funeral.... They all died. Like my father, he died from pneumonia. Walking pneumonia right in the kidneys. His sisters and brothers died from cancer.... It was hard when you go to the funeral, and you walk up to the casket, it would be hard for me to get away from the casket.... On the side, on that side of the family, when I lost someone... when I lost somebody in my family, I wouldn't talk about it.... It really hurt me.... They're throwing up right behind one another.... I was crying so much, that I didn't never believe that you could get sick from crying too much.

Lack of adequate health care was the reason that Ross lost many family members in his early childhood. But there is also another dimension to this great loss in Ross's early years. In Coleman's (1985) incomplete mourning theory, drug abuse results from a state of unresolved mourning for a deceased member by the family. Unresolved conflict in a previous relationship with a deceased relative is also carried over into other relationships.

Drug abuse and suicide are seen as similar. A number of authors have argued that addiction is an option or a counterpart of suicide (Coleman and Stanton 1978). This theory may be extended to include drug dealing because drug dealing greatly increases the risk of death and can be interpreted as possibly an unconscious wish for death. Like the addict, the dealer's lifestyle also reflects an unusual degree of involvement with death. Death is not a lone process. It occurs in relationship to others, particularly family and friends (Coleman and Stanton 1978). It has very long-term effects.

Coleman examined death as a participatory phenomenon in families of drug abusers. Because drug use/sale is a life-threatening behavior, she sees the impact of past death as having an impact upon the present. Many deviant behaviors are a by-product of loss at a most critical period of development. Ross's words express feelings of hostility toward loved ones that impact on other areas in an individual's life:

> I wouldn't bring Dad ... I wouldn't bring my daddy back. 'Cause he punched me in the mouth and made my nose bleed one time. I remember that. I wouldn't wanna bring him back. I remember he punched me in my mouth and made my nose bleed 'cause I wouldn't eat my pork and beans. And I don't eat no pork and beans up to this day. And ever since then, you punch me on my mouth and my nose bleed. I was sitting on his lap and he punched me on my mouth and made my nose bleed. I left him there and started crying and went to my mother. . . . And up to this day I don't eat no pork and beans.

This conflict in Ross's relations with his father was never resolved. Coleman stipulates that this kind of unfinished business with deceased ones is the basis for incomplete mourning. Individuals develop a variety of attitudes and behaviors to cope with the death. Reilly (1976) considers incomplete mourning as preventing families from expressing affection to each other (a major problem addressed below).

After the death of Ross's father and stepfather, Island worked as a nurse's aid. Her inability to adequately support the family on her wages forced the family to receive welfare stipends. This was unacceptable to Ross. He disliked the whole process of receiving food stamps and getting supplemental food.

> My mom gave me food stamps to go to the store. No! I take a whooping. And she never whooped me though. That's what I said. Ma, I take a whooping, rather than take the food stamps to the store. . . . I have got a conscience then, I don't know. . . . It's just ... it's just something that came into me. Until today I never know why. . . . And my mother always asks me that [why he doesn't like welfare and food stamps]. . . . I don't know why. . . . Oh, when I was a little boy. I remember when we used to get the surplus. . . . And they tell me to pull the wagon. And I said no, I'm not pulling no wagon. I'm not pulling no wagon.

Ross could not adjust to the welfare status of the family. It was a source of guilt and embarrassment during the growing-up years. The constant state of deprivation experienced by the family coupled with Ross's apprehensions about receiving public assistance eventually led him to drop out of school and sell drugs. At the age of 16 his first decision was to leave school; he felt compelled to help his family. At this same age, he became the father of his first child, a son, who died of crib death while Ross was in jail. Thus larger social forces again created death, a crisis situation which re-creates crisis in family life.

Crisis in Family Relations

In 1969, 58 percent of all poor black children were in female-headed families; in 1984, 75 percent of poor black children were in female-headed families. In the course of their childhood, 86 percent of black children compared to 42 percent of white children are likely to spend some time in a single-parent household (Jayne and Williams 1989) where poverty is the highest. Several mechanisms by which chronic poverty creates crisis in female-headed families can be identified in Ross's family. Women earn less than men, so single-parent, women-headed families are more likely to be poor than those with a male head. Young black women who form single-parent households come predominantly from poor households and often lack the requisite skills for high earnings. Ross's family of orientation is a transgenerational female-headed household. Island came from a single-parent household and did not complete high school. After the death of her husband, she worked as a nurse's aid. She was not able to earn enough from outside employment to justify working; she received welfare assistance.

Drug Use and Dealing: The Double-Edged Sword

Drug dealing may aid the economic life of the family, but at the same time it undermines family relationships. Drug use/sale has been a major crisis factor. In 1973, at age 15, Ross began to deal drugs to help his family economically. He dealt angel dust until he was 20 years old, at which time he began to deal heroin. Dealing heroin presented him with many contradictions. He knew and had had to deal with his extended and immediate family members' heroin addiction and the destruction of normal living patterns.

> The only thing I disliked was selling heroin. It was a fast sell, but it wasn't my type of work, though. Every time, every time I would sell to somebody that bag I would feel guilty that I sold that. I would every time ... when I sold so many bags ... first thing that came to my mind ...

first thing I thought about was my family. And first thing come to mind . . . and I would feel bad. 'Cause I'm a family man. And I suppose I had a guilty conscience then. I would hesitate on taking the money.

In 1972, at age 18, Sonya (Ross's older sister) began to use heroin along with other members of the extended family. Being the only son, Ross felt responsible for his family's well-being. Repeatedly, he and the mother tracked Sonya and rescued her from many drug consumption situations. The sister, of course, would resume drug consumption. Treatment programs proved unsuccessful because she was free to leave at will. Each time the family encouraged her to enroll in treatment and escorted her to enroll in programs, she would check herself out. After a few days in various treatment programs, she would be out and consuming drugs again.

> My sister, it took me a long time to beat it out of her, she used to . . . she used to do heroin till I beat it out of her. Now she won't get nowhere near it, she don't want to be by nobody that deals it. As long as I got my sister out of it. Whatever pleases them. Whatever . . . if they like it, I love it. Now that I got my sister away from it. Now that I got my sister away from it, it made me feel better about myself. I'm so proud of her. But my whole family, if they like it, I love it. We [sister] fight like a dog sometimes. We love each other. Sometimes . . . sometimes we argue. We won't talk for weeks in a month . . . and [if] something happened to one of us, we'd be right there. As long as they [other family members] don't push it at my sister. I love it, they can do what they want.

The sister's drug consumption caused many problems for the family. As can be seen, it encouraged violence between family members. Many contradictions of love and hate between family members were present. In the late 1970s, Ross was dealing heroin (and feeling guilty), yet he was resorting to violence to stop his sister from taking the drug. This whole situation led to continual crisis in the family. The sister stole many articles and money from family members in order to acquire drugs. She was also active in crime.

> She got locked up on . . . homicide. She and her friend, they had stuck up a jewelry store. And somehow there was a person there that got killed. And she cried like a baby. I took everything that I had in my job [dealing heroin] to try to help her. And she, I understand, got five years for it. I told my mother, don't put any money down. The money you've got, you need now. You have nobody else to take care of you. You need the money yourself. Now that I'm working, I'll try to help her. All the money I had I put up.

When I began this research in 1989, Sonya had served time and was out of prison. Ross had moved over into dealing crack. He had enjoyed dealing angel dust, but heroin had presented too many problems psychologically for him. He felt that the type of drug sold was an important element. Angel dust was not only seen as a profitable business, but he found amusement in the effect of the drug on individuals. He also felt it was all right to deal this drug because he "indulged."

Seeing crack as a booming business, he began dealing crack. This business also promoted crisis in family relationships. Although he knows crack is harmful, he perceives it as somewhat different from heroin. He is willing to give drugs to family members to keep them from stealing too much from him:

> 'Cause if you don't give it to them, I know they will do it. They're gonna steal some. When I make it up, I make a little smaller batch on the side, for I know they're coming around. Ha, they're coming around. And if they don't come around I'll call 'em. I'll call 'em up and tell 'em I've got something for you. They have it ... they have it, I have it for them to avoid them to getting in trouble? I don't. I don't cut no time with them. I don't trust them. As soon ... as soon as you turn your head, they'll steal from you. No matter how much you give 'em, they just steal from you.

Ross considers himself as different from other members of his family kin-network. He gives a great proportion of the money he makes dealing drugs to his mother. But he claims Island does not know he is dealing or has ever dealt drugs. He keeps this from her because, he says, "I feel that if I let her know I'd be disrespectful to her." These contradictions represent family values, beliefs, norms, and behaviors related to drug dealing. There is an agreed-upon silence. The mother and the son do not openly discuss his major economic activities and major sources of family income. She does not inquire about where he gets the money, and she does not discuss his activities. Nor does Ross discuss these with her.

Most of his relatives are also involved in various criminal activities and drug sales and give money to their parents. Ross displays a double standard.

> [The cousins'] parents think their offspring are children for the rest of their lives. Everything they do is all right and everyone else is wrong. You know how it is, when you're money hungry. As long as you keep bringing the money home you're all right. As long as you bring some money, it's all right. And that was it. A lot of them rob and kill, some deal, and that was it.

> Yeah, that's why I don't bring no drugs home. You know what I'm saying. Not in my house. I have nobody coming looking for me.

As long as he does not let his mother know what he is doing and does not bring drugs into the house where she can see them, then he can feel that she does not know what he is doing and it is all right for her to take the money because she does not know what its source is. As long as Ross and his mother (Island) can pretend with one another, they can respect each other. Ross can see Island as different or not like the rest of the family and kin-network. Ross sees her as not "money hungry" because he feels that she does not know he deals drugs. Since Island supposedly does not know about his drug dealings, she can accept the money he gives her and they both preserve their dignity.

Ross is a major contributor to the economic functioning of his family of orientation. He is also the father of three children. The children are not by his wife, from whom he is presently divorced. He does not keep in contact with his ex-wife but has good relations with the mother of his children. He is not a major economic provider for his family of procreation. He does contribute to his children, but on a marginal basis. The same pattern emerges in the household where his children are being raised. Ross's children are mainly supported by their mother's drug-dealing brothers. Thus they are growing up in a household supported by drug-dealing monies.

> About my daughter's uncles.... And all of them are criminals. You want to talk about the one that has big money? They all have money.... He got one whole avenue to himself.... When I met them, we used to all live there. We stayed around [the corner from the dealing area talked about].... That's the only avenue he got, and he stays out there.... He buys the coke and he cooks it up. All the workers he's got... all of them, he could work with. All of them used to play ball together.... I don't know how he train them. I went up there one day and he had the whole avenue to himself.... He's still out there. He got out of jail.... His baby brother and his older brother's in jail. All of his brothers are in jail. The baby brother was out there with him. The baby brother was his lieutenant.... When he's not up there, he's supplying them.... That's the way it is when he's not there. And when the other brother is out there, they're both out there together. The baby brother's a lieutenant. The older brother is the boss.

Ross and his family kin-network and their relations must continually be seen and viewed in the larger framework laid out at the beginning of this essay. The socioeconomic crisis to which the entire household is responding makes dealing seem like a reasonable economic alternative. Yet dealing only creates other crises and impacts on personal and family relations. Ross and his family kin-network and their relationships also highlight generational transmission of drug dealing in the inner city.

Ross claims to have special relations with his children. Their limited interaction stems from social and economic factors.

> My three children by the same mother. Only the first one was by another woman [this is the son who died from crib death]. My daughter she's gonna... be 15; my son, 11, and one is 12. And they had a fire in their

house. They come over every Sunday, though. Only time . . . only time my kids ask me for something is when they need it. If they don't need nothing they will not ask me for nothing. Me and their mother is real close. . . . And she's real close to her mother. . . . We always had that agreement [financial support]. . . . She don't never want me giving her no money. . . . There are times she says, don't ever give me nothing. The only way I would need something is for the kids need it, and they would come to you and ask you for it. And if they need something, they will come and ask me. . . . They'll come and they say, Daddy, when they come in. I look at them when they come through the door. Oh, oh, money time. Hi, Daddy. What's wrong, Daddy? We don't want nothing today. . . . The only time when they really ask me for something is when they want some records or they want something to go to school, or they're going away. . . . That's the only time they really ask me for something. Or sometime they would come over and ask me when they're going on a trip. But any other time, they won't ask. And my mother she spoils the hell outta them kids.

Clearly his economic obligation is to his family of orientation. The family of procreation is the responsibility of the mother and her family of orientation. He is peripheral to this unit. Although he can provide gifts on holidays and some money during emergencies, he does not provide major support.

The complexity of the situation becomes more apparent when societal expectations for the family are to socialize its members to participate legitimately in the economy. But with drug dealing such an intricate part of their lives, how will children view drug dealing as they grow up, and especially when they too face chronic unemployment? From all indications, they will see it as the only viable alternative to being unemployed. Their father deals, their uncles deal, and their grandparents and parents do not talk about it. It is simply accepted without talking about it.

CRIMINAL JUSTICE SYSTEM AND CRISIS

Crime rates and violent behavior among young black males have become epidemic. In 1986, 47 percent of rape arrestees and 62 percent of robbery arrestees were black. Since 1952, the gap between black and white arrest rates has been widening. In 1978, the arrest rate per 1,000 whites was 35 while the black rate was almost 100. Between 1933 and 1985, homicide arrest rates for whites have been relatively stable while black homicide rates, significantly higher, have fluctuated from year to year. From 1953 until 1978, the arrest rates for rape, robbery, and assault grew as well as economic crimes such as burglary, larceny, and auto theft (Jayne and Williams 1989). Blacks are twice as likely as whites to be victims of robbery, vehicle theft, and aggravated assault. They are disproportionately victims of homicide. Deaths due to homicide among blacks have ranged between six and seven times those for whites during the past fifty years. Blacks are subject more frequently than whites to violent death, injuries, and property losses by criminal actions. Most black criminal offenders victimize other blacks (Madhubuti 1990).

Ross's family has had extensive contact with the criminal justice system. Talking of his family and contact with the criminal justice system, he says:

> I had my cousins. My cousins had fifteen to twenty-five at armed robbery. Then I have another cousin. He was 25, right? Bank job, murder. He did a lot of things. He'd be here today to talk about it.... Some of them, they're still in jail today.... Some of them had armed robbery, some of them had murder. Each one of them had... they all had murders... they had armed robbery... everything they stuck up... everything they rob, they kill.... I'm the one they didn't socialize with. I never really got to know them.... The way I feel they make it bad for me and drag me with them. I know what was going on. I decided... I stay far away as I can from them.

Ross's criminal career began when he was 16 years old. He claims he was falsely accused of robbing a blind man. After this he has a history of frequent contact with the criminal justice system.

> I was in jail when I was 18 years old, after I start working.... Came home when I was 20, then got locked up. Came home when I was 22 and that's when I got shot. Got busted at the job.... I say two years each time.

Acquiring a criminal record further limits his chance of legitimate employment and taking advantage of other opportunities, e.g., armed forces. Ross was one of the "children of crisis" (Coles 1967) as he grew up in the 1960s. These crises have worsened in the past thirty years; his family reflects several common responses to larger social forces that have created other crises of drug dealing and incarceration for Ross and family members.

CONCLUSION

This paper delineated a wide range of social forces at the macro level and showed how they create conditions that lead to stressful situations in inner-city family life. Poverty, unemployment, poor skills, inadequate health care, and crime continuously create crisis conditions that require responses. Many times a person's or family's responses set up a chain reaction of crises, creating more crises. Early in his life, Ross experienced the death of his father and of many family members. Thus he grew up in a single-parent family. His mother had come from a single-parent household and did not have sufficient skills to adequately support the family. The family was in a perpetual state of poverty during his childhood. He left high school before completion and began selling drugs, which in turn got him arrested many times. Acquiring a criminal record limited his chances of getting legal employment. At least Ross avoided heroin and crack addiction, although he "indulges" occasionally. His sister and many kin were addicted on a nearly continuous basis.

Larger social forces also have an impact on the contradictions in family relations. To help his family confront poverty, Ross sells drugs. At one point, he was torn between dealing heroin and watching it destroy his sister and harm his family. This contradiction became too much for him. He later sold crack and tried to resolve the conflict by setting portions aside for family members. He gives his mother money, but she never inquires where the money comes from. At the same time, he scorns his cousins' parents for accepting money they have acquired illegally. This is a state of crisis in values, morals, and practices for Ross. He is very clear about the inappropriateness of the cousins' parents accepting "drug money" but does not connect his activity with his mother's behavior in the same category. Last, the issue of generational drug use/sale is apparent. The adults in Ross's household and his children's household were continuously exposed in childhood to drug use/sale. They see the only nonuser, nondealer in the household, their grandmother, accepting drug money as correct because it is not condemned nor talked about. If their options for getting a good education, gaining legal employment, and earning even a modest legal income are as closed as they were for their mothers, fathers, and uncles, then it is likely that they will also pursue the same career of drug use/sale as the only viable economic alternative.

Note

This research was supported primarily by the National Institute on Drug Abuse grant to study "The Natural History of Crack Distribution" (1 R01 DA05126–02) and in part by the Behavioral Sciences Training in Drug Abuse Research (5 T32 DA07233–07) and the National Institute of Justice grant for "Changing Patterns of Drug Use and Criminality among Crack Cocaine Users" (87–IJ–CX–0064). Additional support was provided by the New York State Division of Substance Abuse Services and National Development and Research Institute, Inc.

References

Bullard, R. D. 1984. "The Black Family Housing Alternatives in the 80s." *Journal of Black Studies* 14, no. 3: 341–51.

Coles, R. 1967. *Children of Crisis: A Study of Courage and Fear*. Boston: Little, Brown.
Coleman, S. B. 1985. "Incomplete Mourning in Substance-Abusing Families: Theory, Research, and Practice," in L. Wolberg and M. Arson, eds., *Group and Family Therapy: An Overview*. New York: Brunner-Mazel.
Coleman, S. B., and M. D. Stanton. 1978. "The Role of Death in the Addict Family." *Journal of Marriage and Family Counseling* 3:79–91.
Davis, K., and D. Rowland. 1983. "Uninsured and Underserved: Inequities in Health Care in the United States." *Milbank Quarterly* 61:149–76.
Friedrichs, D. O. 1980. "Legitimacy Crisis in the United States: A Conceptual Analysis." *Social Problems* 27, no. 5: 540–55.
Habermas, J. 1975. *Legitimation Crisis*. Trans. Thomas McCarthy. Boston: Beacon Press.
Jackson, J. S. 1981. "Urban Black Americans," in A. Harwood, ed., *Ethnicity and Medical Care*. Cambridge: Harvard University Press.
Jackson, J. S. 1985. "Race, National Origin, Ethnicity, and Aging," in R. B. Binstock and E. Shanas, eds., *Handbook of Aging and the Social Sciences*. New York: Van Nostrand Reinhold.
Jayne, G. D., and R. M. Williams Jr. 1989. *Blacks and American Society*. Washington, D.C.: National Academy Press.
Kain, J. 1972. "Housing Market Discrimination, Home Ownership, and Savings Behavior." *American Economic Review* 62, no. 6: 263–77.
Larson, T. E. 1988. "Employment and Unemployment of Young Black Males," in J. T. Gibbs, ed., *Young, Black, and Male in America: An Endangered Species*. Dover, Mass: Auburn House.
Lewis, O. 1966. *La Vida: A Puerto Rican Family in the Culture of Poverty—San Juan and New York*. New York: Random House.
Lyman, S. 1975. "Legitimacy and Consensus in Lipset's America: From Washington to Watergate." *Social Research* 42:729–59.
Madhubuti, H. R. 1990. *Black Men: Obsolete, Single, Dangerous? The Afrikan American Family in Transition*. Chicago: Third World Press.
New York Times. 1987. "Poverty of Blacks Spreads in Cities," January 26.
Reilly, D. M. 1976. "Family Factors in Etiology and Treatment of Youthful Drug Abuse." *Family Therapy* 2, no. 2: 149–71.
Reissman, C. K. 1974. "The Use of Health Services by the Poor." *Social Policy* 5:41–49.
Robinson, J. 1968. "Crisis," in *International Encyclopedia of the Social Sciences*, Vol. 3. New York: Macmillan.
Sexton, P. C. 1965. *Spanish Harlem: Anatomy of Poverty*. New York: Harper & Row.
Time. 1987. "The Ghetto: From Bad to Worse." August 24, 18–19.

7

Urban Regeneration, Economic Restructuring, and Community Response in London Docklands

Andrew Church

Lunchtime in the public plazas of Canary Wharf in the year 2000 will be the test of the classless society and land of opportunity Mr. Major is committed to creating in Britain. Office workers from blue-chip companies—American Express, Texaco, Reuters, Ogilvy and Mather (to name just a few)—will be avidly consuming from the prestige shops whilst casting a casual eye over the lunchtime displays of art and entertainment. A crucial part of this supposedly ideal urban scene will be the young adults from the predominantly working-class areas of East London that surround Canary Wharf. The sons and daughters of former dockers or factory workers will have been recruited as office staff straight from the local schools and colleges. Their path to rewarding employment will have been smoothed by a period of school work experience with one of the large employers twinned with a nearby school. As they rise up well-paid career ladders, their affluence will be typical of the surrounding community. New and existing residents will have become progressively wealthier as Britain's largest urban redevelopment project nears completion. The London Docklands Development Corporation (LDDC), overseers of the regeneration process, will have achieved their 1980 aim of creating a "balanced" harmonious community of different class groups.

But will the new multinational firms even bother recruiting from local schools? The phrase "balanced community" may come to haunt the LDDC. Nowhere in London in the 1990s are class divisions so stark as in London Docklands.

The political stakes are clearly high. A Conservative party political broadcast before the 1987 election was devoted solely to London Docklands as the flagship of Mrs. Thatcher's inner-city initiatives. For Massey (1990, 6), Docklands is "a microcosm of wider social and economic trends," and "the problem is no longer simply one of decline. Today, the problem is, in a way, growth. What is at issue is not just growth or decline but the nature of the growth being promoted. This is the crucial issue for Docklands and the country." Docklands may only contain about 1 percent of London's population, but the changes experienced by these people will be a sharp indication of the social, economic, and political processes determining the lives of many Londoners. For those concerned to develop initiatives for the social and cultural revival of urban communities, Docklands is a reminder that policies have not only to stem decay but also to stimulate and influence patterns of growth.

This essay concentrates on the changing economy and labor market of London Docklands in the 1980s, to illustrate the forces shaping local economies in London during that decade and the consequent effect on people and communities. The discussion of community response by its very nature also examines aspects of local social policy and general attitudes to the regeneration process.

ECONOMIC DECLINE AND THE EMERGENCE OF THE LDDC

Deindustrialization came early to London. Buck et. al. (1986) outlined how the decline of London's manufacturing sector in the 1960s and 1970s was well advanced before the ravages of industrial decline really took hold in the other regions of Britain. Indeed, London performed relatively well in the recession of the late seventies and early eighties. As one of London's main manufacturing areas, Docklands and the surrounding East End experienced marked decline. Between 1971 and 1981, the number of jobs in East London[1] fell by 16 percent compared to 10.5 percent in Greater London. In the manufacturing sector, 75,500 jobs were lost in East London, a decline of 44 percent. The figure for London as a whole was 36 percent (Censuses of Employment 1971 and 1981).

To make matters worse, East London's service sector was performing badly. In 1960, twenty-nine thousand people had worked in the Port of London. Dock closures started in 1967 and, combined with reductions in manning levels, had reduced dock employment to nineteen thousand by 1970 (Docklands Forum/Birkbeck College 1990). In 1982, the closure of London's upstream docks was complete. This contributed to a 40 percent fall in

---

[1] East London is defined as the five local authority boroughs of Tower Hamlets, Newham, Greenwich, Lewisham, and Southwark.

transport and communication employment in East London between 1971 and 1981, compared to a 15 percent decline in London. In addition, public expenditure cuts in the late seventies were mainly responsible for the loss of one in four public sector jobs in East London (Censuses of Employment 1971 and 1981).

In the much smaller area defined as Docklands for policy purposes (see figure 3) the situation was even more severe. In just three years, between 1978 and 1981, the area lost over a quarter of its thirty-seven thousand jobs. The restructuring strategies of multinational manufacturing firms and the Port of London Authority were responsible for many of the job losses. The Docklands communities attempted to resist the decline. Campaigns against dock closures were fought by broad coalitions of trade unions and local community groups (Mayo and Newman 1981). Central and local government tried to design policies to stem decline and stimulate local growth. The Docklands Joint Committee, made up of representatives of central, metropolitan, and local government and the community, devised the London Docklands Strategic Plan in 1976. This envisaged a redevelopment process funded mainly by the public sector that was strategically linked to the economic and social needs of people in East London. Weak powers over land and a lack of money limited the role of the Docklands Joint Committee. The £35 million of extra central government money committed to Docklands between 1977 and 1982 compared poorly to the £33 million made available to the LDDC in 1981–82, its first year of operation (Docklands Forum/ Birkbeck College 1990). Ineffective policy was unable to alleviate the process of economic decline in the 1970s. By 1981, 40 percent of Docklands lay vacant or derelict and unemployment had risen to 22 percent (HMSO 1988).

Regeneration LDDC Style

The Conservative administration of 1979 instigated a typically market-oriented approach to urban decline. The LDDC is now one of eleven urban development corporations responsible for the physical, economic, and social regeneration of depressed and derelict parts of urban Britain. The initial emphasis of the LDDC was firmly on the physical. This model of private-sector-led regeneration—variously labeled "demand-led planning," "leverage planning," and more emotively "a local monetarist experiment"—assumes that once public money has been used to overcome the image of decay and provide infrastructure then private investment will be attracted. The wealth created, in theory, will "trickle down" into the local economy and community, thus alleviating the area's pressing economic and social problems.

According to Conservative central government, the scale of dereliction in

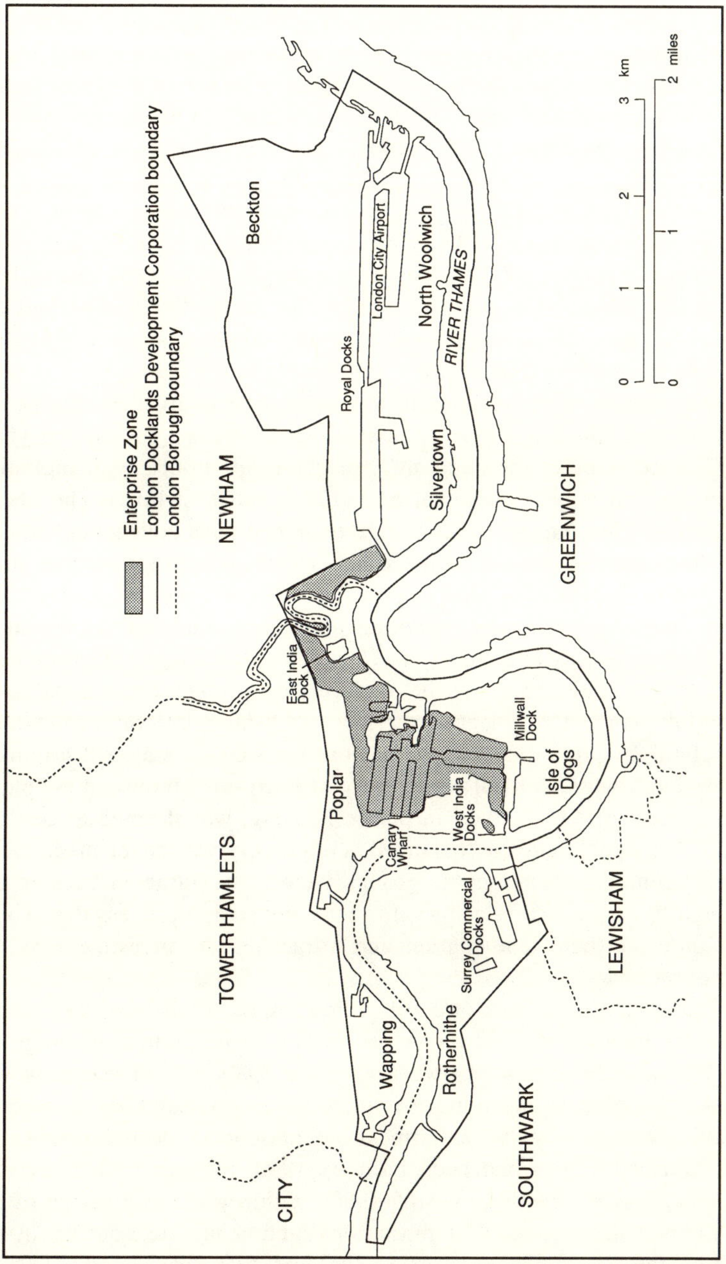

FIGURE 3   London Docklands

an area bordering the City of London made Docklands national priority requiring Treasury funding and a single-minded agency solely concerned with regeneration. Not surprisingly, the local Labour governments' recipe of municipal socialism was deemed to have failed to revive the local industrial and housing base and was viewed as a hindrance to private investment. These arguments, based on Tory ideology, and the large scale of Treasury support—over £6 million a week in 1989–90—were used to justify the central control of the LDDC by the Department of the Environment. Local planning control was removed from the locally elected councils and given to the centrally appointed LDDC. Among the armory of LDDC powers, land acquisition is probably the most important. By 1988, the LDDC had acquired, and in many cases already serviced and released, some 1,975 acres of the 5,000 acres of land and water in the area.

A significant stimulus to economic regeneration was given by the designation of much of the Isle of Dogs as an Enterprise Zone for the ten years after 1982. Incentives in the zone are strongly property-oriented, including tax concessions on property investment and local business taxes. The liberal planning regime of an Enterprise Zone further eroded local government control over the development process, and Canary Wharf, the largest single office development in Britain, was able to proceed without a public inquiry.

LDDC's annual reports and corporate plans have laid out its vision of creating a new economy and society in Docklands. Declining industries were to be allowed to fade away, to be replaced by growth firms capable of competing internationally. Financial services, publishing, telecommunications, and biotechnology were some of the sectors the LDDC imagined might be attracted to Docklands. A local community of thirty-nine thousand people in 1981, 86 percent of whom lived in public housing, was deemed to be "unbalanced." What constitutes a "balanced" community was never made clear. Nevertheless, middle-class income groups were to be attracted back to the area through the construction of private sector housing, a process that would also stimulate the local land market and attract private investment by the volume housebuilders.

The LDDC's preferred measures of policy impact have been well documented in the international media. A private/public investment leverage ratio of 12.5/1 had been achieved between 1981 and 1989. It is unclear, however, whether all government expenditure is included in this calculation, such as the massive investment by the Department of Transport in local road schemes. Thirteen thousand homes had been built by 1990, ranging from converted warehouse apartments costing over £500,000 within walking distance of the City of London to more modest mass construction private housing in the area around the Royal Docks. During the first five years of the LDDC, commercial interest was slow to grow and consisted largely of mixed low-rise high-tech units. Latterly, Docklands was at the center of the London office development boom of the mid-1980s. By 1990, 1.1 million square meters of commercial and industrial space was constructed (LDDC 1990). Canary Wharf and other large-scale development under construction meant that Docklands could contain approximately 2 million square meters of office space by 1993 (LDDC 1989).

At the turn of the decade the LDDC found its grand vision falling apart. The deep property market recession resulted in a series of bankruptcies amongst Docklands developers as the supply of housing and offices far exceeded demand. Estimates claimed that 50 percent of Docklands office space was vacant (Savills 1990). In 1988, criticism of its approach to regeneration started to gather pace with critical reports from House of Commons committees (HMSO 1988, 1989) and adverse comments from developers and even former LDDC board members (Brownill 1990). The lack of a strategic approach had produced a crowded and inadequate transport system (Church 1990). A mass of evidence showed that the social and economic problems of Docklands and East London remained as persistent as ever (see, for example, Docklands Forum 1987 on housing and Docklands Forum/Birkbeck College 1990 on employment). Poverty continued to exist alongside large-scale redevelopment.

The LDDC's response was to develop a belated social agenda. The 1989 corporate plan outlined the LDDC's intention to spend £84 million "developing the social fabric" which would allow the construction of social housing and the enhancement of training and education provision. These good intentions also fell foul of the property recession, and a lack of income from LDDC land sales led to a moratorium on social expenditure (Docklands Forum 1990).

Sorting out the transport chaos required more drastic measures. Approximately £2.5 billion is to be spent on roads in and around Docklands by the end of the 1990s and over £1 billion on public transport. Docklands used to be portrayed as the shining example of the success of free private enterprise. The reality is that private money is backed by colossal sums of public money.

In this boom-and-bust environment, local residents, communities, and politicians have continued to campaign for a different approach to regeneration. Clearly, the attitudes and lives of many local residents will have been significantly affected by the LDDC's policies. The detail of local economic change indicates the background to community response and change in London Docklands.

THE NATURE OF ECONOMIC CHANGE

In 1981, there were 27,000 jobs in Docklands. By 1991, the figure had risen to 60,000, which included 6,000 to 7,000 temporary construction jobs

(Docklands Forum/Birkbeck College 1990). Predictions for the future abound. The LDDC in 1990 envisaged 200,000 jobs in Docklands by the year 2000, whereas property analysts, who believe the take-up of office space will be slow, predict 190,000 by the year 2008 (APR 1989).

Overall figures hide the nature of local economic change. Few of the incoming jobs are new in the sense that they have not been located elsewhere before. Between 1981 and 1987, 20,000 jobs came to Docklands, 75 percent of which were transfers (RISUL 1988). This is indicative of the fact that many firms are moving to Docklands as part of a broader economic restructuring (Church 1988). The significant growth sectors are newspaper printing, retail, and banking, finance, and insurance. A move from Fleet Street to Docklands allowed many national newspaper firms to introduce new technology and changes in management-union relations, leading to substantial increases in profitability. New retail outlets are in part a result of the national competitive strategies of the major companies who dominate the U.K. retail grocery industry. The expansion of financial services stems more from the global process affecting the City of London. Deregulation and internationalization led to the expansion of financial services in London in the mid-1980s. Many of the firms moving to Docklands use this as an opportunity to rationalize their employment levels in the current recession. Ironically, growth in Docklands may be part of an overall decline in this sector in London (SERTUC 1990).

Less attention has been paid to the continuing loss of jobs in Docklands. At least 13,000 jobs were lost in the area between 1981 and 1990. Some losses stem from continued rationalizations and closures by multinational companies. Others are the result of LDDC redevelopment proposals that require firms to move or close down (Docklands Forum/Birkbeck College 1990).

Despite the influx of jobs and the national economic recovery of the mid-1980s, unemployment remains high in Docklands and the surrounding area. The three local authority areas of Tower Hamlets, Newham, and Southwark overlap the LDDC area (see figure 3). Unemployment rates in these three boroughs in October 1990 ranged from 10.6 percent in Newham and Southwark to 13.6 percent in Tower Hamlets. The figure for Greater London was 6.4 percent. Comparisons over time are made difficult by continual changes to the compilation of figures. Total unemployment in these three boroughs was 32,800 in January 1981 and rose to a peak of 55,700 in January 1986. The figure fell to a low of 31,000 in March 1990 before rising sharply to over 34,000 in December 1990. If unemployment was calculated in the same way as in 1981, the 1990 figure would be nearer 46,000 (Docklands Forum/Birkbeck College 1990).

Even in the small LDDC area, the unemployment total at the end of the

1980s was back to over 3,000 compared to 3,500 in July 1981. Numerous research studies have shown that commuting patterns mean that new jobs in areas like Docklands are likely to be taken by people traveling into the area (Hausner and Robson 1985). Of the 20,000 jobs that came to Docklands between 1981 and 1987, 75 percent were taken by residents of areas outside the three Docklands boroughs of Tower Hamlets, Newham, and Southwark (RISUL 1988).

Unemployment in East London, therefore, is a persistent problem. Gordon (1989) outlines how the interactions between housing and labor markets lead to spatial concentrations of disadvantaged groups of workers in London. The result is high levels of unemployment in inner-urban public housing estates. The conclusion of Gordon's analysis is that an increase in labor demand alone will not solve this problem. Policies will be needed to improve the relative competitive position of the most disadvantaged. A report on employment in Docklands (Docklands Forum/Birkbeck College 1990) argued that this required job creation strategies linked to extensive training and education policies and a greater commitment to equal opportunities initiatives to tackle labor market discrimination.

The lack of links between local residents and new jobs suggests that the effects of regeneration on the local community cannot be easily read off from the nature of the redevelopment process. In-depth research is needed to understand the interaction between regeneration, people's lives, and attitudes. By contrast, the local political responses are more easy to identify.

LOCAL AUTHORITIES AND THE LDDC

The relationships between local councils and the LDDC varied throughout the 1980s. Tower Hamlets, which was Liberal controlled between 1986 and 1993, has always been the most conciliatory of the three boroughs. In a draft borough plan, it was prepared to surrender its statutory rights over parts of the Isle of Dogs in an attempt to get the LDDC to agree to the rest of a statutory plan. A councillor from the borough has always been on the LDDC board.

By contrast, Newham claimed that a councillor initially took a seat on the LDDC board only to resign it three years later frustrated by the LDDC's secrecy (HMSO 1988). Newham was prepared to exhibit some flexibility in Docklands. In 1985, it produced its draft South Docklands Local Plan for the area around the Royal Docks. Brownill (1990, 151) argues that this "tried to follow a middle line between a market-led and a needs-led plan in the classic pluralist mode of trying to balance competing uses." The plan accepted LDDC proposals for the development of the short-take-off-and-landing airport, the London City Airport, and other private sector schemes in the Victoria Dock. Despite this, the LDDC was strongly opposed to the plan and at the subsequent public inquiry released details of three massive private sector proposals for the area. The planning inspector sided with the LDDC and deemed the plan inappropriate.

Events south of the river in Southwark illustrated the power behind the LDDC even more starkly. In 1982, a "new left" administration was elected and adopted a policy of noncooperation with the LDDC. It also drew up a needs-based, site-by-site, draft plan for its part of Docklands which emphasized the need for public housing and the maintenance of existing industry. Again the LDDC was the key objector at the public inquiry, and again the public inspector supported many of the LDDC's views. Consequently, Southwark was instructed by central government not to develop the plan any further. The council refused and stated its intention to stick to the plan, whereupon the Minister for the Environment refused to allow Southwark powers to adopt the plan. For the first time ever, central government had prevented a local council from adopting its own local plan. The combined power of the LDDC and the Department of the Environment had proved too much for the local councils, and local plans were simply ignored.

These defeats and the election of a Conservative government for a third term in 1987 led to a shift in the strategies of the local councils. The emphasis was more on what local gains the council could extract from the LDDC and the developers. As Brownill (1990) notes, "local groups and authorities were thus faced with the choice of opposing schemes that would go ahead or negotiating to try and extract some gain and achieve positive results."

In 1987, planning gain deals became the order of the day. The Canary Wharf agreement between Olympia and York and Tower Hamlets was to guarantee two thousand jobs for local residents in Canary Wharf and a £2.5 million trust for training. In addition, the Tower Hamlets Accord between LDDC and the borough meant that the LDDC would pay to rehouse 450 tenants displaced by the construction of the Limehouse Link Road and would provide £30 million for community schemes. The Newham agreement between the LDDC and the borough of Newham set a target of fifteen hundred social housing units, a £60 million community development program, training facilities, and 25 percent of jobs in the future Royal Docks development for local residents. The local councils surrendered their right to oppose the Limehouse Link Road and the developments at Canary Wharf and the Royal Docks.

The implications of these deals are numerous (Docklands Forum 1988; Brownill 1990). Short-term gains have to be offset against possible long-term costs for social and community provision caused by rising land values and development pressure. Many of the community gains involve expenditure that would have occurred anyway and may disguise the effect of other public expenditure cuts. In the Royal Docks, implementation has been slow. Two of the three proposed private sector redevelopment schemes have been withdrawn due to the property slump, and the LDDC is thus short of cash to fulfill its commitments. Furthermore, the basic central ideology of the LDDC's approach still guides development in Docklands. Community gain deals, like earlier advertising and infrastructure expenditure, enable private sector investment in schemes devised by international property developers. The influence of locally elected representatives is marginalized. Perhaps far more important electorally, the alternative strategies of local authorities fade away. Community benefits are extracted but can be portrayed by the LDDC as the outcome of their policies. LDDC press releases have hinted at once opposed councils coming round to their way of thinking. It remains to be seen who reaps any electoral credit associated with the new rented housing and other social facilities.

LDDC AND THE GREATER LONDON COUNCIL

In the early 1980s, attempts to devise alternatives to the LDDC came not only from local councils but also from metropolitan government in the form of the Greater London Council (GLC). The Labour-controlled GLC had established two London-wide initiatives that were in turn focused on the Royal Docks area. The GLC had established the Greater London Enterprise Board (GLEB) with the broad aim of developing projects that would aid the restructuring of production so as to benefit London residents directly. GLEB's method was to target certain industrial sectors, manage a sizeable property portfolio, provide investment capital, develop technology networks, and generally pursue enterprise planning in which social and equal opportunities goals were followed by assisted companies. Elsewhere in the GLC, the Popular Planning Unit aimed to give local communities and trades unions an opportunity to identify local needs and develop community-based proposals for development.

In Docklands, the stimulus for popular planning activity and interest from GLEB was the public planning inquiry in 1983 into the London City Airport. The GLC helped the local community group, the Newham Docklands Forum, establish a People's Planning Centre. The People's Plan for the Royal Docks was produced in which there would be no airport but rather a job mix that recognized existing skills, public housebuilding, better social services, and environment improvements. In discussions over the plan's implementation, there was considerable tension between the centralizing tendencies of the GLC and the local community groups involved (Brownill 1990).

A GLEB team was established in the Royal Docks to try to develop some of the plan's economic proposals. However, the LDDC in 1984 moved quickly to ensure that it purchased the land in the Royal Docks rather than the GLC. Construction of the airport followed soon afterwards. Limited funds meant that GLEB was restricted to small-scale investments in local food and transport firms and establishing a business advice project for disabled people. Not surprisingly, it was unable to exert any influence over the multinational companies that still had plants in the area. The presence of GLEB in Docklands was perhaps also designed to act as a politically inspired pointer to local needs-based planning as a contrast to the LDDC.

The abolition of the GLC in 1986 led to the closure of the GLEB office, but a smaller People's Planning Centre still remains along with a community launderette, a creche, and a local resource center. Massey argues that while the effect of these measures may be limited, they were important in ensuring that alternative approaches to the LDDC remained on the policy agenda. "Docklands has demonstrated through the activity of local groups, through the activity of local communities, the possibilities of an idea of something which is just that bit more democratic, a bit more bottom up, a bit more decentralised. There have been ideas for a different kind of growth, a growth which tries at least to begin to work with local people rather than building simply on land prices and location" (Massey 1990, 13). Nevertheless, the impression is of an all-powerful LDDC and central government gradually breaking the resistance of local opposition.

There are some examples of local community groups successfully taking on the LDDC. Community pressure eventually persuaded the LDDC to allow council housing at Cherry Garden Pier in the Surrey Docks, overturning its former plans for luxury housing. Local groups on the Isle of Dogs campaigned continually for more LDDC expenditure on training, which eventually materialized. These successes may be isolated, but, as Brownill (1990) points out, such pressure and continual criticism from community groups lies behind the emergence of the LDDC's social initiatives and the attempts by more recently established urban development corporations to disassociate themselves from the LDDC's approach.

Understanding the Community Response

The reaction of local politicians and community activists to urban change is, of course, part of a much more complex process of social change and response in Docklands. Academic research has often simplified the nature of social divisions and attitudes in Docklands. For Short, a new social order is emerging in Docklands. "Yuppification involves the destruction of an existing community and its replacement by a new one with consequent changes in the meaning and use of space" (1989, 185). Like other academic studies,

Short (1989) is concerned to show how the "postmodern" built environment and public spaces of Docklands facilitate the dominance of capitalistic middle-class values in the regeneration process. Harvey (1989) describes how the use of space to express corporate and financial power has been central to the strategies of urban governments competing for international investment.

Bird (1990) notes that the local community in Docklands can also utilize visual culture to express its resistance to change. The Docklands Community Poster Project, founded in 1982, organizes a series of photomurals on large billboards in Docklands that act as statements of opposition to LDDC policy. For Bird, these posters indicate "a cultural organisation's efficacy in producing a coherent communal identity and providing a focus for sustained social and political struggle" (1990, 90). These posters articulated the views of many local residents, but the community's identity and attitudes are far from coherent. Ironically, the Community Poster Project later changed its name to Art of Change and was funded mainly by the LDDC.

The influx of wealthier residents as a result of new housing has fundamentally altered the nature of the community. By 1996, 55 percent of households in Docklands will be in privately owned housing as opposed to 5 percent in 1981 (Docklands Forum 1987). Many of the new residents in areas like Wapping are from high-income groups (Crilley et al. 1990). Others in housing around the Royal Docks are first-time buyers from the East End. But for many of the local residents buying a house is not an option. In Tower Hamlets, a council report concluded that the average mortgage repayment for a first-time buyer was four times the average take-home wage in the borough (Malik 1989). However, Docklands residents cannot be neatly divided into haves and have nots. There are major divisions amongst the residents of public housing, and the residents who were living in the area prior to 1981 are certainly not united in their resistance to the LDDC. More detailed research outlines a much more complex relationship between regeneration and the local community.

The Impact of Regeneration and Economic Change on Young Adults

Questionnaire data from a sample of 150 young adults who had formerly been pupils at the only secondary school in Docklands on the Isle of Dogs indicate some of the economic forces affecting local residents (Church and Ainley 1987; Church 1989). The sample was aged seventeen to twenty-one and had left school between 1981 and 1985. The interviews took place in 1986 and were a follow-up to interviews in 1983–84 of a sample of ninety. Untypically for an inner-city locality, the catchment area served by the school at the time was mainly white working class. Parental occupations indicated family backgrounds typical of an area where the local economy had been dominated by manufacturing and dock-related industries. Over half of the respondents' fathers worked in manual jobs, whereas only 13 percent worked in nonmanual occupations.

The nature of the transition from school to adulthood in working-class life has been subject to a series of postwar studies since Ferguson and Cunnison's follow-up of Glasgow school leavers in 1947. The overall picture was clear: the occupational aspirations of working-class school leavers were found to be uniformly limited, influenced as they were by what Jahoda (1952) called the "climate of opinion" regarding certain types of job. Once in work, young working-class adults were discovered to follow a predictable pattern of behavior ranging from initial euphoria to subsequent disillusionment and resentment of authority (Keil et al. 1966). Wilmott (1966) indicated that the subjects of his *Adolescent Boys in East London* were most discontented at age seventeen and eighteen when they had yet to become subject to the social controls of family and community.

Since the sample in Docklands was aged seventeen to twenty-one, some were older than the typical "transition" age groups. The extended labor market experience of the older respondents in an area of high unemployment might be expected to lead to a lowering of occupational aspirations. On average, however, the older groups tended to have more precise aspirations than the younger respondents. Aspirations were less toward manual work and more toward nonmanual. 58 percent of the respondents aspired to nonmanual jobs as opposed to 24 percent aspiring to manual work. The remainder wanted to be self-employed or did not specify. These aspirations differ from those recorded amongst the sample of ninety interviewed in 1983–84. 43 percent of this earlier group aspired to a manual job and 39 percent to nonmanual work. So rather than lowering aspirations, some respondents had transferred them to other areas of work upon realizing the limited opportunities in traditional manual jobs.

Roberts and Parsnell (1988) similarly found young people maintaining aspirations during the 1980s. They argue that this stems from the lack of clearly identifiable adult destinations and the fact that an adjustment based on early labor market experience would involve setting remarkably low goals that many found unacceptable. In the Docklands environment, local labor market factors seemed to be at work. Some of the sample had experienced long periods of unemployment, but 94 percent had worked at some point since leaving school. In addition, despite high local rates of unemployment, the City and the West End are relatively buoyant areas of the London economy. In this environment, it is perhaps possible to maintain aspirations. There was also evidence that peer group communication allowed the least successful to adjust their aspirations since they were always aware of individuals with similar qualifications who obtained reasonable jobs (Church and Ainley 1987).

The observed shift in aspirations suggests an element of adaptation to the changing labor market, and this adaptation is even more pronounced when the type of work done by respondents is examined. The sample were asked about their longest jobs and their current jobs if they had one. Responses showed 74 percent of current jobs and 64 percent of longest jobs were nonmanual, whereas in the first round of interviews, in 1983–84, 59 percent of those in work were in manual jobs and only 41 percent in nonmanual jobs. The traditional concentration of work in manual jobs had weakened. However, the traditional gender division exists in that only four of the forty-six girls currently in work were in manual jobs. Males faced with declining opportunities in manual work are responding by working in increasing numbers in nonmanual jobs. So the changes taking place are based partly around the reduction of gender divisions in work but only in one direction, with young males moving into occupations more often done by females.

There is, therefore, evidence of adaptation to the surrounding labor market. Interestingly, the interviews were undertaken in 1986 when the LDDC's policies were just starting to take effect. Twenty thousand jobs had come to Docklands between 1981 and 1987 (RISUL 1988). If incoming firms in Docklands provide nonmanual office jobs for local young adults, this will not represent some major transformation. Instead it will merely reinforce a process of labor market change that had already begun.

However, for the vast majority of the sample, the influx of firms had not affected their labor market experiences. 35 percent of the sample had worked locally on the Isle of Dogs at some point since leaving school, mostly in the firms that had existed prior to the LDDC's establishment in 1981. Only 13 percent had worked in newly established firms, and over half of them had been employees at the newly opened Asda grocery supermarket. Furthermore, the labor market experiences of some of the group suggest that the economic problems of the local residents will not be tackled by a simple increase in the number of jobs.

Typically for young adults from East London, the sample had low levels of educational attainments; 36 percent had no educational qualifications and 24 percent very few. Despite this, some of the respondents, usually the better qualified, had obtained well-paid secure jobs with prospects. The careers of others, however, had been far from satisfactory.

The survey did not reveal some permanently unemployed subclass. Rather there was a distinct subgroup which, although not permanently unemployed, had experienced regular and lengthy periods without work. One-quarter of the sample had been unemployed for over a third of the time since leaving school. By contrast, 38 percent of the respondents had never been unemployed, and two-thirds had spent less than 20 percent of their time since leaving school in unemployment. The 25 percent of the sample who have performed less well in the labor market had labor market histories that might best be described as disjointed. They had worked on and off since leaving school: 50 percent had been on a training scheme, and they had all experienced long periods of unemployment. None of this group admitted to choosing to follow such a career pattern, and the incidence of work in the informal economy by this group was relatively small. Harris et al. (1987) found similar "chequered" career patterns amongst young people in South Wales.

The differences between the poorly performing 25 percent and the rest of the sample are not simply a matter of qualifications which this group lack. There were many equally poorly qualified respondents who were not part of this group. A comparison between the social characteristics of the poorly performing respondents and other respondents also with no or very few qualifications reveals no clear differences. Family backgrounds are similar, and there were no marked variations between those from different family situations.

This sample is admittedly small, but the disjointed careers of the poorly performing group seem to be more related to the types of jobs they obtained. These were less well paid than those held by the rest of the sample and provided no training. Poor conditions, temporary appointments, and a lack of prospects were also features of their employment. Larger-scale studies have revealed how the transformation of the British economy has led to the recent growth of such jobs in the national youth labor market. Roberts et al. (1987) claim this is "recreating the dead-end youth jobs that became infamous before the Second World War."

It seems that the lower quartile are only obtaining some of the worst jobs available in the changing London economy. Devising policies to break the disjointed career patterns of young people is probably far more of a challenge than developing initiatives to promote physical regeneration in Docklands. Furthermore, the data for the whole sample indicate the diverse labor market experiences of young working-class people from East London in the 1980s. Background and school experience may be shared, but work careers are very diverse. This may further widen some of the divisions within the community that are indicated by attitudes to the redevelopment process.

Attitudes to Change in Docklands

For some of the working-class residents of Docklands, the regeneration policies of the LDDC may have a significant effect on their lives; for others, they are marginal. This range of experiences is reflected in the varying attitudes to change in the area. Wallman's (1987) survey of twenty-two hundred households on the Isle of Dogs found that 16 percent of those interviewed felt they had benefited from developments in Docklands. By contrast, 40 percent felt they had not gained, and 17 percent claimed regeneration had an adverse impact on their lives. The sample of young adults already mentioned expressed diverse opinions. Several young males felt their area was being taken over by new residents and offices. One claimed, "We used to do what we liked round here, we could even go swimming in the docks but that's all stopped now: everywhere you go now there's people stopping you having a laugh" (1987).

Those with stable employment histories tended to be less critical of the redevelopment process. "It's better than the mess before"; "I know quite a few people who've got jobs in new firms"; "at least the buses are better now": these were typical comments of those generally supportive of the changes. Some qualified their support of redevelopment with a sense of cynicism. One male argued, "I support what they're doing. But let's face it, if they couldn't do something down here with the City, then we might as well all give up" (ibid.). Critical opinions were just as prevalent amongst those with stable careers. One female was particularly wide ranging in her comments: "I went to one of their [the LDDC's] public meetings and I asked the bloke why should people round here take all the bad jobs coming to the Island. I mean, you know, jobs in places like Asda pay really badly and I told him that local people didn't want those sorts of jobs.... Anyway, he just stood at the front and said there's no alternative to those jobs. But they're wrong, local people shouldn't just end up with the rubbish jobs" (ibid.).

Comments supporting regeneration were far less likely to be made by the group who had experienced disjointed work histories. Their attitudes were not, however, directly critical; rather they reflected a sense of marginalization from the whole redevelopment process. Some based their views on direct experiences. One female claimed that whilst looking for work, "I must have written about 30 letters to all the new firms, most of them don't even reply. These new firms aren't the sort of place I'm going to get a job" (ibid.). The comments of one male when asked about the impact of redevelopment were more typical of this group. "I don't really know. I suppose it'll do something but not for me. I mean it just won't" (ibid.).

More recent ethnographic research on the Isle of Dogs conducted by Janet Foster from the London School of Economics provides evidence of a similar range of attitudes amongst a sample of more diverse ages. In this case, there seems to be some relationship between attitude and length of residence. The community on the Isle of Dogs contains many individuals whose families have lived there for three or four generations. According to Foster,[2]

---

[2] This evidence was gained from discussions between the author and Janet Foster.

this group are mainly opposed to redevelopment but in a "state of shock" at the way the area has changed. By contrast, many of those who moved into new public housing in Docklands in the 1960s tended to be more positive toward redevelopment even if they were not certain how it would be of direct benefit to them as individuals. In-migrants in the late 1970s were often being moved to "hard-to-let" public estates. For many of this group, daily social stresses tend to lead to a sense of disassociation with redevelopment. They are unable to imagine any significant benefits of regeneration that will ease the problems they face.

Wallman's (1987) statistical survey of twenty-two hundred Isle of Dogs residents provides a less precise link between length of residence and attitudes to regeneration. In keeping with Foster's views, long-standing residents were the most critical of developments to date. They were, however, more optimistic about possible future benefits. The statistical and ethnographic data confirm the diverse views amongst local residents and the extent of social fragmentation. The range of responses stems in part from the past historical economic and social development of this locality.

Docklands has never been a totally homogeneous community, but long-standing kinship networks and the close relationship between the dock work and local residents created closely knit groups within the community (Hill 1976). Wallman's (1987) study indicates that 23 percent of households had always lived on the Isle of Dogs, and 64 percent of their respondents had relatives living in the area. Nevertheless, many residents of public housing are less interlinked with the area. Further evidence of social fragmentation is provided by increasing racial tension.

In 1981, the ethnic minority population in Docklands was only 9 percent. By 1990, the proportion had risen to 20 percent (Docklands Forum 1990). At the same time, the Docklands Forum noted that racial harassment and vicious attacks were increasing alarmingly and that "what has become clear in both Newham and Tower Hamlets, there are disproportionately more attacks in the Docklands area than in other parts of the borough" (1990, 10). Race issues have also emerged over housing allocation. Since 1987, the borough of Tower Hamlets has allocated a proportion of vacant housing on the Isle of Dogs to homeless families, 80 percent of whom are Bangladeshi. The scale of racial harassment and violence has led a few Bangladeshi families to turn down their one chance of public housing rather than go and live on the Isle of Dogs.

More recently, racism has detracted from the community success of persuading the LDDC to allow public housing to be built at Cherry Garden Pier in Southwark. On completion of the housing, there were heated debates at public meetings over whether it should be allocated to residents from the local area who were mainly white or to people with the greatest housing needs in the whole of Southwark, many of whom were black. Racist comments at public meetings were reported extensively in the local press and were one reason why a successful local community group felt driven to disband itself (Docklands Forum 1991).

Racial tension is not just confined to public housing areas. In some private sector housing schemes, developers unable to sell units have been leasing them short term to the local councils for homeless people. Private tenants' associations have been formed to oppose the ensuing influx of mainly Bangladeshi families. Explaining this increased racial tension is far from straightforward. Long-standing East End racism, a "white flight" reaction from those unable to flee, the pressure caused by an intense local housing shortage, inadequate police response, and institutional failure amongst local authorities to explain sympathetically their allocation policies have all been suggested as reasons (Malik 1989; London Alarm against Racism 1990). Whatever the cause, racial tension and racism create further fissures in this already divided community.

CONCLUSION

For Massey, the fragmentation of the Docklands community is not altogether surprising, and "the particular economic strategy in this country at the moment isn't just accidentally leaving some people out. It is built on the notion of two nations. Part and parcel of the economic strategy is inequality.... What's happening in Docklands is in a sense just a heightened, sharpened version of things that are happening nationally. And, in that sense, the divides we have are heightened forms of the divides that exist within the country as a whole" (1990, 11). The labor market experiences of young adults in Docklands seem to bear out these conclusions. The broader economic processes of change in the London labor market seem to have marginalized a significant proportion of the young. Local economic regeneration is unlikely to alter these economic differences.

Devising alternative local policies is far from straightforward. Local councils have been torn between resisting the LDDC and acquiescing to ensure some improvements in housing and social facilities. The latter approach may blur the edges of any alternative vision.

Empowering local councils and communities through some form of community-based planning will be a step in the right direction. But the fragmented nature of the Docklands communities shows the need for more extensive policies. Economic problems and unemployment will require extensive training, education, and advice alongside job creation.

A further problem is developing alternative policies that are wide-ranging and coherent. The persistence of economic and social problems in Docklands generated considerable local criticism of the LDDC. However, it is the inadequacies of the transport system that have really attracted widespread national media attention and shown to a much wider audience the inefficiencies of market-based solutions. The media fragments the issues, and therefore alternative policies can seem like a ragbag of responses to the problems of the market rather than a coherent strategy.

Sadly, the real opportunity that Docklands represented is fast disappearing. Unlike many other areas of London, there was space in Docklands. An area half the size of the City of Cambridge was 40 percent derelict or vacant in 1981. There was room for public and private housing, industry and offices, efficient public transport, social facilities and a pleasant environment. As the land of Docklands was gobbled up in the 1980s, we are left with more of the same in London. Immense poverty alongside immense wealth, intense office development, a mediocre environment, and a congested public transport system.

Postscript

When this essay was first written it was designed to outline the nature of the economic and social changes in London Docklands during the 1980s. Since then a number of significant developments have affected its economy, society, and political environment. The commercial and residential property markets in Docklands have slumped dramatically. Office vacancy rates of about 50 percent were attributed to the national economic recession of the early 1990s and the over-supply of office space in London that had been created during the 1980s property boom. Olympia and York, the developers of Canary Wharf, went into receivership, and became the most high profile casualty of this property slump. The problems of the Docklands economy, in part, explain the fact that unemployment in Docklands in 1993 was still as high as when the LDDC was first set up in 1980. Consequently, the LDDC no longer occupies such a privileged political position as the government's leading, highly publicized inner-city initiative. Indeed, the LDDC is now implementing a program of phased withdrawal of its powers from Docklands by March 1998. Socially, the area remains highly fragmented and racial tension reached a peak when in 1993 a member of the extreme right British National Party was elected as a councillor for part of the Isle of Dogs. However, large scale political mobilization of the local community in the 1994 elections saw to his replacement by a Labor councillor. These recent developments tend to confirm the conclusions of this essay that the market-led regeneration of the 1980s did not provide a solution to the deep-rooted economic and social problems of London Docklands.

References

APR. 1989. *The Employment Potential of London Docklands.* London: Applied Property Research.
Bird, J. 1990. "Dystopia on the Thames." *Art in America,* July, 89–97.
Brownill, S. 1990. *Developing London's Docklands.* London: Paul Chapman.
Buck, N., I. Gordon, and K. Young. 1986. *The London Employment Problem.* Oxford: Clarendon.
Church, A. 1988. "Urban Regeneration in London Docklands: A Five-Year Policy Review." *Environment and Planning C,* 6:187–208.
Church, A. 1989. *The Economic Regeneration of London Docklands.* London University Ph.D.
Church, A. 1990. "Transport and Urban Regeneration in London Docklands." *Cities, the International Journal of Urban Policy and Planning* 7, no. 4:289–303.
Church, A., and P. Ainley 1987. "Inner-City Decline and Regeneration: Young People and the Labour Market in London Docklands," in P. Brown and D. Ashton, eds., *Education, Unemployment and Labour Markets.* Sussex: Falmer Press.
Crilley, D., C. Bryce, and P. Ogden. 1990. *New Migrants in London Docklands.* Department of Geography, Queen Mary and Westfield College, University of London.
Docklands Forum. 1987. *Housing in Docklands.* London: Docklands Forum.
Docklands Forum. 1988. *Does the Community Benefit?* London: Docklands Forum.
Docklands Forum. 1990. *Minutes of November Meeting.* London: Docklands Forum.
Docklands Forum. 1991. *Minutes of May Meeting.* London: Docklands Forum.
Docklands Forum/Birkbeck College. 1990. *Employment in Docklands.* London: Docklands Forum.
Ferguson, T., and J. Cunnison. 1952. *The Young Wage Earner.* Oxford: Oxford University Press.
Gordon, I. 1989. "Urban Unemployment," in D. Herbert and D. Smith, eds., *Social Problems and the City.* Oxford: Oxford University Press.
Harris, C., et al. (1987). "Young Adults in South Wales," in P. Brown and D. Ashton, eds., *Education, Unemployment and Labor Markets.* Sussex: Falmer Press.
Harvey, D. 1989. *The Condition of Postmodernity.* Oxford: Blackwell.
Hausner, V., and B. Robson. 1985. *Changing Cities.* London: Economic and Social Research Council.
Hill, S. 1976. *The Dockers: Class and Tradition in London.* London: Heinemann.
HMSO. 1988. *The Employment Effects of Urban Development Corporations.* Employment Committee, House of Commons, *Third Report.* HC 327–1 and 327–11. London: HMSO.
HMSO. 1989. *Urban Development Corporations.* Public Accounts Committee, House of Commons. HC-385. London: HMSO.
Jahoda, G. 1952. "Job Attitudes and Job Choice among Secondary Modern School Leavers." *Occupational Psychology* 26:125–40, 206–24.
Keil, E., C. Riddell, and B. Green. 1966. "Youth Work, Problems and Perspectives." *Sociological Review* 14, no. 2:117–37.
LDDC. 1989. *Corporate Plan.* London: London Docklands Development Corporation.
LDDC. 1990. *Annual Report.* London: London Docklands Development Corporation.
London Alarm against Racism. 1990. "Racism Gone to the Dogs: Racial Harassment on the Isle of Dogs." *London Alarm against Racism Bulletin* 3, 6–7.
Malik, K. 1989. "The Making of Eastenders." *Living Marxism,* September, 8–10.

Massey, D. 1990. *Docklands—A Microcosm of Wider Social and Economic Trends?* London: Docklands Forum.

Mayo, M., and I. Newman. 1981. "Docklands." *International Journal of Urban and Regional Research* 5, no. 4:529–45.

RISUL. 1988. *LDDC Census of Employment.* London: R. I. Specialist Units Ltd., London Docklands Development Corporation.

Roberts, K., S. Dench, and D. Richardson. 1987. "Youth Rates of Pay and Employment," in P. Brown and D. Ashton, eds., *Education, Unemployment, and Labour Markets.* Sussex: Falmer Press.

Roberts, K., and G. Parsnell. 1988. "Opportunity Structures and Career Trajectories from Age 16–19." Department of Sociology, University of Liverpool.

Savills. 1990. *Docklands Office Report 1990.* London: Savills.

SERTUC. 1990. *Wall Street on the Water: Employment Patterns in London Docklands.* London: South East Regional Council TUC.

Short, J. 1989. "Yuppies, Yuffies, and the New Urban Order." *Transactions of the Institute of British Geographers* 14:173–88.

Wallman, S. 1987. *Report on the Isle of Dogs: Millwall Survey.* Department of Geography, University College, London.

Wilmott, P. 1966. *Adolescent Boys in East London.* London: Routledge.

8

Bust, Baby, Bust: Coming of Age in America with Inflated Expectations and Diminished Options

Donna Gaines

In the 1950s and early 1960s, most public discussion of American youth was framed in the rhetoric of "social problems." There were kids who conformed and kids who slipped by, but mainly adults were concerned with juvenile delinquents, gangs, bad kids. Sometimes experts attributed kids' badness to poverty. If middle-class kids were acting difficult, sociologists might point a finger at the sterility of the middle-class family. But we worried mainly about the victims, not the perpetrators. By the mid-1960s, American scholars shifted gears. So did the media, and in the public view the collective activities of young people seemed important to us. By 1970, such discussions were almost always framed in a political rhetoric, as intergenerational politics. If we spoke about young people, it was in terms of the impact they had upon society as a historical force. Kids in the streets en masse meant the world was changing.

During those years, young people enjoyed a certain prestige. They inspired awe as well as fear among adults. Progressive-minded members of the prevailing adult authority structure viewed youth as the harbingers of social change. Teachers believed they could learn something from their students. Some adults became reflexive, others repressive, reactionary, and resentful. But the impact of youth on the adult imagination remained significant through the middle of the 1970s. After that, British scholars noted with great interest the political significance of the cultural productions and processes of punks, rude boys, and skinheads (Chambers 1986; Frith 1981; Hebdige 1979; for example).

But as the impact of the baby bust began to fade, with a few notable exceptions (for example, Ralph Larkin's *Suburban Youth in Cultural Crisis*, published in 1979, and Leon Sheleff's *Generations Apart* in 1981) most American scholarship on youth moved from the sociopolitical and cultural to the medical and psychoanalytic.

To be sure, American rock critics took note of the cultural activities of young people—punk, disco. But it was increasingly difficult to view these activities as unified or oriented toward any common goal. It was equally tricky to link these practices with the larger society. As our attentions shifted and were fragmented, the political prowess of America's young people began to diminish. Unless they were in trouble, kids grew less visible to adults, and eventually we forgot about them. They were no longer our agents of history.

By the 1980s, America's young people came into view again, in the rhetoric of social problems. In America, according to television, the kids were always screwing up. If experts were brought in to explain what was going on, they were generally psychologists and psychiatrists. The political and sociological sense of youth as a contesting age-caste, a "minority of minorities" up against the hegemonic adult authority structure, was lost. The adult authority structure took every opportunity to atomize and individualize each new "young atrocity." American kids entered the adult imagination as drive-by shoot-'em-up drug dealers, abusive teenage crack moms, Satanic suburban high school dropouts on angel dust. Then there was parricide, suicide, incest, sacrifices, racially motivated killings, date rape, and bad national test scores.

These hapless, hopeless young people came of age in the shadow of a far more fabulous generation. The 1960s had been an era where American kids commanded attention, respect, college loans, grants, and sometimes even free tuition! In addition, the cultural veterans of the 1960s youthquake have never stopped reminding the kids in the 1980s about how great the old days were. In the 1980s, as baby bust kids came of age, some found this depressing and longed for the glory days of Woodstock Nation. Others found it boring and as meaningless as dad's World War II stories sounded to sixties kids. Mostly, the unspoken relationship between sixties relics and eighties kids was based on mutual contempt, ignorance, mistrust, and, at best, benign neglect (see Gaines 1989a for more discussion).

During the 1980s, the kids in America managed to carve out autonomous cultural space with and without the help of adults. Most kids viewed adults as either ineffectual or menacing. Rarely did kids turn to adults for help. During this time, families were hard pressed by economic forces, parents were less available, schools had fewer resources, the kids were less valued as a power bloc because of their diminished status. Meanwhile, peer-regulating norms emerged, and kids taught each other how to survive. Rap groups like Public Enemy and N.W.A. explained about urban street economics, race, and violence. Thrash bands Metallica, Slayer, and Megadeth taught suburban kids how to deal with war, family violence, and suicide. West Coast hardcore bands like MDC and Black Flag spelled it out in complex verbal assault on multinational corporations, boredom, anomie. Radical women's bands like Wilma railed against patriarchal authority. But all this went on out of sight and mind of adults (Gaines 1991). Very rarely did the kids' culture come up in adult explanations of the world, except when they were used to build lawsuits against the kids' heroes—Ozzy Osbourne and Judas Priest, whose lyrics were blamed for teenage suicides.

A Tale of Two Generations

When demographers speak of the "pig in the python," they refer to the glut of Americans born between the years just after World War II ended and 1964—the baby boom. After 1964, birth rates began to drop, and people born between 1965 and 1974 were commonly referred to as members of the baby bust. Two generations were thus identified, solely on the basis of their birth rates. Today, in the United States, seventy-five million people make up the baby boom while only thirty-seven million constitute the baby bust. This demographic identification that distinguishes two generations also metaphorically describes their life experiences. Baby boomers enjoyed unprecedented affluence, indulgence, and prestige, while the baby bust is hitting a brick wall, as dead-end kids in America's suburban and urban teenage wastelands. Under the best of conditions, kids are still fighting harder than ever, for less.

As we know from Karl Mannheim, the media, and our own life experiences, there is much more to a generation than its demographic magnitude. Much like a class or an ethnic group, each generation has a unique character, a mentality, a defining *geist* carved out in the process of living in the world at a particular moment in history.

People of both generations come of age with shared experiences of culture, modes of economic organization, structural and institutional arrangements, legal and moral codes, grand events (wars, migration patterns), evolving technologies, and societal mood. With and without the additional burdens such as sex, race, class, gender preference, religion, or region, each generation must share the task of negotiating the existing adult authority structure.

In addition, there are people born on the cusp of a generation—caught in between. For example, the tail end of the pig, the end of the baby boom, the advance guard of the baby bust, are children born between, say, 1960 and 1965. They may view themselves as Reagan kids, because they were coming of age during that particular moment in American history, and that is their central shared experience. Some kids may have identified as yuppies, coffee achievers, St. Elmo's Fire babies. Others may have held fast to the rebel spirit, posthippies, dead heads. Some may reject it all and spit it back, calling themselves punks. Either way, this puny intermediary generation will have as little in common with their predecessors from Woodstock Nation as they do with their heirs, the hip-hop, heavy metal, hardcore kids of the late 1980s and early 1990s.

At the turn of the 1990s, the oldest among the baby boom were people in their middle forties, and the youngest were just turning twenty-six, placing them outside of the official statistical category for youth, which according to the U.S. government is between fifteen and twenty-four. At the turn of this decade, then, the kids of the baby bust were between sixteen and twenty-five years old.

The baby boom now comprises a good portion of the adult authority structure. The baby bust is subject to this authority structure. At the end of the American century, these two generations interact in economic, cultural, social, political, and legal arenas. Some members of my generation, the baby boom, are now engaged as knowledge workers, situated in various institutions and in roles of authority which impose upon the life chances, economic opportunities, and social experiences of young people. While I am concerned with the societal experiences of young people as an age-caste across the lines of class, race, sex, region, and sexual preference, my own ethnographic work has been focused where I work and live, in suburbia, with white ethnic, non-affluent turnpike kids stuck in low-paying dead-end service sector jobs (for specifications see Gaines 1991.)

Once upon a time in America, when we spoke about "youth" we neglected to differentiate experience along the lines of class, race, sex, etc. In the 1960s, a cultural rebellion erupted, but the media presented us with a monolithic portrait of a homogeneous group sharing common goals, dreams, and visions: a youth sub*culture*. This rupture, viewed as a large aggregate of humanity unified solely on the basis of age, began to fragment. We began to conceptualize feminist, gay, black, and Hispanic identity politics by the 1970s. We saw that we were multicultural, coexisting with varied degrees of social tolerance.

In the 1990s, young people continue to be unified on the basis of their shared experience as an age-caste, but they are now also profoundly aware of, and sometimes uncomfortable with, their differences as members of a multicultural society. But if their grandparents held fast to immigrant traditions, identifying themselves by race, ethnicity, and religion as "Italians," "Jews," or "blacks" out of deference to "roots" (the parent culture), the kids are just as passionate about their scenes, cliques, and subcults. Thrashers hate Jocks, and Guidos hate blacks, and the girls stand outside it all against the boys. All this fragmentation insulates kids from adults and from each other. It undermines any potential they have for self-advocacy on the basis of their shared age status.

By the mid-1990s we see more, not less, cultural fragmentation among young people. As hip-hop, death metal, techno, industrial, Fox Core and Riot Girrrl subcults evolve, young people are yet further from one another and from any sense of shared sociopolitical identity.

CRACK, BABY, CRACK

For contemporary youth, the baby bust kids coming of age in America's cities, suburbs, and rural areas, one experience is common. Young people are entering their majority in an age of inflated expectations based on the baby boom as referent and the diminishing options and economic opportunities all Americans now face. Like the rest of us, the kids have come to expect much more than they will ever get. But this is occurring at a time when they are more powerless than ever before, when they are less likely to be heard by adults and therefore more angry and alienated from adults than ever. Even the language kids use to express their rage and their hopes will be very different than that of any preceding generation: they aren't being heard, and when they are, they aren't being understood. Because of the rupture between adults and youth, in everyday life, cultural exchanges, and meaning systems, it becomes increasingly hard to identify the conditions under which contemporary youth experience their present historical moment and how they interpret it. More often than not, we cannot speak for them and they cannot speak for themselves.

If we discard all the romantic notions attached to the concept of adolescence as an idyllic time where young people, under the guidance and concern of wholesome adults, prepare for life, we see that young people are essentially poor people without rights. They are legally, socially, culturally, and economically dependent upon an adult authority structure which has proven itself incompetent, indifferent, and insignificant. Adults have seemed obsessed with "protecting" kids from sex and violence in their music but indifferent that the minimum wage went up just once in ten years. The same ten years where kids watching the news heard about increases in sexual assaults perpetrated against their peers by parents, clergy, day-care workers, school bus drivers, and everyone else kids were told they should trust.

Since birth rates continued to decline in the United States after 1974, the demographic prowess of young people is not likely to improve anytime soon. As with any minority, fewer members, limited access to power, less resources, the slighter the impact of their collective voice.

The political capacities for self-advocacy among young people are further eroded by the fact that all minors, unless they die, do eventually age out and become "adult". Even more disturbing is the general climate of anomie produced by global transformations in the nature of capitalism, upheavals in the labor force, changing markets, and widespread social dislocation. Clearly, kids face more pain and confusion in the short run. And there is no guarantee, in the long run, that conditions for young people will ever get better. The kids know it. They are angry. You can see it on the street, hear it in the music, and read it in the homicide rates.

The economic portrait of American youth at the last decade of the century is not very promising. While kids are actually dropping out of high school less, fewer are able to afford college, at the same time that the manufacturing jobs in the United States are being farmed out to cheaper labor markets overseas. In a technological, postindustrial economy this leaves a gaping hole in the opportunity structure for kids who do not go on to college.

Beyond nepotism, it is increasingly difficult to find employment if you are young, unskilled, and have no spectacular talents. According to James Wetzel, in *American Youth: A Statistical Snapshot*, there are now more high school graduates from poor families at a time when college costs have risen more rapidly than the cost of living.

As Wetzel reports, in 1988, 22 percent of twenty-five- to twenty-nine-year-olds had completed four or more years of college, up from 11 percent in 1959 and 6 percent in 1940. But in 1977, 24 percent of that age group had completed four or more years of college, a level much higher than recent averages (1989, 12). Wetzel adds that poor kids, net of race, are three to four times more likely to drop out of school than those from more affluent households.

Most kids today work. According to Wetzel, in 1987, more than twenty-nine million young people had individual income. Twelve million teenagers had incomes, bringing home an average of nineteen hundred dollars. By 1989, the jobless rate among youth averaged about 11 percent. Regardless of education, incomes were lower and unemployment rates were higher for minority youths. In 1988, according to Wetzel, the unemployment rate of black youth was 2.3 times the rate for whites and five times the rate for adults. For example, 56 percent of black youth live in central cities, while only 23 percent live in suburbs. Alternatively, 23 percent of young whites live in central cities, while 43 percent live in suburbs (1989, 4).

Up there with the great myth of homogeneity among youth in the 1960s is the notion of monochromatic, classless, comfortable suburbia. While opportunity structures for kids in suburbs are better than they are for kids in cities, they aren't great. In the suburbs "youth employment" opportunities are most available. Kids work in supermarkets, convenience stores, fast food chains, and other service sector jobs. But these jobs are low paying and offer no opportunity for advancement, development of skills, or health benefits. Kids may get after-school jobs at sixteen, and they'll still be working there at nineteen. By twenty-one, they may be parents themselves, unable to support their families, living with in-laws and without health insurance for their own kids.

Meanwhile, underemployed minority kids living in an American city have fewer opportunities for dead-end service sector jobs, higher high school dropout rates, and lower wages. As Terry Williams has shown in his book *Cocaine Kids*, innovative and ambitious kids not wishing to remain in the underclass have created alternative economies. Similarly, suburbia's dead-end kids often supplement their wage earnings with after-hours activity in the sex, drugs, and weapons trades. Wetzel reports that in the fall of 1986, there were 3.7 million eighteen- to twenty-four-year-olds who had quit school before earning a diploma. Most kids who did graduate were white and non-Hispanic. He observes that when compared with kids in 1973, in 1983, dropout rates had actually improved, most significantly among black males. But class and sex had a greater influence on who will be most likely to return to school to finish. Girls, kids from more affluent homes, and homes where parents were more highly educated themselves are more likely to return to finish school if they do drop out.

In general, baby bust girls do somewhat better economically as well as socially. They are more likely to utilize education as a means of upward mobility, and then they have lower expectations to begin with, based on the economics of their gender-caste. Many, too, have the desire for family, although they are marrying later. Girls are more likely to go on to college and to graduate. When they don't, and they are unskilled, they are employed at malls, in retail sales, as receptionists, in jobs that young women who did not go to college have always had. If they drop out, they too work in the same service sector jobs described above.

Suburban baby bust girls may be just as alienated as the boys, but they are less persecuted for it. For example, rarely are high school girls farmed out to special education programs for behavioral problems. These programs are famous for warehousing minority males and uncooperative nonaffluent white boys. In addition, baby bust girls who do not go on to college can be prepared more easily for entry into cosmetics and data processing fields. While teenage pregnancy, date rape, and substance abuse among girls may concern us, it has generally been the activities of boys that have troubled adults: they have higher suicide rates, homicide rates, and rates of recklessness; they rape, and generally they scare us.

The economic opportunities for young people are limited and changing. They innovate when they can and retreat when they have to. In my work on teenage suicide (Gaines 1991) I found that many young people feel hopeless, helpless, and worthless. They feel hopeless because all avenues of escape seem blocked. Helpless, because they are unable, by their own efforts, to transform their fates. Worthless, because they are treated like dirt. We have no place for them to go in the labor force unless they go to college, and we make college unaffordable. With the failure rate of the small business in America, how many can be absorbed into a family business? The civil service lists are frozen, and anyone with a history of substance abuse cannot get into the military, which is streamlining anyway. Unless they are spectacular, break the law, commit suicide, or become scam artists, many kids have no way out.

Still, kids labor on with the American dream dangling before them on a stick. Kids stuck in dead-end jobs, living at home with families barely getting by themselves, will often complain, "I can't live, I can't buy clothes, food, I just exist." Twenty years from now, we can look forward to a two-class society. On top, a hypereducated knowledge-producing elite. On bottom, an unskilled, semiliterate, poorly housed, malnourished, service-providing class. Kids are being tracked in this way already.

These are the social relations between two generations. In most service sector jobs, a needy baby bust serves a greedy baby boom. Young people see the pig in the python as a gluttonous mass, taking up space, housing, resources, jobs, and even culture. In a tale of two generations, young people are subordinated under adult authority at home in the family, at school, at work, on the street, in the courts, under the law.

Culture Vultures

At the cultural level, they are overshadowed by the myth producing of baby boom culture vultures who refuse to acknowledge the individuality and integrity of a historically unique aggregate of people with something new to say. In the words of a twenty-three-year-old college graduate, "I'm just so sick and tired of reading about the musical tastes of some aging rock critic."

During the 1980s, the American media took every opportunity it had to trash the baby bust kids. For example, I remember seeing something on TV in October 1988. "America's Kids: Why They Fail" was an ABC News Special anchored by Barbara Walters. It seems American students are "dumbing down." Up against thirteen of the world's leading industrial nations, our high school kids test near the bottom in physics, chemistry, and biology. They're not too swift in basic math and reading either. They are ignorant of history, even recent history—few know what the Vietnam War was, how a democracy functions, why the Civil War was fought. And forget about Euroculture's grand legacy of art, literature, and music. They never heard of any of that stuff, and they don't care. According to experts, SAT scores are lower now than they were twenty-five years ago. The bottom line is that our youth may grow up to be "undisciplined cultural barbarians."

To underscore this point, an ABC news camera moves to a teenage boy who says he wants to join the Marines. He has a part-time job unloading toxic waste. We see him moving heavy barrels around an open field. He says he's an average student. He likes to watch TV when he's home. When asked about the liberal arts, the classics, he says he sees no point. "How will it make me any money?" he asks.

Then the camera shifts to a group of kids at a Burger King, scratching coupons to win a trip, a *Carnival Cruise* on the Atlantic, a *Pontiac Grand Prix*!! Or maybe even a *cool million*!!! They're playing Triple Jump Checkers over their burgers and fries. It's a commercial (Gaines 1988).

TV zombies, cultural barbarians, stupid kids. That's the mainstream adult rap on American youth today. But even progressive-minded adults, folks who *should* be youths' natural allies in struggle, don't respect 'em. Instead, they fret over how "anti-intellectual" American students are: they don't read, they don't study, and they don't care. I've been a knowledge worker for over a decade: at a university, at scholarly conferences, in the media. In each of these arenas, there has been a persistent tendency—dissing the kids.

Longing for a Beijing be-in in their own back yard, many emancipation merchants wondered why contemporary American students have not emerged as this country's harbingers of change. Why aren't *our kids* committed to democracy, willing to *die for it* like the kids in China? Why aren't America's young people reaching for the brass ring of social possibility, spearheading mass strikes like the Czech kids? What's wrong with them? Are they brain dead? Why are they listening to Axl Rose and Public Enemy? Date rapists, crack babies, garbage pail kids. Are today's youth an emergent nation of ignorant reactionary fascists?

In our recent social history, students at American colleges and universities have provided a fruitful canvas for the carving out of righteous praxis motives. Many 1960s radicals are now members of the adult authority structure. Some are situated in the university, others work as TV producers, publishers, or mental health workers. They interact with young people in institutional settings. Ironically, many sincere, serious, good people—socialists, feminists, lefties, free spirits left over from the 1960s—can be as repressive toward young people as adults who seek to censor the kids' music or blame suicide on the kids' cultural icons. Repressive because we don't take the time to listen to young people on their own terms—linguistically, culturally, historically.

For baby boomers who hope to induce political mentalities among young people, apathy is disturbing. We are perturbed because the kids couldn't care less about what's going on in the third world unless their families come from there. But kids work harder now than they ever did. College students have jobs, and many have to contribute to their families too. There's enough to deal with just getting through each day.

It is true that many of the kids in America are alienated. So are kids in the United Kingdom, China, and the former Soviet Union. Some kids in America are apathetic. They just want to survive the working week like anybody else. But many are in fact engaged as activists, fascists, anarchists, separatists, nationalists, feminists, and Greens (Gaines 1989b).

Unfortunately, even when America's youth are organized in social movements, they often get stuck doing the "shit work." They get to do all the things women once did for the left before feminism: make the coffee, burn the stencils, answer the phones, stuff the envelopes. The only thing new happening is that they get to send faxes. At a scholarly conference in 1990, I spoke on a panel, "Youth in Crisis." By now more young people have begun seizing opportunities to speak for themselves in the print and electronic media, and at youth-organized conferences. It remains our responsibility to open up time and space, to do what we can to include young people who assert their right to speak for themselves on their own terms.

Beyond this, there is quite a lot that we can do for the kids. We can demystify the world of work, help create linkages with employers, impart "cultural capital" when needed, and listen to their reading of the world. They are often visual, postliterate—this does not make them dumb. They are the harbingers of developing mentalities that will someday predominate, long after the verbal cultures we valorize today.

As adults who regulate young people in the family, the universities, the corporation, the legal system, and the media, we have to recognize that the kids have a historical sense of the world vastly different from ours. Understand that every interaction with young people that does not honor and validate this is repressive, hegemonic, reactionary. Acknowledge that we have access to power-knowledges that can be used on behalf of young people, that we can understand them historically, anthropologically and thus support them politically (see Gaines 1989b for a more detailed discussion of this).

Alternatively, young people have organic and formal knowledge of their world that we may not. Whether engaged or uninvolved, every kid in America is fighting every day for what he or she needs to live. Alone and together, kids resist incarceration in mental hospitals, drug addiction, and the lure of local drug economies. They fight against family violence. They struggle for their civil rights as homosexuals and lesbians. They act up against AIDS. They petition for reproductive rights and also for the rights of the unborn. They seek protection from street abuse based on sex, race, and sexual preference. The nonhearing kids at Gallaudet University were American kids who spoke out in a hearing world that was not listening. Other American kids work to protect the environment, on behalf of homeless citizens, and for a livable wage. Some young people boycott and leaflet against cruelty to animals in cosmetic testing and in the fur trade and against the animal Auschwitz of corporate meat and chicken farms (Gaines 1991).

The world is changing. Nation-states are separating and cooperating. Markets are unifying. Americans have never shared a common national identity beyond mass culture. Like the rest of the kids in the world, our kids bear divergent class agendas. They come in all shapes and colors, from different regions, with varied cultural histories and religious orientations. Life in America today is hard for young people. Some are angry, some are sad, some are heroic. In everyday life, our youth aren't that different from the kids who fought and continue to fight in China or South Africa or Belfast. Our kids, too, fight the power. They reach out every day, randomly, violently, passionately, for freedom and for the courage to be.

References

Bensman, D., and R. Lynch. 1987. *Rusted Dreams*. New York: McGraw-Hill.
Chambers, I. 1985. *Urban Rhythms: Pop Music and Popular Culture*. New York: St. Martin's Press.
Chambers, I. 1986. *Popular Culture: The Metropolitan Experience*. New York: Methuen.
Curran, D. 1987. *Adolescent Suicidal Behavior*. New York: Hemisphere.
Empey, L. T. 1980. "Revolution and Counterrevolution: Current Trends in Juvenile Justice," in D. Shicor and D. Kelly, eds., *Critical Issues in Juvenile Delinquency*. Lexington, Mass.: Lexington Books.
Frith, S. 1981. *Sound Effects*. New York: Pantheon Books.
Gaines, D. 1986. "Night Rally: Youth and Fascism Today." *Maximum Rock and Roll* 37:56.
Gaines, D. 1988. "In Search of the New Barbaria: American Youth and the Education Crisis." Paper presented at Italian Cultural Institute of New York, October 25.
Gaines, D. 1989a. "Counter-Cultural Racism: The Case of Guns N' Roses." Paper presented at Socialist Scholars Conference, New York City, April 2.
Gaines, D. 1989b. "The Kids Are All Right." *Village Voice*, December 19.
Gaines, D. 1991. *Teenage Wasteland: Suburbia's Dead End Kids*. New York: Pantheon Books.
Gillis, J. 1981. *Youth and History*. New York: Academic Press.
Granger, L. 1986. *The Magic Feather: The Truth about Special Education*. New York: E. P. Dutton.
Hebdige, D. 1979. *Subculture: The Meaning of Style*. New York: Methuen Press.
Kimmich, M. 1985. *America's Children: Who Cares?* Washington, D.C.: Urban Institute Press.
Larkin, R. 1979. *Suburban Youth in Cultural Crisis*. New York: Oxford University Press.
Mannheim, K. 1936. *Ideology and Utopia*. New York: Harvest Books.
Mannheim, K. 1954. *Essays on the Sociology of Knowledge*. New York: Oxford University Press.

Platt, A. M. 1977. *The Invention of Delinquency*. Chicago: University of Chicago Press.
Roberts, K. 1983. *Youth and Leisure*. London: George Allen and Unwin.
Schneider, K. 1987. "Oklahoma Suicides Show Crisis on Farm Has Not Yet Passed." *New York Times*, v136:13.
Schrag, P., and D. Divoky. 1975. *The Myth of the Hyperactive Child and Other Means of Child Control*. New York: Pantheon Books.
Sebald, H. 1977. *Adolescence*. Englewood Cliffs, N.J.: Prentice-Hall.
Seligman, M. 1975. *Helplessness: On Depression, Development, and Death*. San Francisco: W. H. Freeman.
Sennett, R., and J. Cobb. 1973. *The Hidden Injuries of Class*. New York: Vintage Books.
Sheleff, L. 1981. *Generations Apart: Adult Hostility to Youth*. New York: McGraw-Hill.
Simmons, K. 1987. "Adolescent Suicide: Second Leading Death Cause." *Journal of the American Medical Association* 257:3329–31.
Wetzel, J. 1989. *American Youth: A Statistical Snapshot*. Washington, D.C.: William T. Grant Foundation.
Wideman, J. E. 1984. *Brothers and Keepers*. New York: Holt, Rinehart and Winston.
William T. Grant Foundation. 1988. *The Forgotten Half: Non-College Youth in America*. Washington, D.C.: Commission on Work, Family, and Citizenship.
Williams, T. 1989. *Cocaine Kids*. New York: Columbia University Press.
Willis, P. 1981. *Learning to Labor*. New York: Columbia University Press.

9

Race and Housing: Politics and Policy in London

John Solomos

Few aspects of racial inequality have over the years attracted as much attention as housing. From the earliest stages of the arrival of black migrants in postwar Britain, the disadvantages they suffered in the housing market were a major issue of concern in some localities. Additionally, during this time, antiimmigrant groups found that housing was an emotive issue around which they could attempt to organize political support. One way or another, therefore, it can be said that it is around the question of housing that many local political debates about racial issues have focused.

Systematic research which proved the extent of racial discrimination in public sector housing began to emerge in the mid-1970s (Smith and Whalley 1975). In London, the early work of the Runnymede Trust (1975) provided a stimulus for further detailed local studies. Parker and Dugmore (1976) found widespread discrimination in the allocation process of the Greater London Council (GLC). Research in Islington drew similar conclusions (Islington 1977). Other authorities, such as Wandsworth (1979) and Lewisham (1980), also began an examination of their procedures and practices in the light of these findings.

During the 1980s and 1990s, the housing question became inextricably tied up with wider concerns: about urban decay, unrest, and related "social problems." There has been an increased awareness that housing conditions are an integral element of urban disadvantage and inequality and that black communities have been particularly hard hit by the deteriorating social conditions in many inner-city localities. In this context, the changing role of public housing has been at the center of much political debate during the past decade. Additionally, housing issues have attracted much popular attention from the media and other opinion-forming agencies.

The development of race equality policies in relation to public housing by a sizeable number of local authorities has been a particular focus in recent political debates. These policies have developed over the past decade, by and large, and there is much dispute about their role and impact on patterns of discrimination in public sector housing. They have also been the subject of regular discussion in local political institutions and in the local and national media.

This chapter examines the history of the formulation, implementation, and impact of race equality policies, with reference to public sector housing. The key period we shall focus upon is the 1980s, although inevitably we shall also look backwards and forwards in order to contextualize the developments with which we are concerned.

To help to illustrate the main processes we are concerned with, we shall use as case studies the experience over the past decade of the London boroughs of Hackney and Haringey. In many ways, these boroughs provide useful models of policy change in this field. Both have large black and ethnic minority populations in housing need and public sector housing. Both have a recognized political commitment to establishing race equality within the local government system. And during the 1980s, both saw increased mobilization and political participation by the black and ethnic minorities.

This chapter (1) outlines the policy initiatives which have become identified with a number of local authorities in the field of race and housing; (2) examines the background to policy change and conflict in the two case study authorities; and (3) assesses some of the problems of policy implementation in this field.

Context

In the past thirty years, housing has become an important area of concern in the study of the racialization of politics and policy in British society (Ward 1984; Ratcliffe 1986; Henderson and Karn 1987). This growing interest has been influenced by the increasing recognition that equal access to housing (and other local services) is central to determining the overall life chances of black and ethnic minority groups. Indeed, in his report on the urban unrest of 1981, Lord Scarman pointed out that housing represented one of the most enduring sources of conflict in racial relations in many areas (Scarman 1981; Benyon and Solomos 1987).

Research into racial disadvantage and housing has been available for some time, and there is no need to go through the evidence produced by such studies here. The earliest studies into racial disadvantage in housing were ethnographically based. Concentrating on the tendency of the newly arrived migrants to cluster in inner-city areas, these works emphasized the naturalness of the process. This pattern, it was argued, was voluntaristic, conditioned by migrants' expectations of the host community, and was largely unrelated to racial disadvantage (Phillips 1987).

Coinciding with the growing national importance of race issues during the 1960s and 1970s, new studies attempted to unravel processes of discrimination and exclusion in the housing market. This can be seen in Rex and Moore's (1967) study of the politics of race and housing in Birmingham. This highlighted the mechanisms which regulated the allocation of housing between racial groups within the private and public sectors. Differential access to scarce housing resources, Rex and Moore argued, was related to the existence of differentiated housing classes, which circumscribed the relative position of black and ethnic minorities and the host community within the public and private sector housing markets. This analysis was also supported by other empirical studies of the housing situation (Daniel 1968).

Detailed research into processes which perpetuated racial disadvantage began with an increasing demand by black and ethnic minority groups for a fairer allocation of public sector housing in the mid-1970s and early 1980s. The seminal study in this area was undertaken by the Runnymede Trust into council housing in London. This study stimulated further research. Parker and Dugmore (1976) examined the allocation process of the GLC; and Islington (1977) conducted its own investigation. All these studies provided considerable evidence that the allocation procedures of local councils were discriminatory in their operation toward black applicants. Further evidence that discrimination was systemic was provided by the works of Skellington (1980), Simpson (1981), Phillips (1986), and Henderson and Karn (1987). The Commission for Racial Equality's own investigation into the Hackney Housing Department (CRE 1984) also confirmed these findings. In public sector housing, the Hackney investigation became a cause célèbre, and the recommendations of the CRE on policy changes required of the local authority became a model for good practice in other authorities.

It also seems clear, however, that, despite a number of changes over the past four decades, the housing situation of black and ethnic minority groups has not improved in any substantial sense. Recent research by Deborah Phillips and Susan Smith on the experience of black and ethnic minority communities in public sector housing over the past four decades points to a pessimistic conclusion (Phillips 1987; Smith 1989). Phillips, while noting that black and ethnic minority communities have benefited from the general improvement in housing conditions, observes that this change continues to coexist with a "pattern of entrenched inequalities" (Phillips 1987, 106). She argues:

> Looking back over the post-war period, there is no doubt that there have

been significant changes in the housing conditions of the ethnic minorities, progress in terms of legislation and advances in the formulation of housing policies sensitive to ethnic minority needs.... Such advances are significant, but they are not in themselves indicative of fundamental structural change. There is also no doubt that the ethnic minorities have been and still are in a disadvantaged position within the British housing market. Racial discrimination as manifest through persistent inequalities pervades the housing market. The ethnic minorities know it from their everyday experience. (Phillips 1987, 114)

From a broader historical perspective, Smith has argued that the politics of race and housing has been a central factor in the construction of racialized politics over the past four decades (Smith 1989). She draws attention to the diverse political, social, and economic dimensions of racial relations in contemporary Britain. Smith's analysis highlights the racialization of residential space within urban localities and the political and social responses of agencies, groups, and individuals to this process.

What research such as this seems to show is that despite successive changes in policy and legislation, and some improvements in relation to the allocation of public housing, there are deeply entrenched racial inequalities in housing which continue to be reproduced. It is within this context that we can begin to analyze the development and impact of local authority initiatives on racial inequality in housing.

The Politics of Race and Housing

It was during the early 1980s that the adoption of racial equality policies in relation to housing became part of the local political agenda in London and elsewhere. Against the backdrop of political mobilization by black and ethnic minority groups, urban unrest, and accumulated frustration, a number of local authorities, most notably in London, adopted policies and procedures to promote and effect racial equality in public sector housing.

Such policy initiatives were based on ethnic monitoring of all applicants for public sector housing, ethnic monitoring of all new property allocations, targeting to obtain ethnic proportionality in housing stock, redefinition of council housing access channels on the basis of need, recognition of the special household requirements of black and ethnic minorities, race awareness training for staff of housing departments, and new structures to promote racial equality within local authorities.

Collectively these changes were introduced as part of equal opportunity and race equality programs designed to have a systematic impact within the structure of local government. Such policies were based on two important considerations: first, that there was, and would continue to be, a political commitment to race equality; second, that the collective provision for housing would remain within the control of local government.

As applied in many radical Labour authorities, including Hackney and Haringey, race equality policies in housing since the early 1980s have had three main objectives:

(1) to establish the conditions for allocative equality
(2) to increase the recruitment of black and ethnic minority staff in the relevant departments
(3) to undertake promotional initiatives designed to increase black and ethnic minority participation in, and awareness of, public sector housing

While we cannot go into all the details of the policy models and philosophies that underlie these objectives, it may be helpful to clarify briefly the basic issues that they addressed.

Allocative equality

Under the rubric of allocative equality, the central question addressed has been, who gets what? Do black and other ethnic minority communities receive equal treatment in the allocation of public housing? The emphasis has been on establishing an equality of treatment and equality of outcome in the allocation process. Ethnic records have been introduced to monitor access channels (waiting lists, decants, homeless, and others), mobility within the local housing stock (transfers), and the quality of distribution (property quality indexes).

A central target has been the elimination of procedures that facilitated discretion and contributed to discriminatory outcomes. In many authorities, such procedures have been seen as the main channel through which racial discrimination has been reproduced over time, and much effort has been put into examining and revising discretionary procedures.

Additionally, targeting has been adopted to correct imbalances in black and ethnic minority access and representation. It is around this question that much of the controversy has been concentrated, particularly in the context of a political climate that has in general been unfavorable to positive action measures. We shall return to this issue later on in the chapter.

Employment of black and ethnic minority staff

A parallel feature of initiatives in this field has been the linking of allocative equality with measures aimed at increasing the representation of black and ethnic minority staff in housing departments. Racially discriminatory outcomes, it was argued, were not solely the function of organizational procedures but also related to the underrepresentation or exclusion of black and ethnic minority staff. Consequently, targets have been established to increase the employment of black and ethnic minority staff in housing departments.

Promotional initiatives

These are measures intended to improve communications with, and awareness of, the difficulties faced by black and ethnic minorities. They include such measures as the translation of housing policies into ethnic languages, race awareness training for Housing Department staff, and more effective controls against racial harassment. Compared with allocative equality or employment development, however, promotional initiatives generally have low operational costs.

Overall these three dimensions are neither exclusive nor exhaustive: at best they have represented the general parameters within which race equality initiatives have developed. We now turn to how these elements were identified and the success and difficulties encountered in their implementation.

RACIAL INEQUALITY AND HOUSING POLICY

Broadly, the process of policy formulation and implementation in relation to racial inequality in public sector housing can be seen as going through three stages. First, the issue was identified and became the subject of concern for the local authority. Second, local authorities began to formulate policy agendas and alternatives in dealing with the issue. Third, there has been an evaluation and critical evaluation of local authorities' responses, including suggestions for alternative courses of action.

This process can be illustrated in greater detail if we look at the experience of such initiatives in those authorities at the forefront of policy change in this field. For the purposes of this essay we have chosen to draw on research carried out in the London boroughs of Hackney and Haringey. These authorities provide an illustration of the processes that have shaped racial equality policies in relation to housing and the gap that often exists between policy and practice. Where appropriate, we shall also refer to the experience of other local authorities and broader national trends.

THE LOCAL POLITICAL CONTEXT

As mentioned above, systematic evidence about the extent of racial discrimination and inequality in public sector housing in London began to emerge in the 1970s. The willingness of some London authorities to undertake research was the first recognition that existing policies were perhaps discriminatory. It is not surprising, in this climate, that Hackney and Haringey, with their large black and ethnic minority populations, could not remain insulated from pressures to change their practices in the housing field.

If we look at the origins of policy formulation in the two authorities, we can see more clearly the forces that shaped the political debate in these and other local authorities. Hackney first responded to the issue of race equality in council housing in late 1975 when the Community Relations Commission (CRC) approached the authority with a view to discussing the findings of the Runnymede study of race and housing in London (1975). This report, which was based on 1971 census data, argued that a greater number of families of New Commonwealth origin were living in older property in Hackney than in any other borough in London. The CRC's proposal for a new research project to evaluate the post-1971 situation was withdrawn when the Race Relations Board (RRB) expressed an interest in undertaking an investigation of housing allocations in Hackney under Section 17 of the 1968 Race Relations Act.

During its discussions with Hackney councillors and officials in May 1976, the RRB expressed a need for access to tenants' files and a survey of their ethnic origins. The council's response was emphatic:

> It was made clear to the Race Relations Board that the Council was not prepared to allow the Board to inspect tenants' files and, moreover, that this was the ruling generally applied to all tenants' files which debars access by members or other third parties. In addition, it was made clear that, in the view of the Council, a survey of tenants to ascertain ethnic origin and related matters would not be appropriate at that time. (Hackney 1983)

In 1977, the newly established Commission for Racial Equality (CRE) approached Hackney to undertake a similar investigation to that proposed by the former RRB. Perhaps recognizing the legal difficulty in sustaining further opposition to the CRE's demand, Hackney changed its previous strategy. In response to the CRE request, the council now proposed self-regulation in the form of an internal unit that would liaise with the CRE. The unit, it was suggested, would consist of two officers who would monitor all aspects of the housing service to ensure that it provided fair and equal treatment to the ethnic minorities. The unit would report regularly to the council and the CRE, and the latter was free to monitor its progress and raise matters of concern with the council. Such a structure, Hackney insisted, would meet the council's guidelines regarding tenant confidentiality, overcome staff suspicion, and ensure the staff's cooperation and positive motivation in the project as it progressed. Turning misfortune into triumph, Hackney now boldly proclaimed that such a scheme would act as a pilot for other authorities with similar problems (Hackney 1983).

But the CRE was not convinced by this newfound radicalism. Despite last-minute delaying tactics by the authority, the commission decided upon a formal investigation in May 1978. We shall return to this investigation and its consequences later.

In Haringey similar factors seem to have influenced the initial stages of policy change, though the initial impetus seems to have been pressure from officials. In October 1976, the Borough Housing Officer wrote a detailed report on the increasing concentration of black and ethnic minorities in unpopular estates such as Broadwater Farm. His suggestion for arresting this development, which was held to be the result of a high allocation of homeless and single-parent families to such estates, was a recommendation for a greater social mix (Gifford 1986). Though it is likely that this concern stemmed as much from popular paranoia at the time about black ghettos as from professional concern about racial discrimination, the issue soon became established and could not be ignored.

Policy Agendas and Alternatives

After the initial stage of response, Hackney continued its stance of opposition to the CRE investigation but now combined it with apparent concern. On the one hand, the council resisted CRE calls for access to tenants' files; on the other, it projected an image of concern by creating its own Housing and Race Relations Monitoring Review Unit (HRRMU) and adopting a formal equal opportunities policy. The HRRMU was established in 1978 and headed by a researcher previously employed by the CRE itself.

That Hackney foresaw no evaluative or monitoring role for the HRRMU seems to be borne out by its relative inactivity during the first five years of its existence. Moreover, the intellectually combative Director of Housing lent weight to the authority's unofficial policy of race blindness by drawing on the idea of bargaining power. Some black and ethnic minorities, he argued, were in poor-quality accommodation not because of racial discrimination but because bargaining power between those already in public sector housing and those seeking access was unevenly distributed. Since new and recent tenants tended to be allocated low-quality accommodation, it followed that the black and ethnic minorities who were heavily represented among them would get a disproportionate share of this stock. There was nothing racial about quality differentials, the director insisted: they would be overcome in time as black and ethnic minorities moved up the quality ladder and their bargaining power increased vis-à-vis the excluded and new entrants (CRE 1984).

While the Housing Department continued its opposition to the CRE investigation (permission for access to tenants' files was eventually conceded in September 1979 under the threat of subpoena from the Secretary of State for the Environment), the council leadership seemed more interested in criticizing voluntary groups campaigning for a more explicit race equality policy by the authority. The occasion was a review of the Hackney Council for Racial Equality (HCRE), and the undeclared objective seems to have been to undermine the various groups operating under the umbrella of HCRE.

Unfortunately for the council leadership, HCRE cooperation in the review was only secured after the review team broadened its terms of reference to include the authority's own race relations policies in the context of local and national developments (Hackney 1981). Though this concession led to detailed consideration of parallel developments in other London boroughs— and a recommendation for the creation of a Race Relations Sub-Committee—the review team dismissed the HCRE's demands on housing (such as ethnic monitoring of allocations and an effective racial harassment policy). Indeed, it spoke warmly of the HRRMU, as "an excellent example of a unit working exclusively on race issues" (Hackney 1981).

An indication of the standpoint of the Hackney leadership at the time can be found in an interview given by Sam Springer, a leading black councillor. The interview is worth quoting at length because it is illustrative of the contemporary political climate. "The mere fact the CRE has decided to investigate," commented Springer, "does not mean Hackney is guilty." He continued:

> Hackney has a progressive and fair policy for allocating council homes. We have a firm commitment to equal opportunities and good race relations. If the CRE wish to investigate we have nothing to hide.... So far they have come up with nothing. Quite frankly we are getting a little fed up. The CRE has a right to investigate but we are entitled to ask whether it is misusing its powers by a prolonged investigation with apparently no end in sight. One wonders whether those directing such investigations are simply going on a fishing expedition without knowing what they are looking for. (*Caribbean Times*, June 11, 1982)

Yet despite such protestations from within the council, within a year the outcome of the CRE's formal investigation forced the council to reverse this stance.

Haringey's response to issue identification was only slightly less contradictory. Following the 1978 elections, which led to the success of Bernie Grant and a small group of left councillors, the authority responded to increasing demands for more action on race equality issues by appointing a Principal Race Equality Officer (1979) and creating an Ethnic Minorities Joint Consultative Committee (EMJCC) (1979). This was a consultative forum for the black and ethnic minorities in the borough. Initially the EMJCC was successful in raising policy and service issues such as housing, but it seems to have soon become embroiled in conflicts between the various community representatives. In the context of these developments, steps were taken to promote racial equality in housing, though at the time little seems to have been done to make them effective. Thus ethnic minority housing needs were recognized, but only two officers were appointed to process them. Although ethnic monitoring of housing applicants was introduced, it was voluntary and was of little value in monitoring changes (interview 1988).

As in Hackney, the role of officers in Haringey in the promotion of policy change was limited. Although they seemed to accept the inevitability of change, they were unwilling to lead or encourage it. As a former critic has noted, at the time the leadership "was saying things that sounded okay, but what was said was like jelly: you couldn't get hold of it. To put it bluntly, they were smart bastards who were always so charming and liberal" (interview 1988).

Policy Evaluation and Critique

The final stage of policy formation which culminated in the present policies resulted from critiques of existing policies, the linking of these critiques with wider notions of race equality, and iterative modifications arising from implementation.

By formally committing themselves to race equality soon after the Race Relations Act and taking only limited measures to effect it, both Hackney and Haringey created a policy gap. The discrepancy between formal commitments and reality, between radical rhetoric and the space between the words, was seized upon by those Ken Young defines as policy entrepreneurs and by political activists of the urban left and voluntary groups with an interest in housing in their attempts to define and redefine policies. The development of a radical critique of existing policies was further enhanced by the growth of the unofficial information network—an exchange system where latest initiatives in housing and among local authorities were discussed and analyzed (interview 1988). Hence, when the results of the Hackney investigation were made public, earlier critiques of existing Housing Department policies had extended beyond the prescriptions the CRE was willing to make.

The CRE nondiscrimination notice in Hackney required the authority to fulfil four conditions: to introduce ethnic monitoring for all persons applying for housing and being rehoused (identifiable by quality of accommodation); to reevaluate its procedures and practices in matching applicants and tenants with relevant housing needs; to undertake race training of staff; and to establish a senior post within the Housing Department who would monitor the implementation of the nondiscrimination notice (CRE 1984).

That the CRE's recommendations were seen as too little too late was apparent in the way radical critics of existing policies used the investigation as a resource. These critics, some of whom had been successful in elections to the two authorities in 1982 as followers of the urban left, had always seen housing as an integral part of a holistic conception of race equality. In constructing the two authorities' responses to the new requirements, they were successful in establishing the linkage between the service deprivation encountered by black and ethnic minorities and their underrepresentation within the authorities' staff. The central race relations units in Hackney and Haringey, therefore, became the principal agencies for overseeing black and ethnic minority recruitment into housing departments. Occasionally, as for example in the employment of specialist fieldworkers, the imperative of generic recruitment merged with the requirement to cater for the specialist needs of black and ethnic minorities.

Last, what distinguished this stage in policy formation from previous ones was that it set in motion a dynamic process of review and reformulation. The increase in the recruitment of black and ethnic minority staff within the housing departments, for example, created a constituency of interest—à la Black Workers' Housing Groups—that began to question the exclusion or nonrepresentation of black and ethnic minority people in some grades. Similarly, ethnic monitoring of allocations produced some controversial findings that could only be analyzed by further detailed research. In short, potentially the limits of policy could be continuously called into question.

IMPLEMENTATION STRATEGIES

A number of factors need to be taken into account in looking at the implementation of the policy changes that authorities such as Hackney and Haringey have introduced in relation to housing. As noted above, the recent origin of race equality policies in housing has meant that they have had a limited life span. Further, the complex process of formulation, with its critique of previous policies, was likely to generate its own complexities in the new cycle of implementation. These difficulties have also been compounded by the simultaneous crisis of local government that has powerfully affected the working of left-leaning authorities such as Haringey and Hackney. Consequently, a detailed assessment of implementation is beyond the scope of this paper. What follows is a brief summary of the three dimensions identified at the beginning and some reflection on the factors and processes that may have impeded the fulfillment of radical policy objectives.

The official position regarding allocative equality within the Departments of Housing in Hackney and Haringey today is that, though they have not achieved perfect equality, they are more likely to attain this goal than with previous policies. Both departments have introduced ethnic monitoring and methods of reviewing the results. Both have developed property indexes to identify qualitative differences in allocations. And both undertook reviews of allocations procedures. Officer discretion, the main factor in producing discriminatory outcomes, has, it is argued, been restricted and minimized. In Hackney, even the principle of targeting was applied to allocations for a while to increase quality and quantity of property allocated to black and ethnic minorities. Furthermore, the general change in allocation practices from date order (waiting list) and bargaining power (transfer and homeless) queues to those based on need has enhanced the race equality strategy insofar as black and ethnic minorities tended disproportionately to be represented in the latter queues.

Yet this official position exists uncomfortably with a reluctant acceptance that racial discrepancies and disparities remain in the allocation process—despite the elusive pursuit of perfect equality (interview 1988). For example, a recent monitoring report in Hackney (produced, incidentally, on the termination of the CRE nondiscrimination notice) found significant variations in the offers and acceptance of property between white and black groups, to the latter's disadvantage. Not unexpectedly it provoked a lively debate among black and ethnic minority councillors, some of whom questioned the integrity and commitment of officers and the Labour Group to race equality (Hackney 1988a, 1988b).

More important, it is possible that monitoring evidence for increasing equality on which the official positions are based is related to the homeless initiatives rather than the race equality policies. Since about 1986, almost all the new tenancies in Hackney and Haringey have gone to those in the homeless queue in an effort to reduce the bed-and-breakfast charges in the face of financial crisis. Because black and ethnic minorities have traditionally been more concentrated in this access channel, it is likely that their inclusion has increased the overall representation of the minorities. Certainly the Chair of the Housing Committee in Hackney has drawn this conclusion: "As a direct result," he has observed, of the homeless initiative, "and for the first time in Hackney, black people are getting a fair share of housing" (*Hackney Herald*, May and June 1988).

If implementation of allocative equality has been a mixed success, the emphasis on increasing black and ethnic minority staff within the Departments of Housing presents a different picture. Housing, in line with other service departments, has attempted to achieve proportionality targets of black and ethnic minority employees that are in keeping with their local population figures. The main direction of this element of race equality policy has been undertaken by the central race relations units, for whom the ability to influence recruitment has been an important source of power.

One source of concern is that the overall distribution of black and ethnic minority staff within the two housing departments is unevenly spread among middle and lower officer grades. Relatively few black and ethnic minority staff in both authorities are represented either at senior officer level or among manual workers. Of course, these deficiencies may be due to historical inequalities in the labor market or low staff turnover (Young 1987). However, there is increasing evidence that black and ethnic minority employees are resorting to authority switching in response to the lack of upward mobility within the two housing departments.

Finally, promotional initiatives have occupied an important position in the race equality strategies of Hackney and Haringey. Sometimes, they have been the logical extension of attempts to change awareness of the needs of racial minorities: sometimes, as in the case of the CRE requirement to train housing staff, of necessary legal impositions. Nevertheless, all promotional initiatives have had one thing in common: they are essentially educative and aimed at changing behavior through influencing attitudes rather than the use of sanctions.

Hackney and Haringey, along with other radical authorities, have made regular use of promotional initiatives. These have included conferences, seminars, race training for staff, audiovisual publicity, and the translation of housing policy material into ethnic languages. Specialist agencies working in housing, such as the Association of Metropolitan Authorities, the CRE, the London Housing Unit, and the London Race and Housing Research Unit, have provided valuable contributions to developing this area of policy.

However, like allocative equality and employment development, promotional initiatives have endured mixed fortunes. Occasionally, they have given the appearance of being substitutes for policy. Often, when they have threatened to incur substantial cost or change in overall policy, as in the case of racial harassment, they have been quietly deemphasized. In the mid-1980s both boroughs gave racial harassment a high profile and promised to punish perpetrators of harassment. More recently, however, this policy has mellowed. Indeed, it has been argued that racial harassment is no longer perceived as a major problem in need of urgent attention but instead has become another onerous obligation of complex management (interview 1988).

Indecision and prevarication on the course of policy change have become more apparent in the last few years. Perhaps the most interesting is the training program required by the CRE nondiscrimination notice in Hackney. There seems doubt about the effectiveness of this program. Not only did it take two years to design, but many senior officers were reluctant to participate. To date the manual workers, who comprise an important element within the housing staff, have remained an excluded category in terms of training.

LIMITS TO CHANGE

Yet what also seems clear is that we need to go beyond pointing out the gap between policy and practice and explain why policy change has proved to be so difficult to implement. Are there any common variables that may have influenced the dissonance between radical formulation and radical implementation? In this context, there seem to have been four main processes which have shaped policy change and conflict in the field of housing.

First, it seems necessary to evaluate the relevance of political commitment. This may appear paradoxical given the fact that much policy change in this field is associated with the urban left. However, the urban left is not a monolithic bloc. In both Hackney and Haringey after 1982, political power was located in various combinations of left-wing labor groups. Not all elements within these groups either accepted or were prepared to privilege the eradication of race inequality above class inequality. Housing was not immune to these tendencies. After 1982, which is usually seen as a watershed in the success of the urban left, the Chair of Housing in both authorities was occupied by councillors who were not totally convinced by the need to prioritize race equality strategies.

Second, and equally significant—if not more interesting—is the need to evaluate the contribution of black and ethnic minority politicians and activists involved in housing. If it is accepted that their mobilization was central to the development of a radical critique, it is necessary to understand why this mobilization has not been sustained during the period of political power. There seems to be common agreement that one reason for the recent quiescence in the promotion of racial equality is the fact that former activists have now become less radical in their demands or have lost confidence in the possibility of achieving change (interview 1988).

The change may partially be explained by the regularization of conflict within the system and institutions of local government. Whatever the cause, it is evident that existing institutions and procedures for effective monitoring of all race equality strategies are not being adequately utilized. The Housing and Race Relations Sub-Committee (HRRSC) in Hackney provides a relevant illustration. Created to review and monitor race equality policies in the Department of Housing in Hackney, it generated considerable interest among voluntary groups and experienced high participation from among black and ethnic minority councillors. Today the HRRSC is still in operation, but, apart from providing an occasional platform for the Housing Black Workers Group, it does not seem to play an important role.

Third, there is a clear need to demarcate and specify the measure of organizational resistance that has impeded policy implementation. We need to identify the objectives and the resources underpinning it. Organizational inertia, a reluctance to accept radical change, may be an important consideration. Similarly the sublimation of racial opposition in the guise of technical competence requires to be identified. Certainly the systemic nature of race equality policies instituted new technocratic controls within the Departments of Housing, and these may have provided a useful resource for recalcitrant and obstructionist officers. The development of ethnic monitoring, for example, and the parallel computerization of housing departments, has concentrated considerable knowledge power in the hands of a few senior officers (Mullins 1986). Not unexpectedly one of the arguments put in defense of the HRRSC was the vast amount of complex, elaborate, and technical data that its lay membership (councillors) were expected to comprehend.

Fourth, resource constraint seems to be a relevant indicator for further examination. Most new policy initiatives are contingent on adequate funding for their success; race equality strategies are no exception. As these strategies were not primarily distributive but growth-linked, they have suffered disproportionately from central government limitations on local government expenditure and investment, particularly in public sector housing. For example, the decrease in the rate of addition to existing public sector stock (coupled with rising demand) has necessitated a switch to needs-based policies which, though they have been in favor of black and ethnic minorities, are too insignificant to radically alter the historical disadvantage suffered by these communities.

Recent Housing Legislation and Equal Opportunity

Finally, an important issue that needs to be taken into account in assessing future prospects in this area is the impact of the 1988 Housing Act, the 1989 Local Government and Housing Act, and other related local government legislation of recent years on the ability of local authorities to remain a key actor in the promotion of racial equality in public sector housing.

The housing legislation of the past few years has not been directly influenced by issues related to race. The most important objectives of housing legislation since the 1980s have been (1) the reduction of the role of local authorities as landlords, and (2) encouragement for greater home ownership (Spencer 1989). These objectives formed a core theme in the attempts by the Thatcher governments during the 1980s to change the shape of local authority housing. But whatever the origins of the legislation, it is still important to ask about the extent to which it will have an impact on issues related to racial inequality.

The 1988 Housing Act and the 1989 Local Government and Housing Act were the most comprehensive attempt to implement the objectives of the Thatcher administrations in relation to housing. They have begun to have significant impact, and their full implementation has been a feature of government policy in the early 1990s. But there have already been complaints that, if there is a significant reduction in the role of local authorities in the provision of public housing, some of the worst hit will be those black and ethnic minority households in greatest housing need (Mullins 1989).

A number of black and ethnic minority groups involved in the housing field have begun to mobilize on this issue and to argue that, whatever the future of local authority public housing, there is a need to take the issue of equal opportunity fully into account and to develop race equality strategies that will help to meet the new challenges to be faced in the 1990s. Particular areas of concern are the issues of homelessness and racial harassment. These are already areas of concern among many community groups involved in the housing field, and there are fears that the recent legislation will actually make the situation worse.

Under the provisions of the 1988 Housing Act and the 1989 Local Government and Housing Act, the government envisages that local authorities will no longer be major landlords and will take on the role of being enablers, facilitating the efforts of other agencies to deal with housing problems. The future of equal opportunity initiatives under this system remains unclear, and the government has done little to clarify the situation or to assuage the fears of black and ethnic minority groups. Whatever happens, however, it seems clear that the role of public housing will be subject to major changes during the 1990s and that race equality initiatives will have to take account of these changes if they are to be successful.

Conclusion

The story of race equality strategies in housing offers some sobering reflections for policy development in this area. The process by which these strategies were formulated into policy entailed a long conflictual discourse and raised hopes of radical changes in practice. Their implementation, however, has failed to realize the original stated objectives. True, some processes, such as the pursuit of allocative equality and the recruitment of black and ethnic minority staff, have been set in motion, but their general contribution to race equality has been limited, and they have yet to address historical disadvantage or the housing needs of these groups.

The "implementation gap" is a common feature of public policy at both central and local government levels. But the failure of the urban left to implement racial equality policies in practice raises important issues for the future efficacy of race equality policies and practices. Central to identifying the cause of the failure to bring about radical change is a fuller understanding of the relevance and the interdependence of political commitment, persistence of organizational opposition, and imposed resource constraint. It is only through such an analysis that we can approach the question of how effective strategies of racial equality in housing can be developed in the 1990s.

References

Ball, W., and J. Solomos, eds. 1990. *Race and Local Politics*. London: Macmillan.
Benyon, J., and J. Solomos, eds. 1987. *The Roots of Urban Unrest*. Oxford: Pergamon.
Boddy, M., and C. Fudge, eds. 1984. *Local Socialism?* London: Macmillan.
Commission for Racial Equality. 1984. *Race and Council Housing in Hackney: Report of the Formal Investigation*. London: Commission for Racial Equality.
Daniel, W. 1968. *Racial Discrimination in England*. Harmondsworth: Penguin.
Gifford, Lord, chairman. 1986. *The Broadwater Farm Inquiry*. London: Karia Press.
Gyford, J. 1985. *The Politics of Local Socialism*. London: Allen and Unwin.
Hackney, London Borough of. 1981. "Review of Hackney Council for Racial Equality." Policy Committee, July 1.
Hackney, London Borough of. 1988a. "Commission for Racial Equality Investigation." Housing Services Committee, January 17.
Hackney, London Borough of. 1988b. "Housing Race Relations Sub-Committee," July 11.
Haringey, London Borough of. 1985. "Haringey's Minority Ethnic Communities: Equal Opportunities in Housing," by Tim Davis. Consultation Paper no. 10, November.
Henderson, J., and V. Karn. 1987. *Race, Class, and State Housing: Inequality and the Allocation of Public Housing in Britain*. Aldershot: Gower.
Hogwood, B. W., and L. A. Gunn. 1984. *Policy Analysis for the Real World*. Oxford: Oxford University Press.
Islington, London Borough of. 1977. "Allocation of Islington Housing to Ethnic Minorities." Directorate of Housing, Research Report no. 12.
Lansley, S., S. Goss, and C. Wolmar. 1989. *Councils in Conflict: The Rise and Fall of the Municipal Left*. London: Macmillan.
Lewisham, London Borough of. 1980. "Black People and Housing in Lewisham." Report to Housing Committee.
Mackintosh, M., and H. Wainwright. 1987. *A Taste of Power*. London: Verso.
Mullins, D. 1986. "Ethnic Monitoring in Local Authority Housing Policy." School for Advanced Urban Studies, Bristol, M.Sc. Thesis.
Mullins, D. 1989. "Housing and Urban Policy." *New Community* 16, no. 1:145–52.
Parker, J., and K. Dugmore. 1976. *Colour and Allocation of GLC Housing: The Report of the GLC Letting Survey, 1974–75*. London: Greater London Council.
Phillips, D. 1986. *What Price Equality? A Report on the Allocation of GLC Housing in Tower Hamlets*. London: Greater London Council.
Phillips, D. 1987. "Searching for a Decent Home: Ethnic Minority Progress in the Post-War Housing Market." *New Community* 14, no. 1/2:105–17.
Ratcliffe, P. 1986. *Race, Community, and Conflict*. London: Runnymede Trust.
Rex, J., and R. Moore. 1967. *Race, Community and Conflict*. London: Oxford University Press.
Runnymede Trust. 1975. *Race and Council Housing in London*. London: Runnymede Trust.

Sarre, P., D. Phillips, and R. Skellington. 1989. *Ethnic Minority Housing: Explanations and Policies*. Aldershot: Avebury.

Scarman, Lord. 1981. *The Brixton Disorders, 10–12 April 1981, Report of Inquiry by the Rt. Hon. the Lord Scarman OBE*. London: HMSO.

Simpson, A. 1981. *Stacking the Decks: A Study of Race, Inequality, and Council Housing in Nottingham*. Nottingham: Nottingham Community Relations Council.

Skellington, R. S. 1980. *The Housing of Ethnic Minorities in Bedford*. Milton Keynes: Open University, Faculty of Social Sciences.

Smith, D., and A. Whalley. 1975. *Racial Minorities and Public Housing*. London: Political and Economic Planning.

Smith, S. 1989. *The Politics of Local Government*. London: Macmillan.

Solomos, J. 1989. *Race and Racism in Contemporary Britain*. London: Macmillan.

Spencer, K. 1989. "Local Government and the Housing Reforms," in J. Stewart and G. Stoker eds., *The Future of Local Government*. Basingstoke: Macmillan.

Wandsworth, London Borough of. 1979. "Report by the Director of Housing on Ethnic Monitoring." Department of Housing, Report to Housing Committee.

Ward, R. 1984. *Race and Residence in Britain: Approaches to Differential Treatment in Housing*. Monograph on Ethnic Relations no. 2. University of Warwick, Centre for Research on Ethnic Relations.

Young, K. 1987. "The Space between Words: Local Authorities and the Concept of Equal Opportunities," in R. Jenkins and J. Solomos, eds., *Racism and Equal Opportunity Policies in the 1980s*. Cambridge: Cambridge University Press.

10

Fiscal Crisis and the New Class Politics: Managing Inequality in an Age of Decline

Eric Lichten

> I am an invisible man.... I am a man of substance, of flesh and bone, fiber and liquids—and I might even be said to possess a mind. I am invisible, understand, simply because people refuse to see me. Like the bodiless heads you see sometimes in circus sideshows, it is as though I have been surrounded by mirrors of hard, distorting glass. When they approach me they only see my surroundings, themselves, or figments of their imagination—indeed, everything and anything except me.
>
> <div style="text-align: right">Ralph Ellison, <i>Invisible Man</i></div>

WELCOME TO NEW YORK CITY

I can still feel their presence. The sounds of their voices reverberate in my mind as if they were still standing beside me and I were still reaching into my pocket. I see their eyes in my mind's eye, and I wonder when their suffering and our complacence became expected. I hear the chant, "Spare change, anyone. Spare change," and see the elder's begging hand extending, seeking relief in a silver coin. I search for my own humanity in the lines deeply drawn in that hand.

It is after midnight; my wife and children are asleep, and I suspect I too would be resting had it not been for those beggars haunting my consciousness. The beggars are polarities apart in age: one barely twenty, if that; the other in her seventies, if one can tell beneath the dirt and the terror of homelessness. How can we measure age? Is it merely an accumulation of time, or is it that distinct quality of inflicted experience that we know to be human suffering? I look at the young woman and decide she is much older than I, although I have lived twice her years.

I meet these beggars on a business trip into Manhattan, where I am conducting my research. I have been researching the decline of New York City for nearly twenty years, or about the age of this young homeless woman. She is thin, cheekbones jutting out from under her tired eyes. I pass her as I walk near New York University, and she reaches out to me, paper in hand. I reach for the paper not wanting to ignore her for fear that she will become as invisible to me as she is in American social policy.

We connect at opposite ends of the sheet of paper, and she asks me if I want it. We hold the ends, with me leaning forward even as she grabs the paper backward. "Do ya want it?" she asks. "Give me some money. Do ya think I'm doin' this for my health?" I'm holding this paper in one hand, my expensive leather briefcase in another. I'm aware that the cost of this briefcase could feed this woman for a couple of weeks. Even with food stamps, welfare grants, and WIC (Women, Infants, and Children) vouchers designed to supplement existing food monies, poor families and individuals go hungry; hence, the existence of soup kitchens as a way of life in this affluent nation.

Even as we engage each other in this absurd tug-of-war, I do not recognize the paper that we hold, together. It isn't *Street News*, the paper circulated by the homeless. I let go of the paper, and our eyes meet. There is so much anger in her face, and it is directed at me, the Stranger who represents the anonymity of her suffering. There is no politics here; just her personal nightmares and sufferings. I reach into my pocket and pull out some change. It isn't enough change to hurt me or to help her. I leave her with the paper and a bit of my conscience, wondering if her young life was already wasted by the cruel inhumanity of market capitalism and austere government. Such is life in America, a little more than a decade after the beginning of the Reagan supply-side "miracle" and the "prosperous" 1980s New York City economy.

Decline and Crisis

Walking the streets of New York City, one is struck by the dirt and the decaying infrastructure; by the army of homeless men, women, and children; by the large numbers of poor, desperately begging for your spare change, awaiting their next meal at the neighborhood soup kitchen; by the groups of teenagers hanging out absent from work or school; by the resurgence and prominence of racism and violent hate crimes; by the hustlers and small-time drug merchants finding opportunity where it is available; and by the overall sense of fear and hopelessness which hangs over this city. Walking the streets of America's premier city—where immigrants still arrive in significant numbers searching for the American Dream, an increasingly slippery dream for citizen and newcomer alike—one witnesses the tenuous nature of this nation's social fabric, a social fabric forged in the social contracts which characterized and emerged from the New Deal and the Great Society so very long ago. Where once the politics of hope and idealism thrived to form an unmistakable aura of progress and social change, cynicism and racist hate-mongering now prevail, joined by a political realism drenched in fiscal conservatism which stresses what politics cannot do and what government at all levels cannot afford.

Roughly a decade and a half after the last New York fiscal crisis, a language of limitations dominates the consciousness of city residents, a language which forgoes the possibility of progressive, humane social change in favor of the language of unrestrained capitalism: privatization, prioritizing markets instead of the public sector, austerity in public programs for those most in need along with a devastating assault on the living standards of working- and middle-class people. In simple terms, a renewed acceptance of human suffering and private sector power has taken hold. If the public sector has failed to resolve social problems, or if there is no money to make a significant dent in those social problems, why not unleash the power of markets and the business community? So goes the reasoning, drenched in the ideology of austerity and the harsh reality of economic scarcity for a growing number of Americans.

I could recite the data about what has happened in my city. Its poverty population stands at about 23 percent. That's 1.7 million people of all ages suffering from poverty-level incomes and inadequate social services. One in four children are poor, seven hundred thousand altogether. That, my friends, is 150,000 more than ten years ago. What kind of future can they hope for in a city and country which claim they cannot afford a decent, humane standard of living for each person? What kind of society sacrifices so many of its young, telling them that they are an expense beyond society's financial capacities? With only 240,000 families receiving public assistance, or 62 percent of the total number of poor families, the answer is clear. America sacrifices its poor because it deems them expendable: like all pariah groups they serve a social function. America demands its poor to be poor, with all the attendant suffering, so that money can be made elsewhere. It is classism, the class system, capitalism with an American twist: racism and sexism.

Turn on the news and you hear that the city, state, and federal governments are broke, busted, tapped. The feds had a party in the eighties, and only the rich could come. They danced the decade away, spending great sums of money on military adventures, terrorism abroad (recall the coffins of Nicaraguan babies), terrorism at home (reinvigorated racism and homophobia with hardly a public response), speculative investments, and the savings-and-loan debacle. President Reagan in Washington and Mayor Koch in the city left us with more poverty, a declining middle class, yuppies (some now disavowing their yuppiedom), urban blight, and a huge fiscal crisis. More than half this country's state governments, along with most city halls and, of course, the feds, now grieve over their own fiscal crises. Add a deep recession, a tax system which fails to adequately tax those with wealth, and some war bills, and the national debt cripples the government.

New York City's Fiscal Crisis and the Age of Austerity

New York City has been grappling with a projected budget deficit of approximately $3.5 billion, and that money is being found in such severe service cuts that the city's ability to meet the most marginal needs of its residents has been crippled. The city's infrastructure crumbles, with 40 percent of its bridges in such a serious state of disrepair as to warrant emergency service; its schools leave the kids alienated and undereducated, while their teachers sacrifice their idealism to the city bureaucracy; its welfare system protects poverty and punishes the poor amid the insurmountable problems associated with scarce resources; its litter prevails; its crime terrifies; its kids suffer; its politics ignore real needs. The people of this great city talk of "the old days" or "what could be," while fearing what their city is becoming.

That is the social significance of austerity, the name of the social policies wrought by government scarcity and private privilege. The city, after all, is broke: the rich get power to protect their wealth; the poor get soup kitchens when they're fortunate; the middle classes live with sterilizing fear and one foot already out of the city. And the budget cuts keep rolling along, threatening the dreams of the middle and working classes and making nightmares of the daily routines of the poor. Sacrifice today's children—cut funding for education, housing, nutrition, medical care, job training—and watch what justice awaits our society in the future.

While social order is not always dependent on humane social policy, this society's degree of economic inequality is rapidly growing, and the gaps between the secure and the financially insecure become ever more profound in light of government's complicity in that growing gap. The Reagan boom, predicated on the unleashing of the corporate sector from social responsibility and public accountability, left the top 1 percent of income-earning families far wealthier than they had been previously, after reaping approximately 60 percent of the after-tax income gain of the twelve years from 1977 to 1989.

The broad pattern of income earnings and wealth holdings clearly shows that the portion of income and wealth received by the top 1 percent rose dramatically over the 1980s. Furthermore, the Reagan years saw a decline in the tax obligations of the superrich. In 1977, the top 1 percent (roughly 660,000 families) was assessed approximately 35 percent of their income in taxes, but by 1989 their assessed taxes had sharply dropped to roughly 27 percent (Nasar 1992).

Further evidence of the increasing privileges of the rich and superrich emerges if we look at income deciles.

> Between 1977 and 1988 . . . real incomes declined in every family decile except the highest ones. In the lowest decile, family incomes (which averaged a distressing $3,504) were 14.8 per cent lower in 1988 than in 1977, in constant dollars. In the middle-income brackets—the fifth, sixth, and seventh deciles—average family incomes were lower by about 5 per cent, again in inflation-adjusted terms. Even the eighth and ninth deciles—the upper middle class—saw a slight shrinkage in its real incomes, off 1.8 per cent in the eighth decile, up 1.0 per cent in the ninth.
>
> Not until we reach the tenth decile ($119,635 per family in 1988) is there real growth. Here the ten-year gain, in real terms, is 16.5 per cent. And if we look "inside" the top decile we can see even more plainly how the GNP could rise and the average income fall at the same time. The income of the top 5 per cent of families in 1988 averaged $166,016. This was 23.4 per cent over their real income in 1977. The income of the top 1 per cent in 1988 averaged $404,566. This was up by 49.8 per cent on the same period. (Heilbroner 1991, 6)

There is a great deal of evidence that there now exists a "silent depression." Even while income inequality was exacerbated by the Reagan years and his regressive economic and social policies, the decline of the middle classes and the increased suffering of the poor date back two decades. There is, in other words, a clear pattern of growing inequality and declining standards of living which has come to characterize this "stage" of American capitalism and social policy. For example, by 1990 the real income of American workers had decreased by 19.1 percent since 1973, and generally family income kept pace only because of the entrance into the labor market of working women, mothers and wives whose income barely made up for the lost and declining income of the male American worker (Heilbroner 1991; Peterson 1991; Ehrenreich 1989; Newman 1988; Phillips 1990).

Hard hit, among others, were previously well paid blue-collar workers, the backbone of the traditional labor movement in the United States. As manufacturing eroded and moved overseas with capital's hypermobility of the 1980s, these workers, often young and white, found themselves with declining incomes and poor futures. These workers depended upon jobs in mills and in the auto industry, in factories producing commodities, and saw their way of life slipping along with their hourly wage. "The median real earnings of men between the ages of twenty-five to thirty-four, measured in constant 1985 dollars, were $10.17 an hour in 1973, $9.70 an hour in 1980 and $8.85 in 1987. For men of all ages with nothing more than high school diplomas, the figures were $9.90 in 1973, $9.37 in 1980 and $8.62 in 1987" (Phillips 1990, 18–19).

Poorly positioned to take advantage of the Reagan revolution in trade, investment, and commerce, and without the education to join the elite professions of law, banking, and medicine, these workers experienced the Reagan transformation as a slide toward destitution. With America's economy in a post-industrial transformation, with services and information replacing manufacturing in jobs and upward mobility paths, Reaganism (its corporate, militaristic priorities dominating the budgetary and political process) meant downward mobility for these workers; and with it a way of life disappeared where sons could follow fathers into the factory and perhaps into a secure job.

There is another significant aspect to this downward tumble that is all too often ignored when the popular press discusses economic issues. That is the issue of class and its relationship to power and social policy. These income and wealth data all indicate that the power of labor has decreased, in the workplace and in the political arena as well. In politics and in ideology we are in an age of austerity, and we cannot assume that those human needs ignored by the marketplace will be met by government. Without a powerful labor movement, joined by a human rights movement asserting the economic and social rights of all, there is no counterforce to the enormous and growing power of capital over the national agenda.

During the decade of Reaganist Social Darwinism, governments throughout America accumulated debts by cutting tax rates primarily for the upper decile of income and wealth holders and by doling out subsidies to the corporate sectors. The Reagan revolution accelerated the trend toward greater inequality as a matter of intentional policy, with an ideology of born-again capitalism. With a faith in capitalism unfettered by government "interference," the Reagan movement demanded and instituted policies to strengthen the corporate sector at the expense of the public sector, to weaken labor vis-à-vis management, to discipline workers and punish the poor. Devoid of countervailing power, the Democratic party generally went along with the defunding of the social welfare state and the overall pattern of shifting resources from human resources to the military-industrial complex.

The policies which gave priority to the military-industrial complex were the other side of the coin to domestic economic and budgetary policies which underfunded human services and social programs needed by clients of the state. To further reorganize power relations and "free" business from public constraints, antitrust enforcement was reduced, along with government regulations over business practices. Deregulation was embraced passionately as an answer to America's decline. Get government off the backs of business and the entrepreneur, and, eventually, all others will benefit. That was the credo by which domestic policy was to be made. Privatization was given legitimacy as an answer to government bureaucracy and to the delivery of services. Spurred by conservative think tanks, Reagan's goals were given the air of academic legitimacy—despite the cruel impact on the lives of the poor and the working poor (Charles Murray's *Losing Ground* [1984] and George Gilder's *Wealth and Poverty* [1981] were used resourcefully by the right wing to promote the idea that social welfare programs cause poverty by destroying family stability and by creating economic and emotional dependence on public assistance).

The Reagan administration's economic policies tightened access to money and greatly reduced inflation (thereby saving the value of capital investments), while real interest rates soared (a favorable development for those investing in government and corporate debt). Meanwhile, labor unions found an increasingly hostile government, with the National Labor Relations Board (NLRB) becoming an ineffective vehicle for labor to appeal to in the face of increasing corporate lawlessness as the NLRB became dominated by antilabor Reaganites. Labor union membership declined, and, equally important, the power of labor was seriously eroded across the country. Important federal agencies originally created to protect workers and their rights, such as the Occupational Safety and Health Administration, were limited by design so as to empower management on the shop floor as well as in collective bargaining.

But nowhere were federal policies more clear in their intent than in tax policy. With the top federal income tax rate declining from 70 percent in 1981 to 28 percent by 1988, the wealth and power of the top income and wealth holders vastly increased. With their increasing capital gains, soaring real estate values, increased income from rent and dividends, and reduced tax rates on their increasing wealth, the corporate elite and their wealthy friends managed to turn this economic power into political power.

Federal tax and economic policies led to growing budget deficits, making Ronald Reagan's charge seem ridiculous that the Carter administration had been profligate with the national treasury. Annual budget deficits of $200 or $300 billion became commonplace.

Yet, overlooked has been the effect of these deficits as a vehicle to redistribute income and power. Investing in the national debt is highly profitable as these investments are tax free at the federal, state, and municipal levels. So, a curious cycle was born in the 1980s. The Reagan tax cuts, and expenditures for the military-industrial complex, created huge budget deficits. Those who most benefited from the tax cuts, individuals having substantial capital to invest in the national debt, took the money that they saved in reduced taxes and invested some of it in the national treasury, thereby increasing their wealth with monies that earlier would have been in the public treasury.

What an extraordinary means to increase the wealth of the wealthy. All paid for by those who will eventually bear the burden of the national debt: those who rely on the state for income assistance and on state policy for jobs, along with the middle and working classes. As budget deficits soared, monies for education and human services were sacrificed. "By 1989 federal spending increases in the Reagan era had clearly benefitted Republican constituencies (military producers and defense installations, farmers and agribusiness, bondholders and the elderly), while decreases in federal social programs served to defund Democratic interests and constituencies (the poor, the big cities, subsidized housing, education and many other federal services)" (Phillips 1990, 88).

The federal budget, always a political vehicle for achieving starkly political aims, had become a vehicle for the exacerbation of class inequities and class domination. The politics of the budget became the politics of class in the Reagan years. Gone was the facade that the budget serves all needs by a government attuned to the needs of all classes and, in America, races and regions. The politics of domination was realized in the budgetary austerity for those whose needs were not directly tied to profit.

Austerity as Social Policy

All the while, poverty increased in actual numbers and in the degree of suffering awaiting the everyday lives of the poor. Now, facing huge budget deficits, a major worldwide recession, and the long-term transformation into the postindustrial economy of services and computers, liberal and conservative politicians alike call for government retrenchment, cutbacks in social service programs, and privatization of governmental responsibilities. In public policy and editorial content, the makers of policy and ideology enthusiastically seek to dismantle America's relatively meager social welfare state.

In the "prosperous" eighties the wealthy justified their riches and government largess with trickle-down ideologies. In the recessionary nineties, economic and fiscal crises are used to legitimize prior and continuing subsidies to this same class. Such is the budget-dominated politics of socially created scarcity in a society of comparative abundance. In good times and bad, during boom or bust, the corporate class presses to institute its needs over public policy. Its class-based power has most effectively stifled potential voices of opposition, as its austerity calls serve now as official ideology. What better example than the "liberal" *New York Times* to show how widespread the opinion that a more austere government is necessary and desirable. Speaking of Mayor David Dinkins, whose successful election campaign was dependent on labor and minority support, the *New York Times* wrote:

> The Mayor has yet to make the bold innovations so necessary in times of duress. What an opportunity he has to force changes in wasteful civil service rules and labor practices, to introduce competition by privatizing some services, truly to create a leaner, more efficient government. (January 5, 1992)

As we study New York City, we notice that it is no longer unique in America or in the Western capitalist world. Its deprivations and its "respectable" political solutions reflect a more general and widespread malaise stemming from the failure of mainstream policies—from conservative to liberal—to challenge the domination of society by the interests of capital. Indeed, the decline of America's cities—the latest in a series of urban crises that have characterized America during the decline of liberalism and the ascendence of conservatism—has been exacerbated by government's embrace of capital's needs over all other needs in society. Yet the current crisis is not attributable solely to one man's political policies or, for that matter, one party's. To understand New York City is to comprehend the decline and passing of a *stage* in the history of American capitalism and the transformation to a new stage with an altered pattern of social, political, and class relations.

New York City's current condition provides us with a microcosm of what is occurring throughout urban America. Its fiscal crisis, racial conflicts, state of disrepair, faltering educational system, abundance of poverty—in short, its declining level of government services upon which the quality of life depends—are joined by the relative powerlessness of labor and ordinary poor, working-class, and middle-class city residents vis-à-vis the power of the real estate, banking, and corporate interests. The city's problems and its retrenching public service and social welfare apparatus are duplicated throughout this country, albeit in forms and degrees that are specific to each locality. Services are being cut, some taxes raised (though generally not in a progressive fashion and, more specifically, not to the detriment of the business community), education sacrificed, and infrastructural repairs delayed as politicians endlessly debate to what extent to cut back expenditures and from where to raise revenues. In the process, fiscal crises provide the ideological legitimation for the sacrificing of community needs and the bailout of business sectors in their own economic crisis.

The official debate is not whether to cut back services and reduce the number of public sector employees; instead, the debate is a quantitative one. Assessing Mayor Dinkins at midterm, the *New York Times* applauded his efforts at making "some managerial progress, cutting down on overtime, reducing city cars, and consolidating economic development offices." He was, however, taken to task for not instituting stronger antilabor practices: "But when it comes to the labor force, half the budget, he has never overcome the damaging precedent of an unaffordably high [5 percent, most of which came from teacher pension funds] wage increase to the teachers 15 months ago. He has yet to wrest significant concessions or productivity savings from any city union and has never presented a plausible plan to cut the work force" (September, 1991).

Labor and the poor have few political allies in such a milieu. Reeling from Mayor Dinkins's austerity policies, the city's labor unions considered supporting some other candidate for mayor when his term expired. Yet, the *New York Times* and others demand more givebacks from labor and more control over the labor process for management. Thus, fiscal crisis becomes the legitimator for antilabor policies which go beyond wages and benefits to become an opportunity for capital-management to reassert stronger control over the workplace and over the structure and functioning of government. Meanwhile, conservatives embrace public sector austerity as a cornerstone of their privatization goals, while the few remaining liberals in public office become fiscally conservative as their more humanistic visions become circumscribed by the structural constraints of decline. Fearing class struggle, liberals adopt the framework of "no money, no programs," thereby presiding over the dismantling of the liberal agenda.

The mayor, even where his own political career depends on liberal forces and minority communities, turns to the investment community for advice on fiscal and public policy. Without the support of investment bankers and Wall Street, the mayor faces the wrath of the bond rating services, which carry the power to devalue the city's notes and bonds and to sink the city into ever deeper debt and, perhaps, bankruptcy. A look back at the last fiscal crisis, circa 1975, gives us insight into the structure of power and control that now functions to limit policy options.

In 1975, New York City, facing billions of dollars of short- and long-term debt and a growing gap between planned expenditures and revenues (severely reduced by a long term recession in the city), became the terrain for an experiment with austerity. As the city tumbled toward bankruptcy, its creditors accelerated the tumble by withholding assistance and helping to inhibit the city's access to the public debt markets. These markets were absolutely necessary for the city to borrow funds to meet its expenses and prior debt obligations; without access, bankruptcy seemed inevitable.

By organizing its economic and political resources, powerful members of the financial and corporate community were able to push for an austerity structure which would accomplish four important class-based aims: (1) the city would be rescued from bankruptcy, and the banks' own holding of city bonds and notes would be saved; (2) public sector unions would be disempowered; (3) a formal austerity structure of control over future city policies—as marked by the relationship between resources and expenditures, a relationship dependent on factors exogenous to any one mayor—would be established, staffed by representatives of the business community and elected officials whose administrations depended on a positive business climate; and (4) the city would redesign its policies to encourage a more profitable business climate.

The financial community organized itself and was able to effect the establishment of the Municipal Assistance Corporation (MAC), to borrow money for the city while setting aside a portion of tax revenues to make these borrowings perfectly safe. MAC became an instrument by which investors could guarantee their investments, thereby eliminating risk. Furthering the power and goals of the financial community, the Emergency Financial Control Board (EFCB) was created and had the power to approve or abrogate all significant city contracts; the effect of this was to empower a superstate apparatus over the collective bargaining process. The EFCB effectively removed the city administration from ultimate authority over labor contracts with the city's labor unions and could, indeed did, send back some labor contracts for being "excessive."

What these two bodies effectively represented was the removal of the city government from influence by constituents who would be most hurt by the austerity policies demanded by the business community and instituted by the mayor. Throughout 1975 and 1976, the city budget for wages, social services, transportation, education, etc., was cut relative to need. All the while, labor and affected communities could do little to alter the austerity policies since authority had been removed from City Hall. In their dominance of ideology and in their control over economic resources, the banking and corporate elites were able effectively to limit the power of labor over city policy. Capital had asserted its power in a city known to be a "labor union town." Ultimately, labor's response was to cooperate with austerity, however forced this response might have been (Lichten 1986).

Still today, MAC and the FCB (Emergency was dropped from the Board's title) figure prominently in the decision-making process. They still constitute powerful actors; indeed, they continue to set the structural parameters for the mayor's policies, in the budget-making and policy-setting agenda. In the case of MAC, monies may be made available to the city if "correct" policies are taken—correct as measured by Felix Rohatyn, investment banker superstar and partner in the investment banking firm of Lazard Freres. In the FCB's case, if the city does not balance its budget, the board can authorize itself to take total control over the city's budget, hence over public policy. These possibilities, in effect, empower the rationale and needs of capital over public policy, dooming the poor to suffering on a scale unknown in the United States since the Great Depression, dooming labor to relative powerlessness unless a new labor movement can be formed, and dooming socially progressive agendas unless the structure and logic of austerity are confronted and defeated.

The Austerity State

Elsewhere I have called this *austerity politics* and have theorized about the creation of a new class relationship between the state and its classes (Lichten 1986). This new relationship between the corporate state and America's classes I now call the *austerity state* to denote a turning point in the corporate-labor-state triad. America's governments and corporate sectors are turning away from the Keynesian social contract of its affluent heyday when America dominated the world economy and when the particular accommodations between labor and capital denied the validity of class struggle in a quest for a greater affluence dependent on class cooperation. However, government and capital presently advance the class struggle, prioritizing business interests and reducing the power of labor and the poor in the workplace and within government. Just a brief look back will give us some insight into the changes which characterize the present period.

The New Deal institutionalized a Keynesian social contract among labor, capital, and American government providing labor with political, legal, and social legitimacy. In exchange for recognizing the collective bargaining rights of labor, capital gained the economic advantages of a productive, stable, and highly trained labor force, belonging to cooperative labor unions which would not challenge corporate-managerial domination of the workplace and economy. Over time, as American corporations came to international domination in the postwar economic milieu, the federal government grew more interventionist in its direct management of macroeconomic conditions and in its subsidizing the corporate sector through a growing military-industrial complex.

While the Keynesian welfare state had originated in the economic disasters of the Great Depression and the labor militancy of America's industrial workers, its actual institutionalization marginalized those militant workers who sought major social transformation through the politics of class. In economic crisis, the Democratic administrations of Franklin Delano Roosevelt and those that followed, regardless of party affiliation, had found a vehicle for limiting the effects of working-class militancy while protecting and moving capital to a more advanced position. Thanks in part to an interventionist government and a conservative labor movement, American capital stood ready to stretch its financial and industrial strength throughout the new postwar world.

Two decades after America's Keynesian state had established its international economic and military dominance, domestic order was again challenged by insurgencies of working-class and poor people. America's legacy of racial oppression was met with the moral, economic, and political force of the civil rights movement, which successfully used civil disobedience, economic boycotts, and electoral strategies to alter this country's social structure. America's legacy of class oppression was attacked by the emergence of the poor people's movements, which brought the issues of class and race to the forefront of domestic policy. Together with the War on Poverty, enormous sums of monies flowed into the cities to rehabilitate its housing resources and to allegedly provide economic opportunity to the poor and to racial minorities against whom discrimination was as American as apple pie. With these monies, the institutional relations among city, state, and federal governments were altered, and America's welfare state truly emerged, however feeble it was when compared to the more fully funded and organized European social welfare states.

As the poor mobilized, a parallel development among public sector workers would further impact on governmental structures and power relations. Beginning in the mid-1950s, America's public sector workers militantly organized labor unions demanding collective bargaining rights similar to those already found in the private sector. America's labor movement was previously successful in organizing a large proportion, although certainly not all, of private sector workers, as civil service and public sector employees were excluded from the rights that other laborers exercised in unions. But as American governments expanded, government workers on the local and state levels unionized, resulting in the most successful wave of labor organizing since the Great Depression of the 1930s (Bok and Dunlop 1970; Aronowitz 1973; Bellush and Bellush 1984). This new political force would have significant impact on the utilization of public resources and government monies and on the delivery of services. Equally significant, the jobs created by and for public sector workers would impact on the class system, as more and more professional, white-collar, and blue-collar workers demanded that government provide decent jobs, with good wages and benefits and guaranteed job security.

To gain this, public employees had to use their ultimate weapon—the strike. In the public sector, a strike threatens temporarily the viability of government, and its impact is on the comfort of the community served by government. Hence, as a weapon it is a double-edged sword. Unless it is effective and swift in its desired result against management, a strike may bring as many enemies as allies.

As public sector workers struck again and again during the 1960s and early 1970s, particularly in New York City, the cumulative effect was to make the unions vulnerable to condemnation by conservatives, the business community, and their allies. Charges of special interest politics, of self-interest, and of holding the public hostage combined with antiunion ideologies to create an antiunion atmosphere; a rhetoric developed which allowed for the right to strike but not the actuality of the strike itself.

By the 1980s, these ideologies could be instituted by President Reagan against the striking air traffic controllers, who were fired and their union (PATCO) decertified. In the course of a few decades, public employees militantly unionized, first gaining then losing influence. Fiscal crisis, perceived as the public's ability to pay, was a key to this transformation of ideology and public policy. If the public believes that there is no money that could be tapped by the public sector for its workers and clients, the demand for such will receive little support or legitimacy.

Additionally, the aforementioned progress against poverty promised more progress than delivered. While there were advances made against poverty, with poverty declining by almost one-half during the 1965 to 1980 period, that period roughly coinciding with the growth of the War on Poverty and the arrival of the Reagan decade, the ideological attack against social welfare found sympathetic ears among the political electorate, such that the Great Society programs were discredited in political rhetoric before progressives could shape and programmatically institute a more ambitious agenda.

Less than a decade old, the War on Poverty started to retrench, assisted by the Nixon years and its ideological bent toward the "benign neglect" of the needs of the African American community in particular and the poor in general. By 1972, as the ideological defeat of liberalism began to pick up steam, the real value of Aid to Families with Dependent Children (AFDC), the major program for poor female-headed families, had peaked, and aggressive remediation of poverty had ceased to be a major goal of policy makers (Katz 1989, 112). Indeed, cutting back on AFDC and reducing the welfare rolls became a prideful achievement for American politicians, regardless of party affiliation. Much to the agony of poor families and their children, "the inflation-adjusted median benefit level for [AFDC] for a family of three fell by 39 per cent between 1970 and 1990. At the same time eligibility requirements ... tightened, by 1989 AFDC benefits reached only 58 of every 100 poor children." (Children's Defense Fund 1991, 11)

How are we to explain the decline of America's cities, and specifically New York City, the city with which this nation is identified outside of America's borders? What has occurred to the structures of the welfare state, to America's politics and its economy, such that the poor are poorer now, more destitute, more likely to be homeless and hungry, malnourished and medically underserved, than two decades ago? What has happened to America's social contract forged in the making of its social welfare state such that the

War on Poverty has become a war on the poor, the legitimacy of the labor movement has become a war against labor unions, and the ideologies of abundance and affluence have become those of scarcity and austerity?

The Politics of Austerity and Fiscal Crisis

Today's political and economic climate must therefore be understood from within the context of decline and crisis. Today, America's fiscal crises occur at all levels of government, from the smallest localities to its largest cities, from state governments to the federal government. Being debt ridden is a condition widespread throughout America as roughly half of this country's state and local governments experience some degree of fiscal crisis with the attendant problems of paying for social welfare and other basic governmental services. As debts pile up, so too has interest paid to the investment community on government bonds and notes. The debt service obligation of government is, of course, paid, without discussion about moratoriums on interest payments or other devices to relieve government from an increasingly crushing burden.

The response to fiscal crisis seems to be equally remarkable and everywhere the same: austerity in the public sector through civil service layoffs, public sector job attrition and elimination; deep cuts in social welfare and income maintenance programs resulting in increased suffering for those in need of food, shelter, and basic services; deep cuts in real public education expenditures; and enthusiastic calls for accelerated dismantling of the public sector in the form of privatization of public services. If you cannot pay for an effective government, sell it! Privately owned prisons, intrastate roads, bridges, natural resources found on federally owned and protected lands, rail systems: sell it all, is the political call of the day.

In short, as fiscal crises emerged, the welfare state apparatus and the structure of government became the targets for transformation, leaving business and other conservative forces free to strengthen their attack on perceived bastions of institutionalized liberalism. The very idea of social welfare lost its legitimacy as welfare became another way of saying undeserving, immoral, and parasitic.

As the conservative attack grew from the political center, as well as the right, forces were joined with ideological counterparts in the investment community, the manufacturing and corporate sectors of the capitalist class, and socially conservative Americans calling for a return to "family values." An assault against the poor took place within the context of an assault against the cities, the urban core of this country which was encouraged by Reagan's New Federalism to restructure its priorities to provide for investment incentives. New York's mayor, Edward Koch, formerly a liberal Congressman from

Greenwich Village, followed the federal incentives and brought the city into alignment with federal policies.

> Koch was anxious to show Washington that New York was on a new tack, that it was friendly to business.... The city embarked on programs that granted hundreds of millions of dollars in tax benefits to encourage development. Commercial and residential investors were given tax abatements to refurbish abandoned space or to build anew. Tax allowances were granted to some of the most congested neighborhoods, adding to the Midtown skyline, as well as in the less sought-after terrain of the West Side. City Hall pumped public and private money for development through an alphabetocracy of agencies such as the Industrial and Commercial Incentive Board (CIB), which oversaw tax exemptions, the Economic Capital Corporation (ECC), which coordinated loans to private enterprise, and the Office of Economic Development (OED), which recruited venture capital. To top it off, Koch helped establish the New York City Partnership, whose members included the city's corporate elite and whose design was to promote business growth. (Savitch 1990, 262)

Koch's policies in New York City were symmetrical to those emanating from Washington, D.C., and had the impact of empowering the real estate, investment, and corporate communities at the expense of poor New Yorkers and in hostility to the city's labor force. Yuppies were in; self-interest and the fast buck were glorified. The poor were sacrificed to the politics of greed. Washington led the way by encouraging economic development at the expense of the rest of society, and the mayor obliged. Meanwhile, austerity surfaced again as the lot of the poor. This time fiscal crisis was no longer the excuse; rather, priorities for economic incentives were justified by trickle-down theories and by the politics of hate. Racism flared and grew as the urban poor, predominantly minority, were blamed for their own poverty and for the social pathologies which other New Yorkers feared. White working-class youths found their expectations of success stifled by the economic and technological restructuring of the city. They focused their blame on the black poor while yuppies and the corporate elite escaped condemnation. Reagan's austerity, matched by Koch's, was barely recognized as a factor in this polarized city.

As the 1980s turned into the 1990s, deep recession replaced economic expansion; stories of bankruptcies replaced those of unimaginable success; downward mobility became recognized as the threat that it is; and Reagan's charisma or Koch's chutzpa would no longer suffice as a diversion from economic and social disaster.

Still, austerity is here for the foreseeable future. In this city, MAC and the FCB, as we have already learned, continue to enforce social policies that fail to address the ever more terrible social problems and failed public services. The homeless continue to haunt the streets, begging for spare change. Poor families search for shelter in the cold evenings, while abandoned housing lies unpopulated and barren. Children go to increasingly impoverished schools, as school budgets are restricted by financial exigencies. Students at the city and state universities pay more tuition for larger classes and less educational service. And the list of suffering and declining standards of living goes on. As does the power of the corporate and financial community. Such is the true structure of austerity: power lies in the corporate and financial communities; political elites and economic elites coordinate policy; labor unions and the poor lack influence. And everyone lacks a transformative vision challenging the ideological basis of austerity, that is, socially created and managed scarcity.

That day, in Manhattan, I continued my journey beyond the West Village, uptown to midtown. Standing on 42nd Street, midway between Fifth and Sixth avenues I came upon the elderly woman. "Spare change," she chanted. "Spare change, please." She held out her hand, fingers frail and timeworn, with a cup of change. I reached in and let go of some of my spare change. I knew this woman well. She has been standing at this spot for fifteen years and accepted my change with a nod. I walked some more, hearing "spare change" chanted in the background. It still echoes in my mind reaffirming our common humanity. She is not invisible, but will she be anything more than a metaphor for the success of Reaganomics and the austerity state?

> Power concedes nothing without a demand. It never did, and it never will. Find out just what people will submit to, and you have found out the exact amount of injustice and wrong which will be imposed upon them; and these will continue until they are resisted with either words or blows, or with both. (Frederick Douglass, August 4, 1857)

Afterword

In the interim between the writing of this essay and its publication, Mayor David Dinkins lost his reelection bid to a former federal government prosecutor and Republican, Rudolph Giuliani. Despite lower crime rates, Mayor Dinkins could not convince the middle- and working-class white population that he had earned another four years as the city's mayor. The city further divided along race and class interests and, in the context of advancing calls for austerity, Mayor Dinkins could not deliver on his promises of a better, more stable future.

Soon after assuming office, Mayor Giuliani embarked on instituting his campaign promises of more austerity in the social service sectors of the city's budget, targeting welfare recipients, the homeless, and the board of education for Draconian-like cuts. The new mayor promised to raise the quality of life in the city by strictly enforcing anti-vagrancy laws against the homeless, thereby feeding the growing hostility toward the pauperized poor. In November 1994, faced with a $1.1 billion budget gap in a $31.6 billion budget, and another manifestation of the city's continuing fiscal crisis, Mayor Giuliani proposed more than $1 billion in budget cuts, the harshest of these directed toward city workers, the board of education, and the government-dependent poor. So terrible is the extent of these proposed cuts that even city-subsidized day-care centers and emergency food programs have been scheduled for deep cutbacks.

As I asserted in this essay, the situation in New York City has served as the harbinger of an even harsher turn to the right wing across the United States. In the November 1994 elections, voters across the country elected to the House of Representatives, the Senate, and to state executive and legislative offices right-wing Republican candidates who promised to reduce government and, specifically, to turn back the "welfare state." With these right-wing politicians campaigning for a reduction of government, there is little doubt that policies will be instituted to make a reality of what I conceptualized as the austerity state. As this occurs, capital will be released from what meager public accountability now exists, the power of organized labor will continue to dissipate, the poor will be further pauperized and punished for the "crime" of poverty, the inner cities will continue to be sacrificed, and social Darwinism will enjoy a new life in the political economy and cultural climate of America. It is quite possible that nearly a decade and a half since Reaganism embarked on its reactionary course, we may now suffer through its greater triumph. In the process, the progressive humanitarian movements of the twentieth century will find themselves with greater need for their reinvention; but now, they need to confront a new state formation—the austerity state—demanding a new class politic.

References

Aronowitz, S. 1973. *False Promises: The Shaping of American Working-Class Consciousness*. New York: McGraw-Hill.
Bellush, J., and B. Bellush. 1984. *Union Power and New York*. New York: Praeger.
Bok, D. C., and J. T. Dunlop. 1970. *Labor and the American Community*. New York: Simon and Schuster.
Children's Defense Fund. 1991. "Child Poverty in America." As excerpted in "Growing Up Poor," *Dollars & Sense*, no. 168, September.
Ehrenreich, B. 1989. *Fear of Falling: The Inner Life of the Middle Class*. New York: Pantheon Books.
Gilder, G. 1981. *Wealth and Poverty*. New York: Basic Books.
Heilbroner, R. 1991. "Lifting the Silent Depression." *New York Review of Books*, October 24.

Katz, M. B. 1989. *The Undeserving Poor: From the War on Poverty to the War on Welfare*. New York: Pantheon Books.

Kozol, J. 1991. *Savage Inequalities: Children in America's Schools*. New York: Crown Publishers.

Lichten, E. 1986. *Class, Power, and Austerity: The New York City Fiscal Crisis*. Amherst, Mass.: Greenwood Press, Bergin and Garvey Publishers.

Murray, C. 1984. *Losing Ground*. New York: Basic Books.

Nasar, S. 1992. "The 1980's: A Very Good Time for the Very Rich." *New York Times*, March 5.

Newman, K. S. 1988. *Falling from Grace: The Experience of Downward Mobility in the American Middle Class*. New York: Vintage Books.

Peterson, W. 1991. "The Silent Depression." *Challenge* (July–August): 30–31.

Phillips, K. 1990. *The Politics of Rich and Poor: Wealth and the American Electorate in the Reagan Aftermath*. New York: Random House.

Savitch, H. V. 1984. "The Federal Impact on City Politics," in J. Bellush and D. Netzer, eds., *Urban Politics: New York Style*. Armonk, N.Y., and London: M. E. Sharpe.

11

Enabling or Empowering: Local Democracy in a Fragmenting Society

Sue Goss

The very concept of "empowerment" in a city context is a difficult one. Cities such as London and New York are not single entities, or single communities, but a jumble of different, contrasting, and often clashing communities and interests. The idea of "empowering" all these interests and communities is therefore fraught with difficulties, since it implies a sense that empowering some may mean disempowering others. Perhaps inevitably, because of the unequal distribution of wealth and power, this chapter concentrates on experiments in and concepts of empowering disadvantaged London. But even there, I will suggest, the overlapping of different cultures and histories has created a range of disparate identities and perceptions.

I will argue in this chapter that in this context it is impossible to put forward a single successful "model" of empowering. Below I have tried to examine some of the different strands, by delineating four ideal-typical models, which I refer to as the collective-representative model, the community action model, the individualist-enabling model, and the collectivist-enabling model. It is, however, a perilous attempt, since I do not want to suggest that these are historically distinct or ideologically coherent. Indeed, what is most significant is the way that the elements within them intersect and overlap. I suggest that not only do all four models exist simultaneously but that, given the increasing fragmentation and heterogeneity of social and political life, this should perhaps be encouraged as creating a parallel heterogeneity in routes to empowerment.

Finally, I argue that while there may be lessons to learn from experience in London about the need for a range of collective as well as individualistic forms of "empowerment," there is much to learn from the U.S. experience about the need to extend democratic practice and to create scope for diversity in local government structures.

THE REPRESENTATIVE-COLLECTIVIST TRADITION

There is a powerful myth within local labor movement history of a "golden age" of empowerment through collectivism, describing the winning of power between 1920 and 1960 by local Labour councils on a platform of "representing" the needs and aspirations of homogeneous working-class communities.

A strong political culture, embodied in the growing strength of trades unionism and a homogeneous, close-knit working-class community, was rooted in powerful ideas of solidarity and of "looking after one's own." This solidaristic collectivism nevertheless often muffled the experience of women and excluded new immigrants and those outside "respectable" family structures. The Labour party, especially in the early twenties and thirties, won political support for a vision of "municipal socialism," a project of planned social provision to replace the squalid tenements and ugliness around them and to meet the needs that the private sector could not meet and that local people could not pay for. The provision by the London County Council and Labour authorities of municipal gas and electricity, adequate levels of poor relief, health services, council housing, social services, parks, and minimum wages for council workers was seen in the rhetoric of Herbert Morrison and the London Labour party as "London collectively, taking its own life into its own hands." This then was a collective-representative model of empowerment—one in which local communities would gain access to the services they needed.

The Labour party locally saw itself as "representing" and "standing for" the community and implicitly understanding and organizing on its behalf. There was, therefore, a belief that there was no need for any other sort of "empowerment" other than the election of Labour authorities or a Labour government. Once power was put in their hands, the interests of working people would be safeguarded (Goss 1988).

THE COMMUNITY ACTION MODEL

By the sixties, however, this vision of empowering local communities through party rule began to cloud. In part, this was due to the dislocation between the "governors" and the "governed," the centralization and professionalization of many services, and the belief in the quick "technological fix" which led to acquiescence in the nightmare of high-rise housing. But it was also in large part due to the fragmentation of what had previously been homogeneous communities. Immigration, greater mobility, changing work patterns, deindustrialization, and changing lifestyles all began to break up what had been close-knit and solidaristic communities. The continuation of belief by Labour party die-hards that they, and only they, "represented" the community often meant that little or no attempt was made to respond to the, by now, diverging interests of London's poor areas. By the 1970s, disillusion with bureaucratic and paternalistic local authorities spawned community action campaigns over housing, road building, and redevelopment in many London boroughs. A new language of empowerment emerged, rooted in ideas of communities "empowering themselves" and of demanding a voice in ways which had previously been denied by very closed political structures.

Caution should be exercised, however, before treating these as struggles between "the people" and the "state" or even "local communities" versus "the planners." Many of the campaigns were waged by traditional working-class activists against those seen as outsiders—gypsies, squatters, immigrants. The community had begun to divide against itself, and local politicians were no longer able to simply "represent" the views and aspirations of their constituents in an undifferentiated way. The community action campaigns had a very important role to play, however, in challenging the elitist and professional direction of politics and in demanding that the views of local communities be taken into account in decision making. Many of the campaigns were single issue and short-lived but did result in a growing political concern with participation, especially in planning, the beginnings of the housing cooperative and housing association movements, and an expanding voluntary sector, including law centers, community centers, and neighborhood councils.

By the 1980s, however, the collectivist model of empowerment was under attack from both the left and the right. From the left came accusations of paternalism and of the exclusion of minority groups from public provision. From the right came an attack on the "nanny state" and an appeal to choice and freedom for the individual consumer. This led to the development of two further models of empowerment.

The Individualist-Enabling Model

During the 1980s, the Thatcher government launched an attack on all forms of collectivism, advocating in its place the empowering of individuals through the marketplace. Collective provision was to be replaced by competition between public and private services, by deregulation and competitive tendering of services, to offer consumers maximum choice. Stress was particularly placed on changing the role of local government. In future, local authorities were no longer necessarily expected to provide public services; instead they would take on a new role of "enabling." Importantly, however, this message, in contrast to attacks on the welfare state made by the right in the past, was not simply aimed at powerful business interests and the wealthy sections of the community forced to fund high levels of public spending; it was addressed directly to those who depended on public provision. The government's appeal was made in the form of an attack on waste, bureaucracy, and paternalism and a demand "on behalf" of those most reliant on public provision for choice and freedom for the individual consumer.

The attempt to win political support for a market approach was symbolized most successfully by the policy of selling council houses. This proved hugely popular with working-class people (although, in fact, it involved a huge state-subsidized transfer of wealth in a very nonmarket way). This was followed by a number of policies with a high profile but far less actual impact on the public sector, including measures to unleash competition within public services through competitive tendering, new rules for Direct Labour Organizations, and the powers which allowed tenants and parents to "opt out" of local-authority-provided housing and schools. The latest moves to generate quasi-markets in the Health Service and in Community Care take the "enabling" and "choice-based" strategies further.

These strategies have had a mixed reception. The introduction of competition and opt-out arrangements has not provided for the wholesale privatization of services. Privatization has been uneven, and initiatives such as Housing Action Trusts and "tenant's opt-out" have proved embarrassing failures. Ironically, however, on the left, while there have been serious misgivings about the dangers of competition from "cowboys," falling standards, and neglect of social values, there has also been a recognition of the incentive that competition has given to the improvement and modernization of public services. The effects of competition have in some cases spurred local councils to a radical reexamination of the way they provide services and led to the evolution of new strategies based on "public service orientation," consumer sensitivity, and choice within public organizations and to the creation of alternative models of an "enabling" local authority.

The right-wing rhetoric of "enabling," particularly in London, sits uncomfortably with the rest of government strategy. Other factors have considerably reduced the power and choices available to Londoners.

The first, and most serious, has been the impoverishment of the public sector in London and the withdrawal of public resources from communities which have some of the highest levels of deprivation in Britain. This has led to a widening gap in the quality of life between rich and poor London and between London and other parts of Britain, in relation to transport, environment, housing quality, and safety. It has led to an increasing sense of powerlessness in the face of growing public squalor, failing public transport and traffic chaos, and the horror of a spreading cardboard city. Increasingly, the very poorest have been disempowered through lack of income, housing, and care, as both voluntary and statutory provision have been cut back. Young single homeless people, people with alcohol or drug abuse problems, or those discharged from the Victorian mental hospitals can no longer rely on the existence of a safety net.

The second has been the increasingly draconian control over London government from the center. A promise to "roll back the state" has been translated into a massive reduction in the powers and opportunities for local government to influence events in their localities but a major increase in the power and influence of central government. Over forty acts of Parliament have been passed over ten years which constrain and regulate the powers of local authorities. Ultimately, the ratecapping legislation of 1982 introduced a fundamental constitutional change, taking away for the first time since 1601 the right of local authorities to set their own rates. The only effects of reductions in government grant in the early eighties had been to shift the financial burden of local spending to local communities, as many Labour councils replaced lost government grant with increased local taxation. In many cases total spending actually increased. The introduction of ratecapping, and then the poll tax, however, finally led to real cuts in the level of local authority provision in London. In 1986, London government was itself abolished and its powers transferred to local authorities, joint boards, and the London residuary body.

Third, central government has imposed a number of economic development and "inner-city" policies which bypass local authorities altogether and create a plethora of new measures and agencies, semiautonomous or accountable to government, which do not have a good record of "listening" to the public or providing choice. These have included Urban Development Corporations, Enterprise Zones, Task Forces, Simplified Planning Zones, City Technology Colleges, Housing Action, Trusts and Estate Action, and new grants such as City Grant and Urban Development Grant. Some commentators have seen this as the "Americanization" of British local government. Certainly, there is little doubt that the intention behind some of the changes has been to emulate the strategies adopted in a number of key American cities. Urban Development Grant, for example, was an idea borrowed from the United States and the London Docklands Development Corporation, and other initiatives were an attempt to copy the "boosterism" of American cities and to replace a concern with poverty and deprivation with policies to attract business and create wealth. Certainly, there has been little sense that local people have felt empowered or enabled by the new private-sector-led economic development models. There is little evidence that local people in

Docklands have benefited from the expensive new restaurants, five-star hotels, city finance jobs, and the New York–style lofts costing a quarter of a million pounds or more.

Problems encountered in the United States have been replicated. There is no evidence that wealth easily "trickles down" to the most deprived people in the community. The removal of planning and regulation has simply created development chaos. Government departments have failed to coordinate their efforts and have created a scattering of inconsistent and ineffective initiatives. Government intervention has been used to enforce the removal of constraints on the private sector and to abandon social purpose in favor of private sector profit, while local authorities have been prevented from providing any coordinated investment strategy.

The "New London Left" and the Collectivist-Enabling Model

The critique within the left of the representative-collectivist approach came from a new radical left within the Labour party, primarily white and middle class but concerned with issues of sexism and racism and with a more libertarian politics. During the 1980s, a number of Labour local authorities in London were won by new administrations committed to changing the face of local government. While there was no coherent ideology behind the changes, and much happened by accident or as a result of a confusion of objectives, a number of strands can be identified. First, there was a determination to bring politics back into local government, to use the resources of local authorities to campaign on political issues—and, during most of the 1980s, to wage a campaign of opposition to the government's policies of reducing local spending and local authority powers. This culminated in the campaigns against the government's powers to ratecap local authorities, in which many London councils tottered on the brink of bankruptcy and surcharge, and one, Lambeth, toppled over. While not successful, the campaigns, particularly the glittering Greater London Council (GLC) campaign against abolition, taught a lot about the scope for local authorities to use publicity and PR to communicate with the public. The lessons were learned by the Thatcher government too, which promptly tried to legislate against political campaigning.

Second, there was a commitment to opening up local government and involving the public far more in decision making. County Hall, the home of the GLC, became a giant meeting hall for women's groups, black groups, community organizations, and Labour party activists. Experiments in community planning, such as Coin Street in Lambeth, allowed local people to plan the development of their areas. Southwark Council caused a stir in planning circles by printing its North Southwark Plan on one large colored and annotated map instead of producing hundreds of pages of inaccessible documents.

Services were decentralized, brought closer to local people, and in some cases made accountable to local neighborhood committees. Local councils, such as Islington, decentralized their housing and social services to twenty-four neighborhood offices. Tenants were given more say over their housing, were consulted over the details of new improvement or repair programs, obtained seats on local district housing committees, and were given the right to form tenant management co-ops if they wanted to.

There was also concern to involve groups seen as previously excluded from local government and to repair the decades of neglect of the needs of women and minority groups. Women's committees, black and ethnic minority committees, gay rights committees, and forums for carers, pensioners, and single parents were all established. Many of these committees tried hard to overcome the obstacles put in the way of low-income or immigrant households by providing interpreters, transport, and child care and by trying to make meetings less intimidating. Voluntary organizations were invited into partnerships, and councils spent time and money on informing and providing facilities for the local community. In Lewisham in South London, neighborhood managers taking over new local offices found that their first job was to work with the community representatives to whom they were accountable to give them enough information and courage to make decisions.

Councils tried to change the nature of the services they provided, to end the paternalism of traditional municipal services, and to experiment with new ideas. Services were altered to give greater priority to black people and members of ethnic minorities. Councils attempted to expand their activity into new areas, investing in economic development, training, job creation schemes, and cultural and environmental initiatives.

It must be said that many of these experiments were dangerous failures. Economic strategies were often ill conceived; equal opportunities policies often relied more on gesture than reality; attempts to involve the community occasionally handed important decisions over to the unrepresentative groups from the far left. The preoccupation with political campaigning often distracted attention from the business of providing services and representing communities. Industrial relations problems mushroomed, and the suspicion that many councillors felt for management meant that they often generated hundreds of policy initiatives with little clear idea of how to implement them. At times, the new administrations provided less efficient services and were less able to meet the needs of local people than their predecessors.

In recent years, however, hard lessons have been learned, and many Labor councillors have recognized the damage done by neglecting service delivery to stage set-piece battles with the government. The last few years have seen a renewed interest from the left in modern management, in consumer-responsive strategies, and in evaluating performance, which promises to combine the best of the new initiatives with a new stress on effective delivery. Sadly, this has come at a time when the draconian financial constraints created by the introduction of the poll tax and then the council tax have led to painful cuts in service provision and reduced the energy and the capacity of London authorities to innovate.

A number of writers, including myself, John Stewart, and Gerry Stoker, have argued that from these initiatives it is possible to develop a less limited idea of an "enabling" authority. Stewart and Stoker have argued that the enabling role should be widened to see local authorities as responsible for the needs of their communities, not simply providing services but using a range of influences as major employers, purchasers, and investors. They argue that this wider role as enablers should be enshrined in a general power of competence (Stewart and Stoker 1991).

COMMUNITY IN LONDON

What is clear, however, is that there is no single route to "empowerment." No single one of these models has captured the sense of political identity, or the political support, of London's inner-city communities. The sense in which London can be said, now, to have distinct communities is itself open to challenge. The close-knit industrial working communities have been broken open even in those areas where manual workers predominate.

There are no longer single interests, and seldom straightforward political allegiances. Even in previously Labour voting areas, there are now strong pockets of Liberal support.

At the same time, there has been a growing tendency to talk about communities, not in the sense of localities, but to talk about women, parents, or council tenants as sharing common interests; to talk about the "black community" or the "gay community." While it may help to think about people relating to each other through networks rather than centers, and through shared interests in certain sorts of service provision or positive action, it would be difficult to locate or to try to "empower" such a community, given the wide differences in life chances, lifestyles, and perceptions that exist. It would be dangerous to "represent" the black community or women, or to try and stick together a rainbow alliance of the unemployed, the young homeless, gays, and other minority groups and expect a sense of solidarity and shared interests to emerge.

The overlayering of the different models of empowering has generated uneven access to power and uneven patterns of representation. While it is clear that some sections of the population were left out of traditional collective models of provision, and that, for the better-off sections of the working population, market models have created a sense of choice and flexibility, it is equally clear that market models fail those with the least purchasing power, for whom there is no longer a functioning "safety net."

There is perhaps a need to examine patterns of access and to try to identify which sections of the communities are most "enabled" and "empowered" by which route. It is unlikely that this would produce neat categories or that political perception can simply be used to label interests. What is clear is that social fragmentation makes empowerment a very complex idea. There are, however, some lessons which have been learned from the London context, which may have wider applicability.

First, it must be true that there is a collective, as well as an individualist, dimension to the provision of public services. It cannot be sufficient simply to adopt strategies which maximize consumer satisfaction. It is evident that, in the public sector, the collective dimension is never absent. While it may appear that choices in public provision are made by individual consumers, they are constrained by the collective choices made by ratepayers and voters about levels of funding and the nature and extent of public provision. Collective decision making, in the form of government actions, remains paramount. It remains an important aspect of social accountability that the trade-offs between service consumers and those who pay for them, between those who are entitled to rationed services and those who are not, are played out within the political agenda. The total level of resources made available must remain part of that agenda.

Local authorities can never simply become businesses in competition with others. Such a concept would make little sense in the European context, where local authorities are seen primarily as local government, speaking for and governing the activities of the local community. There are many areas of decision making which properly relate to the role of government not simply in providing services but in regulating and protecting citizens, through planning and traffic control, the police force, pollution control, consumer protection, etc., which are part of the process of democratic accountability.

It is important, therefore, to reassert the important democratic aspects of empowerment which stem from the powers representative local government derives from its electorate to act on its behalf to control interests more powerful than the individual, such as large companies, nationalized industries, and criminal gangs.

The second issue is related to the extent to which London authorities have learned to work in partnership with local communities, devolving control over certain aspects of provision, setting up joint initiatives with the private sector, working alongside other statutory bodies, funding voluntary bodies, and inviting participation from service users.

John Gyford has centered attention on a key role for local authorities in empowering communities in ways which deliberately stimulate and encourage groups of people to express their needs, support them in their collective actions, and help them with projects and schemes. He sees local authorities as functioning more as a "training agency, resource centre and support service for local community groups" (Gyford 1990, 6) promoting active citizenship. Such an approach involves recognizing the tensions between sections of the communities, the differential levels of access to influence and power, and deliberately attempting to compensate, by reaching out to women, to black people, to tenants' associations, and to local groups. The irony is, of course, that those local authorities that have attempted to do this have found themselves at the center of major rows—precisely because they have courted and uncovered some of the conflicting demands which may remain buried where there is less public participation. Well-intentioned attempts to involve minority groups have often led to ineffectual gestures, to the domination of meetings by unrepresentative organizations, or to a backlash when the newly "empowered" realize the insignificant level of assistance offered. At the same time, traditionally influential sections of the community have been quick to voice their sense of a relative loss of power, and their worries that their own access to scarce jobs, homes, and resources may be in jeopardy.

None of this means that this approach should be abandoned. In many cases these conflicts can be negotiated and resolved. Increasingly, however, the enabling role of elected authorities could include that of "holding the ring," balancing competing needs and using the legitimacy of direct election to decide between competing demands.

It may be necessary to develop a multiplicity of ways of empowering citizens and consumers, to respond to the challenge of social fragmentation. This could well include a combination of aspects from the traditional representational-collectivist model, from the community action tradition, and from the individualist-enabling and collectivist-enabling approaches. Local authorities could learn to manage markets, encourage competition between public and private providers, and establish internal "markets" within the public sector, at the same time extending choice and flexibility within entirely public sector settings. Consideration should be given to extending the rights of individual citizens to information, redress and consultation, and opportunities to take part in decisions about service planning and delivery. Encouragement could be given to the development of user-managed services and voluntary organizations capable of providing services on a contractual basis to commissioning local authorities. Public, private, and voluntary organizations could be required to create vehicles for consumer consultation and involvement in management issues. Local people should be given resources and skills to enable them to "empower themselves."

At the same time, democratically elected authorities should remain capable of setting strategic direction and providing a sense of coherent social purpose and should have the powers and resources to plan, regulate, and control the activities of the private sector, to create opportunities in economic development, land use, and environment enhancement, and to directly provide services where there are gaps in provision or to provide "best practice" models. Councils should also be expected to provide a balance which represents the views of the entire community to the outside world, to industry and commerce, to government, perhaps to regions, and, increasingly, to Europe.

There is a case, then, for introducing proportional representation and for establishing the sense of continuity and parallel working with other levels of government that exists elsewhere in Europe.

In the 1990s, however, two important constraints limit the scope for empowerment. Much of the academic and political discussion has hitherto taken place within the terrain of localities and therefore of local government. But, at least in Britain, the power of local government has always been severely limited and, particularly in Britain, is undergoing a process of continuing diminution. The stress over the past ten years has been on removing powers from local government and transferring them to Whitehall and Westminster. The level of government where most experimentation has taken place is most under attack. After all, the GLC paid the ultimate price for its commitment to innovation and empowerment.

That means that, at best, the limits of empowerment are the limits of local government power. Individuals and communities can have a voice only in those authorities where ideas of empowerment have been advanced and only in decisions over which a local authority has control. But as resources and powers of local authorities are further and further reduced, many of the major decisions which affect a local area are taken by multinationals, by government, by quangos, by privately owned utility companies, and by powerful individuals. There are no equivalent debates about creating accountability in relation to these organizations. Certainly, there has been no willingness on behalf of national government to generate innovative means of empowering its citizens and those dependent on national policy making and service provision.

If, as I am suggesting, concepts of empowerment must recognize the impact of collective as well as market decisions on individuals, then there is a strong case for extending collective means of empowerment beyond the scope of local government.

Central government bodies should similarly be expected to provide open, easily accessible information, to make service contracts with the public, to provide rights of redress, and to report regularly on progress. Regional offices of government departments, quangos, and government-funded bodies should be socially accountable, not simply to Parliament but to the populations which they serve. Social accountability could be extended to the private sector, both through the role that local and central government has in enforcing employment practices, equal opportunities, health and safety, and environmental control, and perhaps directly, by requiring the socially responsible firm to report directly to the public on its activities.

Much of this may seem incomprehensible to a U.S. audience, which is accustomed to a far greater freedom of information and open government. Perhaps the most important point, therefore, on which to end is to draw attention to the lessons Britain can learn from the American commitment to democracy. There may be many aspects of American cities which we do not wish to import. But there is a range and diversity in city government in the United States which creates scope for experimentation, for new initiatives, and for best practice and which strengthens the powers and responsibilities of municipalities. Some of these experiments may have been imported with mixed results. Some of those results may stem from trying to impose experiments top down in a powerfully centralized state. But it is almost impossible to think seriously about empowering local communities within the present British political and constitutional context. Britain is virtually unique in the extent to which power is centralized, in the absence of city government in the capital, in the large size of its smallest local authorities, and in the extent to which local authorities are controlled and constrained. If the complexities of empowerment in the modern city are to be tackled, it can only be done within a strong tradition of local government, with adequate resources and with relative freedom for local areas to use their energies and capacities to develop new approaches.

References

Goss, S. 1988. *Local Labour and Local Government, 1918–1982*. Edinburgh: Edinburgh University Press.

Gyford, J. 1990. *The Enabling Council: A Third Model*. London: University College.

Stewart, J., and G. Stoker, 1991. *From Local Administration to Community Government*. Fabian Research Series no. 351.

12

Turning the Clock Back One Hundred Years: The Problems of Getting Reliable Information and of Developing New Social Policies in the New Economic Order

Peter Townsend

Casual and sweated labor; the homeless class; insanitary housing; neglected children; out-work and irregular low earnings; unemployment; degrading poverty; even the wide gulf "which separates the poor from such a degree of confident comfort as civilisation calls for"—these were among the themes developed by Charles Booth about the London of the 1880s and 1890s. The irony in recalling this a hundred years later is not of his—or our—making. It belongs unquestionably to the Thatcher and then Major governments.

These governments have wrought social havoc in the years of office since 1979. Problems long believed to have been banished were reintroduced. To the people sleeping rough and the beggars on the streets were added the polarization of social classes, the marginalization of labor, the growth of forms of multiple deprivation, the destruction of public administration and service, and the deepening as well as the growth of mass poverty. And much of this has to do with the changing management and power relations of the capital city.

Many elites simply do not accept that such havoc has been caused. Mrs. Thatcher believed passionately that the poor gained during her premiership. That belief lay at the heart of her self-deception about her entire range of policies and is variously related to the "trickle-down" benefits supposed to have been derived from neomonetarist theories and the successive "caring" policies smugly announced by government ministers. In its different forms her central belief was dutifully reiterated by a thousand commentators.

Mrs. Thatcher's final speech to Parliament as Prime Minister contained not one but two significant restatements of that belief. She rounded on two MPs, Simon Hughes and Jim Sillars, for daring to suggest the poor were poorer. "People on all levels of income are better off than they were in 1979.... The Honourable Gentleman is saying that he would rather the poor were poorer, provided that the rich were less rich."

TRENDS IN THE 1980s IN LOW INCOMES

Was she right, or wrong? The grudging production of official information is revealing. At the time it explains the reduced and delayed political impact of growing poverty. This statistical story needs to be conveyed to the reader. The quality of information required to reach sound judgments about social developments is as critical as the analyses of these developments. I shall try to explore each in turn.

Even in 1991 the reports on trends stopped with the year 1987. This was true of the annual report by the Central Statistical Office, *Social Trends*, which attracted press reviews in mid-January 1991. Yet information for 1988 and 1989 was already available to those compiling that annual report (Townsend 1991a). There were delays in putting up-to-date information into the public domain. There were delays also because a familiar statistical series on low incomes was abandoned by the government and another series (Households Below Average Incomes, or HBAI) was substituted. I believe that discontinuities in the statistical series were exploited by ministers to conceal the real trends in poverty.

The Social Security Committee of the House of Commons stepped in to produce a consistent version of low-income data for the year 1988. The committee was critical of the failure of the Department of Social Security (DSS) to maintain the government's previous low-income statistical series—but probably because of the mixed party composition of that committee it did not offer sufficiently telling criticisms of the alternative series that was then instituted (the HBAI series) (Social Security Committee 1991; Townsend 1991b).

Nonetheless, statistical data on the distribution of income were available in Department of Employment reports of the Family Expenditure Survey (FES), and not only in the reorganized form produced in the DSS. The problem was that little attention was paid to this evidence by government ministers, the press, and even knowledgeable commentators. All the attention was concentrated through departmental press releases on the Households below Average Incomes data, which were not only reorganized on the basis of assumptions which are now fiercely debated but were also seriously delayed.

What do the "neglected" official data reveal? Developments in 1988 and 1989 are particularly important, since these were the years of the then Chancellor of the Exchequer Nigel Lawson's unparalleled beneficence to the rich, and also of the introduction of Income Support and the Social Fund in replacement of supplementary benefit (means-tested income support for the poor). These measures affected the incomes of many millions of people.

Taken in conjunction with all the annual reports since 1979, the 1989 FES report showed that the poorest fifth of households in the United Kingdom—representing seven million—experienced no improvement in real income at all between 1979 and 1989, while the richest fifth gained 40 percent. Indeed, the raw figures showed that the poorest fifth lost by some 5 percent. If that figure of around 5 percent had to be adjusted downwards to take full technical account of housing benefit changes in the early 1980s, it also had to be adjusted upwards to take full account of a fall in indirect benefits, like the number and value of free school meals, and for factors like the rise in extent of homelessness (for a discussion of the problems of measurement and representativeness see Townsend 1991b). Overall assessment of trends in income leads to the conclusion that major categories of the poor had smaller real incomes at the end of the 1980s than similar categories in 1979.

All this was reported in March 1991, but it was nearly another two years before the DSS (DSS 1993) published its version of low income statistics which allowed cautious analysts to accept impoverishment as incontrovertible. The media have been slow to react. Yet the data up to 1987 are available publicly (Walker and Walker 1987; Johnson and Webb 1990). The data from the New Earnings Survey about the earnings of both men and women, together with a voluminous set of reports on trends in taxation and social security benefits, have built up a comprehensive picture. The Child Poverty Action Group and the Institute for Fiscal Studies have plotted developments and demonstrated the huge growth in numbers of people at and below the state's minimum benefit rates.

By 1989, the average household in the richest 20 percent had an income after tax which was nearly nine times greater than the average household in the poorest 20 percent, compared with less than six times in 1979 and with eight times in 1987.

The advantage of measuring the trend in relation to the richest and poorest 20 percent of households is that quibbles about definition, measurement, and selected minorities, which so engage the attention of many professionals and mightily relieve ministers, are submerged into the predominant reality. In each case, a fifth of the nation's 22 million households are represented, and each fifth involves a total of 11.5 million people.

Some expressions of this reality are very telling. In 1989, the average household had a disposable annual income of £13,084, compared with £10,561 (at 1989 prices) in 1979—a gain of £2,523. But over the same ten years, the average household in the richest 20 percent gained £7,986 annually and the average household in the poorest 20 percent lost, yes, lost, £160. At 1989 prices, the average poor household had, on average, £3,442 in 1979 but £3,282 in 1989.

The reality can also be expressed in aggregate. The poorest 20 percent accounted for 6.5 percent of total disposable income in 1979. If they had maintained that figure (instead of finding it reduced to just over 5 percent) they would have had approximately £4.3 billion more than they did have in 1989. This is a measure of the collective loss which they experienced. By contrast, the richest 20 percent gained £16 billion more than they would have gained in the same period, if their share had not increased from 38 percent to 43 percent of the total.

This is one measure of Mrs. Thatcher's collected works. It contradicts all the presuppositions of "trickle-down" and certainly represents the biggest shift in resources from poor to rich of the twentieth century.

THE UNITED KINGDOM AND THE UNITED STATES

The miserable trend which I have reported for Britain is important to compare with that for the United States. There are close similarities. In 1990, over thirty million in the United States, or about 13 percent, were reported to live below the poverty line. Between 1979 and 1987, "the more than 40 million Americans who made up the poorest fifth of the population suffered a 10 percent decline in income after taking inflation into account. The richest fifth reaped a 16 percent increase over the same period" (Russell Sage Foundation 1990, 1–3). There was also a deterioration in the situation of those living at the lowest standards in both societies—with a doubling, according to some estimates, of the extremely poor (for example, as prepared by Peter Rossi of the University of Massachusetts), a big growth in homelessness, and an intensification of poverty in certain tracts of large cities.

What the evidence from the United States also confirms is that assumptions about the "trickle-down" effects of economic growth no longer apply, as in Britain, to major sections of the population. Indeed, social scientists have been producing analyses in recent years which point clearly to a paradox that countries which introduce stronger "welfare state" measures improve economic growth at the same time as they diminish poverty (Newman and Thomson 1989).

CHANGES IN LONDON

How do the national changes briefly outlined above apply in major cities—especially London? The differential between the average income in London and in the United Kingdom generally has widened rapidly, but it is the rich, not the poor, who have had the rise which accounts for this. The poorest 20 percent of London households have fared as badly as, and in some respects worse than, the poorest in the rest of the United Kingdom. The average household among the richest 20 percent has a disposable income of more than £30,000 a year, compared with an average of £3,300 among the poorest.

This has been due partly to the collapse of manufacturing employment, the reappearance of casual labor, the emergence of many vulnerable small businesses and growth in the number of self-employed in response to heavy long-term unemployment, the consequences of privatization and deregulation in the loss of employment rights and the upward swing of injury and accident rates, the fall in young people's earnings, and even the sporadic appearance of unlawful child labor (Buck, Gordon, and Young 1986; Buck 1991). It has been due to the application of successive cuts in social security. But it has also been due to the City's "Big Bang" and the growth of financial services like banking and insurance, as well as the property boom of the late 1980s.

London has become a service center for multinational companies and for international agencies. The political problems of the control of vast wealth and of multinational exploitation have outgrown the capacities of national parties and governments to deal with them.

There is the problem of the restructuring of capital in London (see, for example, Murray 1985; Thrift, Leyshon, and Daniels 1987; Greater London Council 1986). There is the problem of the power conferred upon, as well as the power represented by, what might be called the pedestal elites of London. Socially some are becoming more remote, less patriotic, and certainly less considerate and benevolent than their predecessors among the propertied classes of the capital (Scott 1990, 1994; Townsend with Corrigan and Kowarzik 1987, chapter 7).

This might be illustrated from the London property pages in the *Times, Observer,* and *Sunday Times.* Even in the midst of a deep recession, when a conspicuous fall in such advertisements can be observed, there was powerful evidence of continuing affluence. On Sunday, January 20, 1991, there were 125 advertisements in the *Sunday Times* for London properties valued at over £250,000, several of them more than £500,000 and one at £2.3 million. Again, press reports have consistently shown sharper rises in top salaries than in middle or low salaries in the 1980s. The *Financial Times* reported that, including the value of the company car, average remuneration of a wide range of senior employees is above £100,000. At the upper quartile the figure approaches or exceeds £150,000 (*Financial Times*, November 16, 1990).

This is captured by a *Sunday Times* review of "Britain's Richest 500." Those at the top had become much richer. "Five years ago the top 200 were worth £38 billion between them. Today [they] are worth 36 percent more or £54.3 billions. So much for the recession" (Fallon 1994, 4).

The abandonment of public administration in London has had a pervasive effect. It has reduced resources for public services in the poorest areas. Without investment in housing and local authority services, the inner cities have mouldered.

In the seventeenth concluding volume of his *Life and Labour of the People in London*, Charles Booth applauded collective municipal action. "In 1888 the Conservative Government, by establishing the London County Council, took a great step in the development of the sense of local responsibility." He did not foresee the cynical abolition of the Greater London Council and of the Inner London Education Authority. Was it inevitable subsequently that metropolitan borough councils like Westminster evolved practices to preserve Conservative electoral majorities that were described in 1994 as corrupt?

INDEPENDENCE OF STATISTICAL INFORMATION

One problem is, how independent of political influence are official statistics? The relationship between political and scientific or statistical interests seems to be even more incestuous in the United Kingdom than in the United States. Part of the problem is the deliberate delay in publishing the information, part of it the distortion and misrepresentation of the statistical trends. Developing alternative, and innocuous, versions of the facts has become quite a profitable professional industry. The DSS has developed a new method of measuring low incomes which takes little or no account of internationally expressed reservations about the "equivalence" scales adopted for the purpose (for example, Buhmann, Rainwater, Schmaus, and Smeeding 1989; Edwards and Whiteford 1988; Whiteford 1985; Rainwater 1988; Bradbury 1989; Townsend 1979, chapter 6). Government statisticians also take insufficient notice of the undercounting of very high incomes as well as the undercounting of very low incomes. They need to take more seriously such undercounting, and also alternative definitions of income unit and income and, above all, necessary comparative data on wealth and indirect benefits obtained through employment. There is little public grasp of real inequalities in living standards.

Increasingly, it is important to seek out scattered reports on family case studies, as in the recent examples from Barnados (Craig and Glendinning 1990) or from groups like Church Action against Poverty, to interpret and assess official statistics and make good the paucity of independent research studies, in order to arrive at a scientific and balanced assessment of trends in living standards (see also Bradshaw and Holmes 1989).

The national dispute which has to be waged on behalf of the poor is one which has to be waged against ministers but also against the statistical bureaucracy. For example, the Central Statistical Office (CSO 1988, 1990) has issued injunctions to readers of the FES reports to refrain from comparing one year's figures with another's, thereby inhibiting appropriate interpretation of trends, even allowing for minor technical conundrums, and denying the principal purpose of developing such a statistical series in the first place.

Perhaps it would be helpful for me to give chapter and verse. One review article contains the following: "The figures in each year's article are freestanding and are not intended to be used as part of a time series with figures from earlier articles. The FES changes each year, and no special effort has been made in the past to ensure a fully consistent time series." The figures for 1987 "are completely incompatible with those for earlier years" (CSO 1990, 85). Earlier review articles contain careful detailed accounts of technical changes from year to year in definition and measurement but are completely different in the interpretation advised or encouraged. Thus, there are specific references to the reliability and consistency of the annual survey data drawn from the national samples. There are also sections of those review articles which offer statistical summaries of trends for periods of several years.

Throughout the early 1980s (as in the 1960s and 1970s) our statistical Dukes of York led their men to the top of the hill in support of the reliability, utility, and continuity of the data produced in their annual surveys of income distribution. The most recent reviews of income trends (as in the DSS Households below Average Incomes reports) show them to be leading their troops down the hill, toward technical nihilism and confusion.

On January 9, 1991, the journalist Melanie Phillips reported interviews with senior civil servants, in which one former statistician said: "I discovered an inconsistency in some figures which meant the poor were worse off but I was told it wouldn't be helpful to do anything about it because it would cost the Government money" (*Guardian*, January 9, 1991, and see also the correspondence between the Chief Statistician and others, *Independent*, August 28–30, 1991, and Melanie Phillips, *Guardian*, August 30, 1991).

The role of the Select Committees in the House of Commons is of great interest. At times, these committees appear to be attempting to speak for Parliament on behalf of the people, and even the rights of the people to obtain independent information. More often, they seem to confine their activities to the cross-examination and minor amendment of government policies. High-minded aspirations are abandoned. Meetings generally move toward political party compromise over marginal issues, reflecting the irritations of backbenchers against ministers or a mild political consensus of the parties represented on the committees. In late 1989, members of the House of Commons Social Services Committee seemed to lose interest at the very moment when they had drawn blood in their criticisms of procedures in measuring low income. An important initiative in obtaining independent information about the adequacy of social security benefits (Social Services Committee 1989) was abandoned. The production of facts has become as political as their analysis.

The International Causes

In the United Kingdom, the deregulation laws and programs introduced by the Thatcher government, and the attempts to reduce public expenditure to reduce private sector costs and restore the free market, have been widely condemned. They are assumed by many commentators to have been partially responsible for greater inequality of employment incomes, static or even diminishing real social security benefits, and hence greater inequality of the whole pattern of income distribution. The measures are, however, implicit in the structure and mode of operation of the European Community itself.

The modern history of the European Community, now the European Union, goes back to the Iron and Steel Community and the efforts of the original six members to establish the primacy of market operations in a more international mode of operation. Fair competition implied deregulation of protective state laws which applied only to individual countries. Thus, when Britain joined the Community in 1972, the British Government undertook to abandon its own regional employment subsidies, including the regional employment premium. This also suited its increasingly monetarist policies. Regional employment subsidies have been substituted by much smaller E.U. subsidies, which are also more widely dispersed. One consequence has been a drift upwards in the rates of unemployment in regions with already high rates of unemployment.

The restructuring of the international economy rather than merely Conservative policies must therefore be regarded as lying behind the changes introduced by the British government, and especially the Thatcher government, in the last two decades, much as it also lies behind the creation of the European Union. The awkward question is whether the social policies of *both* member states *and* the European Union as a whole are being weakened as a consequence, and what has to be done to resolve the conflict between profit and social justice. Events surrounding the introduction and piecemeal specification and implementation of the Social Charter have to be scrutinized to reveal not just why the British Conservative government has been so implacably opposed to the Social Charter but whether that Charter and its corresponding Social Action program are likely to result in a general decline in public welfare in the nation-states of Europe. Are *national* social policies to be withdrawn one by one and a much less costly European social policy substituted?

The single market has had an increasing influence on the management by the U.K. government of its social policies. The neomonetarist policies adopted by the Thatcher government included large-scale privatization, abolition or wholesale diminution of the powers of the bigger local authorities, the institutionalization of low wages and job insecurity, and depreciation of public service and of scientific and intellectual activity, as well as cuts in public expenditure and erosion of employee and trade union rights. The shift from "public" to "private" implies a greater structural inequality, loss of citizenship rights, more variable standards, less institutional accountability, and more institutional secrecy.

The new economic order is restructuring social classes as well. If an underclass is being created by labor market changes and new economic institutions, then so is an "overclass" (Townsend 1993b). Some among the elites in the United Kingdom feel threatened by the emergence of the single market of Europe. Wealth is indeed related to sovereignty, and wealth which is not multinational may now seem vulnerable. This is very understandable, and it helps to explain expressions of "Little Englander" mentality in the objections made to the rapid development of the European Union. The British, it is argued, must preserve their power to determine their own destiny rather than submit to the collective political decisions of their European partners. But the rapid growth of internationalism in its manifold forms cuts across this expression of independence or isolationism and exposes its absurdity.

Behind the argument against Europe lies a different reality. Class privilege or wealth is dressed up as sovereignty. Long-established elites want to resist the threats, as they see it, of a more participative style of business management, and different forms of external financial and multicultural control. They also fear stronger public services, greater regulation of the labor market, and better social insurance—though these may turn out to be small if not empty threats. Old-style class management is preferred to the uncertainties of European interdependence and the growing powers of those in control of giant multinational corporations.

In the speeches and formal statements of the present U.K. Conservative government lies a remarkable paradox. On the one hand, that government has been responding more swiftly, and more radically, to international market forces than any of its European neighbors. The policies have often been applied in the teeth of opposition from a majority of public opinion. This may explain the government's objections to the attempts by the majority of the members of the European Union to maintain old-style welfare states during the restructuring of the European economy.

On the other hand, the government has reiterated its faith in the sovereignty of the nation-state, when that is the logical casualty of developments in the world's economy. I believe this helps to explain the Conservative government's indifference to external causes of new, or deepening, social problems at home and its ignorance of the need for new strategies and policies, which involve European institutions, to meet U.K. problems.

Other members of the European Union have a similar problem. The question is not whether, but how, different member countries can live together. External collective relationships must now begin to take precedence over internal relationships. It will take time to shift the balance from internal to external relationships. Internal safeguards, especially welfare safeguards, are seriously threatened by the "single" European market. Few governments yet appreciate how to adjust to them.

New international policies depend on recognizing (and meeting) three rather different problems. The first is that many of the obstacles to market operations on the part of large corporations and multinational companies have already been swept away. Second, democratic institutions are too weak and contradictory to maintain some sort of control over economic forces during the erosion and even collapse of national welfare states. And, third, European social policy is too fragmented and poorly backed to fill the gaps left by losses of control over national welfare.

THE FREE MARKET CREATES PROBLEMS

Let me briefly illustrate the three. First is the introduction of a single market. This can be traced from the early postwar years. The Rome Treaty sought the removal not just of national tariffs but of national subsidies and regulatory devices. This was calculated to please multinational corporations but pays insufficient heed to employment and other problems of particular regions and populations. Nor did or does the process safeguard employees who have previously acquired particularly good employment rights.

The U.K. government strategy has been evident since 1979. It has consistently pursued a policy of deregulation. Nigel Lawson, as Chancellor of the Exchequer, said that the object of policy was to "remove obstacles to the effective working of markets in general and of the labour market in particular" (*Hansard*, 1985, col. 792). The labor market changes were substantial. "Part time employment at low rates of pay, self-employment and various forms of casual work have also increased at the expense of full-time regular employment." There had been a "widening of pay inequalities and a lowering of labour standards," the "removal of the legal floor of rights to wages and employment," and the "inducement, through the tax and social security system, of low wage employment" (Deakin and Wilkinson 1989, 1).

There are problems of population control and movement of workers. The Social Charter embodies intentions which some member countries see as overtaking and perhaps leading to the replacement of already well established employment rights in single nation-states. But much depends on what is compulsory (and enforceable) in law, and what is open to national interpretation, and delay, in implementation. This is made crystal clear in works such as that by Wedderburn (1990). One of the major political problems is whether, at a time when membership might grow rapidly because of developments in Eastern Europe, the employment and other rights already enjoyed by the richer members can be made available to the poorer members or whether a "two-tier" Europe, or a Europe of the lowest common denominator, may become the norm.

The tasks of establishing common employment rights and of implementing single-market rules of competition will be difficult to reconcile. This problem is compounded by the problem of immigrant workers. Action is being taken to harmonize immigration control. Britain anticipated 1992 with the Nationality Act 1981 and the Immigration Act 1988, with the effect of nearly stopping entry to the United Kingdom from the Indian subcontinent. Visa requirements have been imposed on visitors from Ghana, Nigeria, India, Pakistan, and Bangladesh. The Trevi group of interior and justice ministers has been secretly preparing ground rules for the treatment of non–European Union nationals in member countries, including policing, repatriation, and deportation. The Benelux countries and Germany and France have reached an "accord" which includes the requirement that one country's bar on a refugee applicant will be backed up by all the other signatories of the accord and deals generally with the consequences of the abolition of internal border controls for immigration, visiting, and asylum procedures. This accord has been delayed from being passed into law only by the complications of adjusting to the accommodation of migrants from eastern Germany seeking work and social security benefits (Arnott 1990). Many refugees from Eastern Europe are trying to reach Western Europe but are being held up in countries like Hungary and Czechoslovakia—which are experiencing severe problems as a consequence. Many of these refugees are unlikely to obtain entry clearance without more generous concessions than the member states seem disposed to make.

It is estimated that in more than fifty countries—from Africa, Asia, and Eastern Europe in particular—residents will require entry clearance with visa.

In the twelve member countries there are expected to be sixteen million non-E.U. nationals, mostly black people from third world countries. The pressure is on to coordinate rules on entry, residency, access to employment, and entitlement to civic rights. The major effect of such harmonization of immigration control both before and after entry will inevitably be a levelling down process, with controls becoming stricter not more liberal.

The scale of the problem and its implications for domestic workers are being played down. Immigrants are said to be less necessary in the next twenty years than in the period of Europe's postwar development. On the contrary, member countries are continuing to rely heavily on cheap and flexible labor, and some appear to be preparing for the substitution of nationals from the so-called Latin rim of Europe for domestic workers. There is also the emergence of a low-paid and casual labor force from within the midst of the original core of six members. So it is not just the emergence of a two-tier Europe in place of labor market dependence upon the third world but also social polarization in most of the member countries which is at issue. The speed of the restructuring of industry is remarkable. In the steel, tire, trucking, and shipbuilding industries, the number of companies is likely to be halved before the year 2000 (Ward 1991).

This is why the Social Charter and its Action Programme deserve a very mixed reception. It is tentative, restrictive in scope, and needs to be bolstered in close conformity with continued protection of national social rights. Thus, while recognizing certain vulnerable groups and demanding equal treatment for men and women, the Charter contains no corresponding call to outlaw racial discrimination. And the expression of generalized principle is not yet backed up by adequate law and E.U. funding. The process of deregulation in the 1980s has weakened the status of some minority groups of workers and has erected barriers to visitors, immigrants, and refugees from outside. A development plan with political backing and authority is badly needed.

THE NEED TO IMPROVE
DEMOCRATIC INSTITUTIONS

Second, democratic principles and practices are at issue. The development of the European Union has put the market first and democracy second. Democratic accountability is badly served by E.U. institutions. The European Commission is the executive of the European Union and has the right to propose policy and frame legislation. Currently there are seventeen members (one for each of the twelve member states plus an additional five nominated by the five most populous states). They are nominated by member states but are not responsible either to them or to the elected European

Parliament. The members of the European Parliament play little more than an advisory role in relation to legislation although they can, if they operate collectively, make difficulties for the Commission unless their advice is heeded. The Council of Ministers consists of relevant existing ministers from the different member countries, coming together to discuss and approve the Commission's proposals. There is a system of qualified voting: member states are allocated votes according to size.

The new international market is not matched by a new European or international democracy. For example, the measures adopted by the Council of Ministers and the Commission are legally binding under the Treaty of Rome. There are three groups of measures: regulations which apply in all member countries; decisions which bind those to whom they are addressed (companies and organizations as well as member states); and directives, which are compulsory but which permit member states to introduce their own legislation to implement them. The third is the one which allows too much variety of both interpretation and action.

As the European Union evolves, much depends on the balance between sanctioned laws or rules and exhortations. There are all too many signs of the Commission, and the Council of Ministers, resorting to an apparatus of unspecific and unenforceable directives to disguise the fact that democratic control, and therefore social responsibility, has been cynically left with enfeebled nation-states. The Action Programme published with the Social Charter indicates proposals for twenty-three directives.

The growing dependence on an apparatus of "directives" is bolstered by the principle of "subsidiarity." This principle states that action should not be taken at E.U. level if it can be taken as effectively at a lower level. Let me give an example. In an otherwise hostile commentary on the Social Charter, the Confederation of British Industry (CBI) supports the Commission's principle of subsidiarity. The CBI opposes new restrictive legislation which "would damage the economy and hence jobs in the longer term. In a free market economy, companies must offer appropriate conditions to recruit, retain and motivate their employees... a moral or ideological basis for action would be dangerous. . . . Employers believe that the real social dimension depends on sustainable economic growth acting as the engine for secure and increased employment and improved working conditions. They do not see a formal link between creating a single product market and a single EC labour market (CBI 1989, 3, 9). There are powerful forces, therefore, which have already weakened the programs for the social development of Europe.

Subsidiarity can be interpreted as a pretense of restoring sovereignty. Having removed the power of nation-states to act effectively to protect interests threatened by multinational corporations and agencies, the European Union is now turning back difficult issues to member states and leading them to believe they can exercise powers when such powers are hollow or are at most very weak.

How can employment and other rights which already exist in some of the laws of member states be accommodated by the Social Charter? How can a minimum degree of social protection for the poorer states be guaranteed? And how can a sufficient body of practice as well as principle be devised to allow a European welfare state to be established—and the further impoverishment of millions in Europe be prevented?

THE NEED TO STRENGTHEN SOCIAL POLICY INSTITUTIONS

These are the economic and political problems of the emergence of the European Union. There is a third problem. This is the lack of coherent policy to achieve minimal social development. European social policies are already skimpy, as I have said. Few observers expect the Social Charter to have much influence on differential earnings, and even less on the adequacy of social security benefits. In 1989, the E.C. budget was 44.8 billion ECUs. This was less than half the social security budget, and less than the National Health Service budget, of the United Kingdom. And social policy comprised only 7.2 percent of that budget (with regional policy, which covered some of the employment subsidies, accounting for a further 9.6 percent). The Common Agricultural Policy budget accounted for 67 percent of the total. The budget for the entire antipoverty program of the European Community, covering four years, was less than the annual social services budget of the average county in the United Kingdom.

On all three counts, E.U. institutions need to be transformed. Otherwise the process of impoverishment described for New York and London is going to apply not only more generally to the two countries but to the whole of Europe as well. In Europe we need: constitutional reform to enable democracy to operate coherently; constitutional reform to confer human and social rights; and legislation on social development and organization, with a corresponding upward surge in budgetary provision. None of these things have much hope of early fulfilment. I have argued that, among other things, the European Union is operating in fact as a negative power, threatening to dismantle the national welfare states without establishing much of a European equivalent in their place.

References

Arnott, H. 1990. "Fortress Europe." *Poverty, Journal of the Child Poverty Action Group*, no. 75, spring.

Atkinson, A. B. 1990. *The Department of Social Security Report on Households Below Average Income, 1981–87*. Welfare State Programme Research Note no. 22, Suntory-Toyota International Centre for Economics and Related Disciplines, London School of Economics, October.

Bradbury, B. 1989. "Family Size Equivalence Scales and Survey Evaluations of Income and Well-Being." *Journal of Social Policy* 18, no. 3: 383–408.

Bradshaw, J., and H. Holmes. 1989. *Living on the Edge*. London: Tyneside Child Poverty Action Group.

Buck, N. 1991. "Social Polarisation in the Inner City: An Analysis of the Impact of Labor Market and Household Change." in M. Cross and G. Payne, eds., *Social Inequality and the Enterprise Culture*. London: Falmer Press.

Buck, N., I. Gordon, and K. Young, with J. Ermisch and L. Mills. 1986. *The London Employment Problem*. Oxford: Oxford University Press.

Buhmann, B., L. Rainwater, G. Schmaus, and T. Smeeding. 1989. "Equivalence Scales, Well-Being, Inequality, and Poverty: Sensitivity Estimates across Ten Countries Using the Luxembourg Income Study (LIS) Database." *Review of Income and Wealth*, 115–42.

Central Statistical Office. 1988. "The Effects of Taxes and Benefits on Household Income, 1986." *Economic Trends*, no. 422 (December): 89–117.

Central Statistical Office. 1990. "The Effects of Taxes and Benefits on Household Income, 1987." *Economic Trends*, May.

Confederation of British Industry. 1989. *Submission by the Confederation of British Industry to the House of Lords European Communities Committee, Sub-Committee C (Social and Consumer Affairs) on the Community Charter of Fundamental Social Rights*. London: CBI.

Cooke, K. R., and S. Baldwin. 1984. *How Much Is Enough? A Review of Supplementary Benefit Scale Rates*. London: Family Policy Studies Centre.

Craig, G., and C. Glendinning. 1990. *The Impact of Social Security Changes: 1. The Views of Families Living in Disadvantaged Areas; 2. The Views of Families Using Barnado Pre-School Services; and 3. The Views of Young People*. Ilford, Essex: Barnados Research and Development Section, August.

Deakin, S., and F. Wilkinson. 1989. *Labour Law, Social Security, and Economic Inequality*. London: Institute of Employment Rights.

Department of Health and Social Security. 1985. *Reform of Social Security: Programme for Change*. Cmnd. 9517. London: HMSO.

Department of Health and Social Security. 1988. *Low Income Statistics, Report of a Technical Review*. London: DHSS.

Department of Social Security. 1988a. *Social Services Select Committee: Benefit Levels and a Minimum Income*. London: DSS.

Department of Social Security. 1988b. *The Measurement of Living Standards for Households below Average Income, Reply by the Government to the Fourth Report from the Select Committee on Social Services*. Cm 523. London: HMSO.

Department of Social Security. 1990a. *Households below Average Income: A Statistical Analysis, 1981–87*. London: Government Statistical Service.

Department of Social Security. 1990b. *The Measurement of Living Standards for Households below Average Income*. Cm. 1162. London: HMSO.

Department of Social Security. 1993. *Households below Average Income: A Statistical Analysis, 1979–90/91*. London: HMSO.

Edwards, M., and P. Whiteford. 1988. *The Development of Government Policies on Poverty and Income Distribution*. Canberra: Department of Social Security.

Fallon, I. 1994. "Seriously Richer," in P. Beresford with S. Boyd, *Britain's Richest 500*. London: Sunday Times.
Government Statistical Service. 1988. *Households below Average Income: A Statistical Analysis, 1981–1985*. London: Department of Health and Social Security.
Greater London Council. 1986. *The London Financial Strategy*. London: GLC.
Jenkins, S. P. 1989. *Recent Trends in U.K. Income Inequality*. Centre for Fiscal Studies, University of Bath.
Johnson, P., and S. Webb. 1990. *Low-Income Families, 1979–87*. London: Institute for Fiscal Studies.
Murray, R. 1985. "London and the Greater London Council: Restructuring the Capital of Capital." *IDS Bulletin* 16, no. 1.
Newman, B. A., and R. J. Thomson. 1989. "Economic Growth and Social Development: A Longitudinal Analysis of Causal Priority." *World Development*, pp. 461–71.
Oppenheim, C. 1990. *Poverty: The Facts*. London: Child Poverty Action Group.
Rainwater, L. 1988. "Inequalities in the Economic Well-Being of Children and Adults in Ten Nations." ISA Research Committee 19, Stockholm, August 25–28, LIS Working Paper no. 19.
Royal Commission on the Distribution of Income and Wealth (the Diamond Commission). 1978. *Report No. 6: Lower Incomes*. Cmnd. 7175. London: HMSO.
Russell Sage Foundation. 1990. "The Social Analysis of Poverty." *Reporting from the Russell Sage Foundation*, no. 12, June.
Sawyer, M. 1976. *Income Distribution in OECD Countries*. Paris: OECD Occasional Study.
Scott, J. 1992. *Citizenship and Privilege*. Leicester: University of Leicester.
Scott, J. 1994. *Poverty and Wealth: Citizenship, Deprivation and Privilege*. London: Longmans.
Smeeding, T. S., M. O'Higgins, L. Rainwater, and A. B. Atkinson. 1989. *Poverty, Inequality, and Income Distribution in Comparative Perspective*. London: Simon and Schuster.
Social Security Committee. 1991. *Low Income Statistics: Households below Average Income: Tables 1988, First Report*. Session 1990–91, House of Commons 401. London: HMSO.
Social Services Committee. 1988. *Families on Low Income: Low-Income Statistics, Fourth Report*. Session 1987–88, House of Commons 565. London: HMSO.
Social Services Committee. 1989. *Minimum Income, Memoranda Laid before the Committee*. Session 1988–89, House of Commons 579. London: HMSO.
Social Services Committee. 1990. *Low-Income Statistics, Fourth Report, 1989–90*. London: HMSO.
Social Welfare Policy Secretariat, Australia. 1981. *Report on Poverty Measurement*. Canberra: Australian Government Publishing Service.
Stark, M. 1988. *An A to Z of Income and Wealth*. London: Fabian Society.
Thrift, N., A. Leyshon, and P. Daniels. 1987. "Sexy Greedy: The New International Financial System, the City of London and the South East of England." Working Papers on Producer Services, Centre for the Study of Britain and the World Economy, Department of Geography, University of Bristol.
Townsend, P. 1979. *Poverty in the United Kingdom*. Harmondsworth: Allen Lane and Penguin Books.
Townsend, P. 1991a. *The Poor Are Poorer: A Statistical Report on Changes in the Living Standards of Rich and Poor in the United Kingdom, 1979–1989*. Report

from the Statistical Monitoring Unit, Department of Social Policy and Social Planning, University of Bristol.

Townsend, P. 1991b. *Meaningful Statistics on Poverty, 1991*. Report no. 2 from the Statistical Monitoring Unit, Department of Social Policy and Social Planning, University of Bristol.

Townsend, P. 1993a. *The International Analysis of Poverty*. Milton Keynes: Harvester Wheatsheaf.

Townsend, P. 1993b. "Underclass and Overclass: The Widening Gulf between Social Classes in Britain in the 1980s," in G. Payne and M. Cross, eds., *Sociology in Action*. London: Macmillan.

Townsend, P., with P. Corrigan and U. Kowarzik. 1987. *Poverty and Labour in London: Interim Report on a Centenary Survey*. London: Low Pay Unit.

U.S. Department of Health, Education, and Welfare. 1976. *The Measure of Poverty: A Report to Congress as Mandated by the Education Amendments of 1974*. Washington, D.C.: USGPO.

Vogler, C. 1989. "Labour Market Change and Patterns of Financial Allocation within Households." ESRC Social Change and Economic Life Initiative Working Paper no. 12, Oxford, Nuffield College.

Walker, A., and C. Walker. 1987. *The Growing Divide*. London: Child Poverty Action Group.

Ward, M. 1991. "The Role of Local Government in Social Policy." Barcelona: European Congress on Social Welfare.

Wedderburn, Lord. 1990. *The Social Charter, European Company and Employment Rights: An Outline Agenda*. London: Institute of Employment Rights.

Whiteford, P. 1985. *A Family's Needs: Equivalence Scales, Poverty, and Social Security*. Research Paper no. 27. Canberra: Development Division, Department of Social Security.

CONTRIBUTORS

SUSANNE MACGREGOR is Professor of Sociology and Social Policy at Middlesex University, London. Her publications include *The Politics of Poverty* (1981), *Dealing with Drug Misuse: Crisis Intervention in the City* (1984), *The Poll Tax: Flagships or Folly?* (1991), and *Tackling the Inner Cities: The 1980s Reviewed, Prospects for the 1990s* (1991). She has researched and written extensively on social problems and social policy in Britain, and is joint London coordinator of the Mega-Cities Project Network.

ANDREW CHURCH is Lecturer in Geography at Birkbeck College, University of London, and author of papers on London Docklands and economic development. He was advisor to the House of Commons Select Committee on Employment in 1989–90 for their enquiry into the employment effects of Urban Development Corporations.

WILLIAM DIFAZIO is Professor of Sociology at St. John's University, New York, and author of *Longshoremen: Community and Resistance on the Brooklyn Waterfront* (1985). He is currently researching the impact of technological change on work patterns and social life.

ELOISE DUNLAP is coinvestigator and Director of Research on the project "The Natural History of Crack Distribution" at National Development and Research Institutes, Inc. (formerly Narcotic and Drug Research, Inc.). This ongoing ethnographic study looks at issues of drug distribution careers and family life.

DONNA GAINES is the author of *Teenage Suicide* (1991) and a regular contributor to *Village Voice* and other newspapers and journals.

SUE GOSS is Development Director at the Office for Public Management, London. She was formerly a committee chair in a London borough and is the author of *Local Labour and Local Government* (1988) and *Councils in Conflict* (1989).

WILLIAM KORNBLUM is Professor of Sociology at the City University of New York and Director of the Center for Social Research at the Graduate Center, CUNY. He is the author of a text on social problems now in its seventh edition, *Blue Collar Community* (1974) and *Growing up Poor* (1985), and numerous studies of social life in New York.

ERIC LICHTEN is Professor of Sociology at Long Island University, C. W. Post Campus, Brookville, New York, and author of *Class Power and Austerity: the New York City Fiscal Crisis* (1986).

ARTHUR LIPOW is Director of the Michael Harrington Centre at Birkbeck College, University of London. He is the author of *Authoritarian Socialism* (1991).

CAREY OPPENHEIM is Director of Research at the Child Poverty Action Group in

London. She now lectures at South Bank University, London, and is the author of numerous publications on poverty including *Poverty: the Facts* (1993 edition) and studies of the impact of the poll tax on the poor in Britain.

GEOFFREY PEARSON is Wates Professor of Social Work at Goldsmiths' College, University of London, and author of *Hooligan: a History of Respectable Fears* (1983), *The New Heroin Users* (1987), and other publications on youth culture, crime, and drug taking.

JOHN SOLOMOS is Professor of Social Policy at Southampton University. He is the author of numerous publications on race and public policy including *Black Youth, Racism, and the State* (1988) and *Race and Racism in Contemporary Britain* (1987). He has edited *Roots of Urban Unrest* (1987), *Race and Local Politics* (1990), and *Racism and Equal Opportunity Policies* (1987; 1989).

PETER TOWNSEND is Emeritus Professor of Social Policy at the University of Bristol. In 1991–92 he was Michael Harrington Distinguished Professor of Social Science at City University of New York (Queens College). His publications include *Poverty in the United Kingdom* (1979), *The Poor and the Poorest* (1965), *Health and Deprivation* (1987), *Poverty and Labour in London* (1987), and *The International Analysis of Poverty* (1993).

AUTHOR INDEX

Arnold, M., 88

Baden-Powell, R., 91
Bird, J., 143
Blauner, B., 55
Block, F., 57
Bourgois, P., 13
Bray, R., 91
Brown, C., 77
Brownill, S., 139–142
Bruegel, I., 75–79
Buck, N., 133

Coleman, S., 122–23
Coles, R., 116

Dahrendorf, R., 9, 24, 25
Davidson, N., 80
Douglass, F., 199
Dugmore, K., 165, 167
Dreze, J., 20

Engels, F., 2

Fielding, H., 88
Foster, J., 147

Gilder, G., 189
Gordon, I., 139
Gyford, J., 211

Hall, S., 96
Hanmer, J., 95
Harvey, D., 143
Hoagland, H., 119
Hoggart, R., 90
Hirschhorn, L., 57

Jahoda, M., 144
Jayne, G. D., 122

Kennedy, R., 6–8
Kornblum, W., 25–26

Lewis, O., 116
Logan, A., 22
London, J., 90

Mannheim, K., 155
Marmor, T., 17–18
Massey, D., 133, 142, 149
Masterman, C., 90
Moore, R., 167
Murray, C., 52–54, 189

Parker, J., 165, 167
Parsnell, G., 144
Phillips, D., 167–68
Plowden, W., 17–18

Rex, J., 167
Roberts, K., 144
Rorty, R., 42–43
Rossi, P., 217

Sassen, S., 1, 5
Scarman, Lord, 99, 166
Sen, A., 20
Sexton, P., 119
Short, J., 142–43
Sidel, R., 46, 49
Smith, D., 165
Smith, S., 167–68
Stanko, E., 95
Stewart, J., 209
Stoker, G., 209
Sudjic, D., 1

Townsend, P., 11, 75, 80

Wallman, S., 146

Wedderburn, Lord, 224
Wetzel, J., 158, 159
West, C., 57
Whalley, A., 165
Wiener, M., 88–89
Williams, T., 159
Williams, R., 87, 106

Williams, R. M., 122
Wilmott, P., 144
Wilson, W. J., 12–13, 54–56

Young, J., 95
Young, K., 174

SUBJECT INDEX

American Dream, 33, 160, 185
anomie (alienation), 158, 162
austerity: age of, 25, 185; economy, 59, 186–90; and social policy, 190–94; state, 194–97, 200

begging, 183–84
Brixton, 7, 15, 97
Broadwater Farm, 7, 99–100, 172
Bush, George, 3, 33, 41, 51, 52; administration, 28, 31, 33, 43

Canary Wharf, 132, 136, 140
Carter administration, 45, 189
children: and AFDC, 46; and poverty in America, 43–44; and poverty in Britain, 62, 63–64, 66
cities: global, 1; world, 4–6
Clinton, Bill, 19, 41, 51
communities: black, 165; community policing, 37; inner city, 209; in London, 142–43; in New York, 34–39
Child Poverty Action Group (CPAG), 23, 216
crack, 7, 44, 108; dealing, 117; epidemic in New York, 37; in London, 103
crime: fear of, 94–95; and hooliganism, 92–94; and policing, 94–100; and poverty, 94; recorded crime in UK, 7; surveys, 94–96
crisis: definitions of, 115; and drugs, 115; and family life, 117; fiscal, 176, 185–90; housing, 50; of local government, 175; personal, 122; urban, 29, 191
culture: Americanization of, 88–89; of Englishness, 89–91; popular, 89

democracy, local, 39
demography: birth rates, 155, 157; population of London, 6, 68; population of New York, 7, 22, 31, 32
Dinkins, David, 50, 87, 191–92, 199
discourses: changing, 17; language of empowerment, 204; language of limitations, 185; of social problems, 153–54 vocabulary shifts, 43–44, 57, 59, 106
Docklands, London, 67, 132, 143; attitudes of local community, 147–49; Development Corporation, 132, 136, 140
drugs: and crime, 96, 101, 105, 107; dealing, 124, 127; heroin, 44, 101; policy, 20–21; surveys, 104–106

economic change: in Britain, 63; and de-industrialisation, 45, 133; in global cities, xv; and inequality, 187–89; in London, 66–68, 137–139; and occupational aspirations, 144–145, 158–160; and social dislocation, 55
education: and mobility, 159; policies, 31; public schooling in New York, 29–32; school performance in New York, 30–31
empowerment, 202; models of, 202, 203–209
ethnic minorities, in London, 68–69, 72–74
European Community (European Union), 221–27

Farrakhan, L., 14

Grant, Bernie, 173
Greater London Council (GLC),

141–42, 167, 207, 212, 219
Guiliani, Rudolph, 199

Hackney, 79–80, 166, 167, 170–80
Haringey, 166, 170–80
Harlem, 15
Horton, Willie, 3
Households Below Average Income Statistics, 63, 215
housing: allocation policies, 149; classes, 167; market, 167; policies, 179–80; public housing in London, 148, 166; public housing in New York, 32–34; and racial discrimination, 165–68
hunger, in New York, 48

immigration: impact in Europe, 224–25; impact on New York, 29–30
income support (supplementary benefits), 69–70, 216
inequality: explanations of, 218, 221–225; problems of measurement, 219–21; social, xiv
inner cities, 61, 166; and family life, 114

King, Rodney, 3
Koch, Ed, 186, 197

labor force: in London, 6, 145; in New York, 7
local government (city council): in London, 139–42, 166, 168, 179; in New York, 22; role of, 204, 206, 211–213

Major, John, 19
Manhattan, 3, 184
market: approach to urban decline, 134, 150, 205, 210; capitalism, 184; free, xiv, xv, 43, 52, 62, 92, 223
media, and images, 15, 33, 37, 160–61, 165–66
multinational corporations, 222–23, 226
Murray, Charles, 18

Olympia and York, 1, 140, 150

politics: campaigns, 134, 137, 142–43, 150, 200, 204, 207, 208; and ethnic minorities, 166, 168; and labor unions, 188–89, 192, 194; strategy of Labour party, 19, 203
post-industrial society, 18–19, 188, 190; and poverty, 40–42, 57
poverty (deprivation): causes of, 62–63; and children in London, 70–71; concepts and definitions, 11, 13, 15; consequences of, 79–80; facts of in Britain, 62–66; facts of in New York, 185; and health, 79–80; increasing, xv, 8, 62, 64, 75; indicators of, 69–75; risks of, 64–66, 75; trends, 215–17; and unemployment in London, 72; and women, 70
privatization, 197, 222; and UK housing policy, 11, 205; and US housing policy, 33
public policy, 16–17, 20–21, 139; equal opportunities policies, 208; initiatives and implementation, 166, 170, 178; and planning, 141–42, 149; and public services, 210; race equality policies, 166–70

race: and crime, 95–97, 128–29; and inequality, 165; and politics, 168; and poverty, 76, 158
racism: in London, 99; in New York, 3, 198; racial harassment, 148, 170, 177; and tension, 149
Reagan: administration, 32, 43, 45, 46, 52, 184, 186, 189, 196; ideology, xv
recession: impact on London, 4, 67, 133; impact on New York, 30; property-market, 137
redistribution: attitudes to, 82; related policies, 19–20, 38, 43, 82, 189
riots: in London, 7, 94, 97; Los Angeles, xv, 3, 33, 39
Rohatyn, Felix, 193

social change: in Britain, 63; in London, 68–69
socialism: municipal, 136, 203
social policy, 43, 184; and AFDC, 53, 196; and democracy, 227; and

young people, 146
social problems, in London and New York, 7–9, 14
social security reforms, 82

taxation, 38, 189–90
tenants councils (tenants associations), 34
Thatcher, Mrs., 23, 214–15, 217
Thatcher: administration, 204, 207; ideology, xv, 92, 96; and inner cities, 133
transport, systems, 5, 137, 150
"trickle-down" policies, 58, 134, 190, 198, 207, 214, 217

underclass: concepts of, 12–13, 25–26, 32, 86; explanations of, 52–56, 58, 159, 222; and overclass, 222

unemployment: in London and New York, 7; and poverty, 66; rates, 138, 145–46, 158; and women, 74
urban: development corporations, 134; enterprise zones, 136; left, 174–75, 180, 207; partnerships, 210; policy, 29, 133, 149–50, 206

wealth, 61, 74, 143, 186–87, 190, 216, 219
welfare state: changes in, xv, 188, 190, 200, 227; role of, 24, 92, 194–95, 217, 223
women: female headed families, 49, 124, 172; and unemployment, 75–79

youth: American, 153; culture, 87, 90, 93–94, 156; impact of change on, 143–46; teenage suicides, 155, 159